THE UKRAINIAN REVOLUTION, 1917-1920

A STUDY IN NATIONALISM

By JOHN S. RESHETAR, JR.

PRINCETON, NEW JERSEY

PRINCETON UNIVERSITY PRESS

1952

Publication of this book has been aided by a grant from the
Princeton University Research Fund

Printed in the United States of America by
Princeton University Press, Princeton, New Jersey

TO MY

MOTHER AND FATHER

Preface

THIS study is an attempt to do justice to a sorely neglected aspect of the Russian Revolution—the Ukrainian effort to attain independent statehood which commenced in 1917 and ended in failure in 1920. English and American students have described and analyzed with adequate care events which occurred in Moscow and Petrograd, but there have been no comparable efforts to study the peripheries of the Russian Empire. In the case of Ukraine this negligence was due to a general unawareness of the existence of a people in Southern Russia distinct from those in the North. The fact that both the Ukrainians and the Russians claim the same early history has been a source of considerable consternation to the uninitiated observer. In the past various Russian writers, among them Prince Alexander Volkonsky and Prince Serge Obolensky, have written polemics based on the thesis that there is no Ukrainian nation but only a Little Russian branch of the Russian nation. Ukrainian historians and polemicists have countered with the assertion that the Muscovite tsars usurped Ukraine's ancient name of Rus.

An attempt to disentangle the various claims and counterclaims advanced by the Russian and Ukrainian historians would go beyond the scope of this study and would be of no practical value because the distinctiveness of the Ukrainians is now generally recognized. The fact that Ukraine enjoys the status of a separate republic as well as membership in the United Nations is indicative of the recognition which has been accorded it. The four years of painful suffering and bloodshed, of chaos and anarchy, and of understandable but harmful compromises described in the following pages did not lead to independent statehood. There is much in this story that is heroic, and there is also the shabby, the tragic, and the ironic. In a narrow sense this is the study of a failure because the men who led the Ukrainian movement were defeated. Yet when viewed in its historical perspective, the Ukrainian Revolution of 1917-1920 was not without effect for it compelled Russia's Communist rulers to acknowledge the existence of the Ukrainian people. This was no mean achievement.

The person who undertakes to describe and evaluate the events of this period of civil war and revolution cannot but be aware of the large number of works with an anti-Ukrainian bias which have come from the pens of Soviet and anti-Bolshevik Russian writers. Yet if the story of the national movement is to be told accurately it must be based primarily on the accounts of the men who made it possible. There are many questions which cannot be fully answered. Personal animosities and the usual desire of participants to avoid responsibility for errors have contributed to the difficulties encountered in this enquiry. Human motives and the causes of failures are not easily determined. If the present writer has been unjust to any of the participants in the events dealt with in this study he requests only that those who would pass harsh judgment upon him recall the complexity of this period before doing so.

Transliteration is invariably a problem because those who are philologically inclined demand a system which incorporates every subtlety while for the average scholar the main function of a system of transliteration is to enable the reader who knows the language to consult a specific source. This writer has not distinguished between the Ukrainian "и" and "i" by rendering one as "y" and the other as "i"; nor has he transliterated "ï" as "yi" or "є" as "ye." This has been done in order to maintain simplicity and also for aesthetic reasons since if "ï" were to be rendered as "yi" it would necessitate spelling "Ukraina" as "Ukrayina." In the case of names of Ukrainians who have been living in exile for a considerable period of time an attempt has been made to render the person's name in the form which he himself has employed more or less consistently in his writings in the Western European languages.

Whatever merit this work may possess is due in no small measure to the aid and encouragement which I have received from my former teachers and from my associates and colleagues. The Social Science Research Council in granting me a pre-doctoral fellowship enabled me to be released from a considerable portion of my teaching duties. I am heavily indebted to Professor Rupert Emerson of the Department of Government at Harvard University and to Professor Philip E. Mosely of the Russian Institute at Columbia University, without whose generous support this study could not have been undertaken. Professor Mykola Haydak placed his excellent private library of rare Ukrainian materials at my disposal, and the since deceased Professor Dmitro Doroshenko, during two delightful summer afternoons and evenings in Winnipeg, provided me with invaluable reminiscences. Professor Harold Sprout and Professor George Graham, my colleagues at Princeton, graciously consented to the lightening of my teaching duties. My former teachers—Professors Merle Fainsod and Michael Karpovich—contributed, each in his own way, to my graduate education and to the preparation which preceded the writing of my doctoral dissertation from which this study emerged.

I should like to express my gratitude to the staff members of the Widener Library at Harvard, the Columbia University Library, the Princeton University Library, the New York Public Library, the Library of Congress, and the Hoover Library at Stanford University for the many services rendered in connection with the research for this study. In addition, the publications gathered by the late Harold Weinstein, and bequeathed to Columbia University following his death in World War II, were of inestimable value to me.

The many persons who have contributed in so many different ways to this study are too numerous to be fully acknowledged. I do, however, wish to express my appreciation to Professor Hans Kohn for providing me with certain background information with regard to various of the Jewish groups in Ukraine; to Katherine Reshetar and Marie Kalina for their typing of the manuscript with such care and efficiency and for their aid in the preparation of the index; to Miriam Brokaw of the Princeton University Press who made innumerable suggestions in connection with the preparation of the manuscript for publication; to Helen Van Zandt for preparing the map; and to Marianne Ehrenborg for aiding in the proofreading.

In accordance with custom, I must state that I alone bear full responsibility for the conclusions expressed and for any errors of fact or interpretation which may have occurred.

Publication of this study was aided substantially by a generous subvention from the Princeton University Research Fund for which I am very grateful.

JOHN S. RESHETAR, JR.

Princeton
December, 1951

Table of Contents

A map of Ukraine will be found on pages 220 and 221.

CHAPTER I
Incipient Nationhood

And Ukraine shall rise from her grave and shall again appeal to all brethren Slavs, and they shall heed her call, and Slavdom shall rise and there shall remain neither tsar nor tsarevich, neither tsarina nor prince, neither count nor duke, neither Illustrious Highness nor Excellency, neither sir nor nobleman, neither serf nor servant; neither in Muscovy nor in Poland, neither in Ukraine nor in Czechia, neither in Croatia nor in Serbia nor in Bulgaria.—NICHOLAS KOSTOMAROV, *The Book of Genesis of the Ukrainian People* (1846)

We know that the struggle will be long and bitter, that the enemy is strong and unsparing. But we also know that this is the final conflict, not to be followed by another opportune moment for a new struggle. The night has been long, but the dawn has approached and we shall not allow the rays of national freedom to shine on our chains: we shall break them before the rising of the sun of liberty. For the last time we shall enter the arena of history and either succeed or die. . . . We no longer wish to bear foreign rule and indignities in our own land. Numerically we are small, but in our love of Ukraine we are strong! . . .

Let the cowards and renegades go, as they have in the past, to the camp of our enemies. They have no place among us, and we shall denounce them as enemies of the Fatherland.

All in Ukraine who are not for us are against us. Ukraine for the Ukrainians! So long as a single foreign enemy remains on our territory we do not have the right to lay down our arms.—NICHOLAS MIKHNOVSKY, *Independent Ukraine* (1900)

THE collapse of the Russian Empire in February 1917 led to one of the richest and most costly periods of political experimentation in modern history—costly in human as well as in material terms. Innumerable parties, governments, and nationalities advanced their programs in the four years of political flux which followed. During most of that crucial period the dominance of the Bolshevik regime, which had established itself in the North, was by no means a foregone conclusion.

While the Bolsheviks were returning from exile or imprisonment in 1917, the Ukrainians were organizing their first government in modern times—that of the Central Rada. Tortuous negotiations between the Rada and the Russian Provisional Government in Petrograd soon revealed serious disagreements regarding the future political status of Ukraine. The Bolshevik coup which destroyed the Provisional Government in November 1917 compelled the Ukrainians to proclaim the independence of their nation. However, this was done only when it became evident that the Bolsheviks were prepared to destroy the Rada by force of arms. Compromise became impossible when the Bolsheviks, while still paying lip service to the right of nationalities to secede, heaped scorn and abuse upon the Rada and proceeded to invade Ukraine in January 1918. The Ukrainian People's Republic sent its own delegation to the peace conference with the Central Powers at Brest-Litovsk when it became obvious that the Bolsheviks had gone there with the intention of representing all parts of the former Russian Empire although Ukraine now had its own government. The Red troops succeeded in taking Kiev, but the Ukrainian Republic was saved when it obtained recognition from the Central Powers at Brest and signed a peace treaty with them.

The military occupation of Ukraine by the Central Powers resulted in the expulsion of the Bolshevik forces but also led to the demise of the Rada and the paradoxical reestablishment of the Ukrainian monarchy by means of

3

a coup. This colorful government headed by Hetman Paul Skoropadsky was somewhat out of step with the times, but it began to take forceful measures to restore order although on an anti-socialist basis. However, it was overthrown by force late in 1918 when the troops of the Central Powers were being withdrawn from Ukraine as a result of the termination of World War I.

The men who overthrew the Hetman were those who had played a prominent role in the Rada, but with the significant difference that in 1919 military action was to play a much more important role than it had during the preceding two years. The Bolshevik Government in Moscow moved its troops against the Ukrainian Republic and its executive organ, the Directory, and succeeded in taking Kiev although under the guise of a nominally Ukrainian Soviet Government. Some of the men in the Directory Government attempted to negotiate with Moscow but soon discovered that negotiation meant capitulation. There was no alternative but to give battle to the Bolshevik invaders. However, the defense of Ukraine was hampered by the Polish attack on the newly-established West Ukrainian Government which had united with the Directory to form a single Ukrainian state.

In early February 1919 Kiev fell to the Bolsheviks, and the Directory was compelled to flee. France had intervened half-heartedly and had landed troops on the Black Sea coast, but her officers and diplomats failed to adopt a definite policy of support for the Ukrainian Republic. Then France and the Allies suddenly withdrew their forces in April 1919 following more than three months of intervention. The Directory was plagued with many very difficult problems: it was unable to control all of its military commanders; it was faced with crucial economic and social issues; and behind its lines anti-Jewish pogroms broke out. Short-lived victories followed defeats, but they enabled the Directory's armed forces, under the command of Petliura, to continue the struggle against the Bolsheviks. However, numerous attempts to obtain recognition and

4

aid in foreign capitals and at the Paris Peace Conference ended in failure, and the government of the Ukrainian People's Republic was compelled to go into exile in 1920 but only after a heroic and costly struggle.

What were the strengths and the weaknesses of the Ukrainian national government during this, the most crucial period in its history? Why were there several Ukrainian governments and what were the causes of the downfall of each? What factors enabled the Bolshevik regime to impose its rule upon Ukraine? How did the Ukrainians attempt to combat this threat to their independence? Before an attempt can be made to offer some answers to these and other questions it is necessary to review briefly some of the significant events which constitute the matrix from which the leaders of the Ukrainian national revolution emerged and from which they derived their ideals and objectives.

The Ukrainian national movement of the first years of the twentieth century rested on an historical heritage which had been accumulated during the preceding eleven decades in spite of Russian rule. In large measure this was a cultural rather than a political legacy. Prior to this, during the eighteenth century, a vast, inert, and characteristically traditionalist peasantry had clung to its native tongue until the literati were able to utilize it in their writings. The first of these was Ivan Kotliarevsky (1769-1838), often referred to as the father of modern Ukrainian literature, who had the courage to write in the vernacular rather than in the old Church Slavonic.[1] This epoch-making step, symbolized by the publication of his *Eneida* in 1798, initiated a transformation which for Ukraine was as significant as the elimination in the West of Latin as the literary medium.

Yet Ukrainian was not used with full effectiveness until the middle of the nineteenth century when Taras Shev-

[1] According to the nationalist literary historians ancient Ukrainian literature includes the chronicles of Kievan Rus as well as the *Tale of the Host of Igor.*

5

chenko, the nation's greatest poet, pleaded for human liberation. Born a serf and having experienced a miserable childhood and an adulthood which contained but nine short years of freedom, Shevchenko grieved not only over the plight of his fellow Ukrainians but also over that of the Russian peasant. Possibly in order to escape the horrible present, he turned to the exploits of the freedom-loving Cossacks of the seventeenth century and found in them numerous poetic themes. In his glorification of the Cossack traditions and in his treatment of their heroic struggle against the Poles and Turks, Shevchenko reflected the romanticism of his century.

Although he kept his diary in Russian and was very much at ease in the company of Russian intellectuals and enlightened aristocrats, he wrote all of his literary works in Ukrainian. It is probable that he first acquired a real appreciation of the beauty of his native land and his people's language in 1832. While accompanying his master in the capacity of a serf-valet he had occasion to visit Vilna, where he made the acquaintance of a nationalistically inclined Polish girl who refused to speak any language other than her own. Later when his freedom was purchased and he took up residence in Saint Petersburg he often expressed nostalgic sentiments for Ukraine. A recurring theme in the writings of this bachelor-poet is that of the injustice caused by the Russian youth, usually a nobleman or soldier, who seduces a supposedly innocent Ukrainian maiden and then leaves her with the unborn child. Yet Shevchenko's attacks on nobility and on landowners seem to have been more frequent than his attacks on Russians, and it may not be incorrect to conclude that he was indicting a whole social order rather than a nation and holding it responsible for permitting unwed mothers, poverty, hunger, and military conscription.

This conviction prompted him to join with other like-minded Ukrainians, such as Nicholas Kostomarov and Panteleimon Kulish, in founding the Society of Saints Cyril and Methodius in Kiev in 1846. This group of rather typical nineteenth century liberals had as its cardinal principle the establishment of a federation of self-governing Slavic republics composed of legally equal units; such a program had been advocated by the organization's ideologist, Kostomarov, and at the time was regarded as subversive. Its platform also included the abolition of serfdom, corporal punishment, and illiteracy, and the guarantee of freedom of conscience, press, and speech—objectives which indicate that the Society was not in any sense exclusively nationalist. It is also significant that it did not select an exclusively Ukrainian saint as patron but chose instead two saints common to all Slavic peoples. The Society was Christian in principle but called for an end to religious animosities and advocated love, meekness, and patience. Membership was secret, with all Slavs eligible; the families of members who fell into the hands of the enemy were to be cared for by the organization.[2] The activities of these revolutionary idealists were abruptly terminated in April of 1847 with a series of arrests, and Shevchenko was sentenced to ten years in exile on the Kirghiz steppe of Central Asia. The first modern political movement that can be termed Ukrainian thus came to an early end and was not to be succeeded by any similar endeavor for several decades.

This retardation can be attributed in large part to the restrictive measures which the Imperial Russian Government imposed upon the use of the Ukrainian language. These were introduced in 1863 and were made more severe in May of 1876, when an edict was issued prohibiting the importation of Ukrainian publications from abroad and permitting only historical documents and belles-lettres to be printed, and these only in Russian orthography. Lectures and theatrical presentations in Ukrainian were also forbidden. In the course of the same year the southwestern section of the Russian Geographic Society was ordered closed because of its alleged Ukrainophilism.

[2] For the by-laws of the Society see N. Storozhenko, "Kirillo-Mefodievskie Zagovorshchiki," *Kievskaia Starina*, xcii (February, 1906), pp. 138ff.

The strength and the weakness of the Ukrainian movement during the greater part of this dark period were probably best symbolized by the work of Michael P. Drahomaniv (1841-1895), who was somewhat unique in that he did not confine himself to cultural matters. His history instructor in the gymnasium had impressed upon him the significance of the revolutionary movements of 1848, and it was here that he acquired his first knowledge of liberalism and the phenomenon of nationality. Later, as a student in the University of Kiev, he studied Roman history, giving special attention to the social struggle which characterized the end of the republic. It was at the university, where he had a reputation for cosmopolitanism, that he became acquainted with the nationally conscious Ukrainian students and commenced to take an interest in their activities. Soon after being appointed as a privat-docent in history at Kiev, Drahomaniv wrote a critical article on Russian textbooks which were employed in the village schools and advocated the use of Ukrainian as an introductory language in the educational system. This forthright stand caused many Ukrainians who had acquired Russian nationality to denounce him as a "separatist," and it was this charge that caused his initial interest in things Ukrainian to develop into a lifelong association.

For a period of several years beginning in 1871 Drahomaniv carried on research in Germany, Italy, Austria, and Switzerland and had an opportunity to meet Galician Ukrainians who were under Austrian rule. In 1875, following further denunciation of his "separatism," he left Kiev and went into exile. He first took up residence in Vienna but in 1876 moved to Geneva, where he published a Ukrainian periodical, *Hromada*, as well as writings on folklore. The last six years of his life were spent in Sofia where he was engaged in teaching history at the university and in conducting ethnographic research. Here he also published a history of old constitutions beginning with a treatment of the Magna Carta which was indicative of his respect for the British political system.

8

Drahomaniv's attitude toward the realization of practical political objectives was evident in the advice which he tendered to his students when he warned them not to regard themselves as men of action but rather as those who were laying the groundwork for future activity. Yet this did not prevent him from believing, together with Alexander Herzen, that the Russian Empire had to be reorganized as a federation of free and equal peoples. A few of the most extreme nationalists in later years interpreted this as a Russophile tendency, but actually it was part of a dualism since Drahomaniv was also disturbed by the Russification of young Ukrainians. At the same time a trace of the initial cosmopolitanism always remained in his mental make-up and caused him to oppose Ukrainian provincialism in literature and to favor collaboration with Russian liberals. However, the very fact of Drahomaniv's self-imposed exile demonstrated the impracticability of his moderate program in the autocratic Russia of the 1870's.

In marked contrast to this were events in Galician or West Ukraine where, despite Austrian rule, the national movement gained momentum and established its center at Lviv or Lemberg. Here in 1873 the Shevchenko Society was founded for the promotion of Ukrainian culture. It proved to be the parent organization of the Shevchenko Scientific Society, which was organized in 1898 with three faculties: history, jurisprudence and philosophy, and medicine and the natural sciences. In that year this center of Ukrainian scholarship also commenced publication of its *Literary and Scientific Herald (Literaturno-Naukovi Vistnik)*. It sponsored the publication of Ukrainian literary classics, historical monographs, and sourcebooks as well as ethnographic, legal, and medical works. In 1894 the Galician Ukrainians obtained a professorship of Eastern European history in the Polish-dominated University of Lviv, and its first occupant was the eminent historian, Michael Hrushevsky (1866-1934), who at that time was a subject of the tsar.

In 1894 Hrushevsky took up residence in Lviv, staying

9

there for twelve years because of the stifling restrictions imposed on Ukrainian activities in the Russian Empire. At Lviv he commenced the writing of his monumental *Istoriia Ukraini-Rusi* (History of Ukraine-Rus). Hrushevsky was followed by other Russian Ukrainians who played not a small part in the emergence of Lviv as the center of the national movement at the close of the nineteenth century, an emergence which was made possible by the sympathetic attitude which certain Austrian officials held regarding the movement. They were not unaware of its potentialities as a dissolvent of the Russian Empire, and Vienna also found it useful as a counter-balance to the restless Poles. The growth of national consciousness in East Galicia was also facilitated by the ethnic duality of the region. The clash and contrast between Poles and Ukrainians in this border area served to accentuate linguistic, religious, and cultural differences and promote a sense of nationality or consciousness of being unique.

Another factor which contributed to the growth of the national movement in West Ukraine was the western cultural orientation of Lviv. Its inhabitants, as citizens of the Dual Empire, enjoyed access to the intellectual life of Western Europe; those who wished to advance themselves found it necessary to acquire fluency in German. German had been the language of instruction in the university until the latter half of the nineteenth century, when it was largely supplanted by Polish. A considerable number of Galicians and East Ukrainians preferred to study in Vienna, Berlin, and Heidelberg, and they undoubtedly were influenced by the growth of German nationalism. As early as 1870 Nicholas Lysenko (1842-1912), the most prominent Ukrainian composer and a subject of the tsar, had graduated from the Leipzig Conservatory of Music. In 1894, at the age of thirty-eight, Ivan Franko, the greatest Galician poet and novelist, received his doctorate from the University of Vienna. Somewhat earlier, Fedir Vovk, a prominent East Ukrainian archaeologist and ethnographer, received his doctorate in France and then spent a total of thirty years in exile.

One of the first English students of nationalism, and the most astute, observed as early as 1862 that "exile is the nursery of nationality."[3] The severance of ties with the homeland not only caused nostalgia but also stimulated awareness of group peculiarities. What was undoubtedly true of Ukrainians who studied and lived in Western Europe was also applicable to those who went to Northern Russia or Muscovy to receive academic training. Volodimir Leontovich, a landowner who became an active supporter of Ukrainian journalism after the 1905 Revolution in Russia, commenced to perceive the differences between the Russians and Ukrainians and developed a preference for the latter only when he became a student in the University of Moscow.[4] Yet there were many others who experienced a reaction which was the reverse of this.

Assimilation took a tremendous toll among Ukrainians in the course of the nineteenth century. Old Ukrainian families became Russified; these included those of Kochubei, Skoropadsky, Kapnist, Rodzianko, Iavorsky, Gogol, Prokopovich, Korolenko, and Bezborodko. When Volodimir B. Antonovich (1834-1907), Hrushevsky's mentor in Cossack history, arrived in Kiev for the first time in 1850 he found only five nationally conscious Ukrainians in the whole city. The census of 1900 placed the Ukrainian population of Saint Petersburg at 1,500 persons while the data pertaining to place of birth indicated that the capital contained more than 14,000 individuals who came from Ukrainian provinces.[5] Some of these denationalized persons suffered from a spiritual schism since they revealed on occasion that they were conscious of their descent, but for the most part they were incapable of undoing the as-

[3] Lord Acton, *The History of Freedom and Other Essays* (London, 1922), p. 286.

[4] See his "Spohadi pro moi Zustrichi z Ukrainskimi Diachami Starshoho Pokolinnia" in *Z Minuloho*, edited by Prof. Roman Smal-Stocki (Warsaw, 1938), p. 76.

[5] Alexander Lototsky, *Storinki Minuloho* (Warsaw, 1933), II, p. 432

similatory process and remained in a state of somewhat disturbed apathy.

Those who discovered the existence of a Ukrainian past, centered in Kiev and distinct from that of the Russians or Muscovites, spearheaded the Ukrainophile movement of the 1880's which was exclusively cultural and was conducted within the limits of the laws of the Russian Empire. In 1882 the first issue of *Kievskaia Starina* (Kievan Antiquity) appeared and proved to be the beginning of a quarter century of fruitful publication. This monthly was an historical journal in the broad sense of the word which envisages history as the queen of the sciences. It included materials on peasant folklore and customs, archaeology, ethnography, biography, and numismatics as well as historical documents and reviews of current books. The writings of the Ukrainophiles, although done mostly in Russian (with the exception of contemporary literature which was in Ukrainian), constituted a necessary phase prerequisite to the elevation of the national movement to the political plane.

This vital last step could be undertaken only by the men who, like Lenin, were in their youth in the 1890's at the time when political parties were coming into existence within the Russian Empire. Probably the first such Ukrainian group was the secret Taras Brotherhood (*Bratstvo Tarasivtsiv*) which was founded in 1891 on Shevchenko's grave at Kaniv by men who did not wish to enter Russian political parties. The organizers were four youths from Kharkiv: Ivan Lipa, Nicholas Baizdrenko, Michael Bazkevich, and Vitaly Borovik. In 1893 the Brotherhood adopted a *profession de foi* which it had published in *Pravda*, a newspaper in Lviv. It called for the liberation of all peoples in Russia from despotism and centralism and the granting of autonomy, promotion of the public welfare, and establishment of a social system having neither exploiters nor exploited. Although the members advocated the development of Ukrainian national consciousness among both the intelligentsia and the

people, they were not sufficiently acquainted with the no-
menclature of the new creed to call themselves nationalists
instead of "nationals." Before the police liquidated the
Brotherhood in 1893, several branches were established
among Ukrainian students.

The local unit in the Russian Saint Vladimir's University of Kiev had among its members a fearless and outspoken priest's son from the district of Priluki, Nicholas
Ivanovich Mikhnovsky (1873-1924). After completing his
legal training in 1899 Mikhnovsky took up residence in
Kharkiv, where he opened a law office. His contribution
to the national movement was his courageous willingness
to adhere to a position which ran counter to the prevailing attitude of the time. He did not hesitate to attack both
the old Ukrainophiles, who were content to study antiquity and confine themselves to educational matters, and
the Ukrainian socialists, who, being under the influence
of their Russian comrades, were more concerned with international socialism and the coming all-Russian revolution which would embrace the whole Empire. Mikhnovsky
insisted that the Ukrainian movement cease being exclusively cultural, and embrace political objectives instead
of concerning itself solely with folk music and peasant art.

The young histrionic and anti-Semitic lawyer was soon
approached by a group of Ukrainian students in Kharkiv
who on February 11, 1900, had founded the Revolutionary
Ukrainian party (R.U.P). These novices organized their
own party because they were dissatisfied with the apolitical
nature of the national movement and did not wish to
collaborate with Russian revolutionary groups in Ukraine.
The group, which contained Marxian socialists as well as
pure national revolutionaries, was at a loss as to how to
draw up a program, and turned in desperation to Mikhnovsky. He had written a brochure entitled *Independent
Ukraine (Samostiina Ukraina)* which the students unhesi-
tatingly adopted as their program and had published in
Lviv in the same year. At the time neither the party nor
its platform was of much immediate significance, but

13

within fifteen years many of its members, including Volodimir Vinnichenko, Simon Petliura, and Volodimir Chekhovsky, were to participate in the attempt to create an independent Ukrainian state.

Mikhnovsky was profoundly influenced by the Boer movement, the liberation of Cuba from Spanish rule, and the desire of the Armenians for independence. He was convinced that the national question throughout the world was rapidly approaching a crisis which made its settlement inevitable. Ukraine as a dependent nation could not be isolated from this inexorable liberating development. Much of Mikhnovsky's argument was based on an analysis of the Pereiaslav Treaty which the Zaporozhian Cossack Hetman, Bohdan Khmelnitsky, concluded with the Muscovite Tsar Alexei Mikhailovich early in 1654. At that time Ukraine had something of the character of a vast no-man's land across which Poles, Muscovites, and Crimean Tartars moved with or without the consent of the Cossack inhabitants. Poland was the primary enemy of the Cossacks, and it was to the Muscovites that they ultimately turned for aid. This fateful decision was facilitated by their common Eastern Orthodox faith which at the same time tended to militate against any alliance with the Turkish Sultan or his vassal, the Khan of the Crimea, and also contributed to existing Ukrainian-Polish antagonism.

Mikhnovsky's demand for a reassertion of Ukraine's rights under the treaty rested on the assumption that the seventeenth century Cossack state was really sovereign when in actuality it was caught between three stronger political entities: Poland, Muscovy, and the Crimean Khanate. The Polish king had been able in 1649 and in 1651 to limit the maximum number of registered Cossacks and to compel the surplus to return to the land and labor for the Polonized gentry. In 1649 the Khan betrayed Khmelnitsky during a joint attack on Poland by concluding a separate peace. Thus the Cossack community was more in the nature of an uncertain autonomous political entity rather than a truly sovereign independent state.

14

The agreement with Tsar Alexei obligated him to protect the Ukrainian frontiers but also placed definite restrictions on the Cossacks in that it included recognition of the tsar's suzerainty and committed Ukraine not to engage in relations with the Sultan or the king of Poland without an ukase from His Tsarist Majesty.[6]

These obligations were supplemented by a statement of rights which the Cossacks believed future tsars would respect. These included the right to maintain separate legislative and administrative authorities as well as an army of sixty thousand men, the privilege of electing the Hetman, and retention of public offices and the administration of justice in Ukrainian hands. The Hetman and the Zaporozhian army were also permitted to receive ambassadors from all foreign countries except Turkey and Poland: "Ambassadors who are bearers of good messages will be received and sent on their way, and the Great Sovereign will be advised as to what business they came upon and with what manner of answer they were dismissed; but Ambassadors who shall have been sent on business which is detrimental to the interests of the Great Sovereign will not be dismissed." In violation of and despite these alleged rights Ukraine of the Left Bank became an integral part of the Russian Empire, and Mikhnovsky, writing two and one-half centuries after the conclusion of the treaty, could only restate them and claim that the Cossack state had done no more than enter into a confederation (*Staatenbund* or *spilka derzhav*) with Muscovy.[7]

[6] For English translations of the documents pertaining to the agreement see Professor George Vernadsky's *Bohdan, Hetman of Ukraine* (New Haven, 1941), pp. 131ff This biographical study contains an excellent account of the numerous shifts in the foreign policy of the Cossacks

[7] The exact nature of the relationship between Muscovy and Ukraine which was established under the Pereiaslav Treaty has been the subject of protracted disputes between Russian and Ukrainian historians One of the latter, Viacheslav Lipinsky, claimed that it was nothing more than a military alliance and a protectorate, while some Russian historians, such as Gennadi F. Karpov of the University of Kharkiv, insisted that it was an annexation resulting from the tsar's favorable reply to Khmelnitsky's petition (*chelobitye*). V. A. Miakotin contended that it was not a real treaty between equals and that Ukraine became a vassal-state of Muscovy. See his

Mikhnovsky claimed that Ukraine as the injured high contracting party could obtain redress only by insisting upon the fulfillment of the original provisions or by renouncing the treaty and severing relations with the violator. He advocated a struggle for the restoration of the lost rights and threatened that the Ukrainians would seize forcibly what was due them legally.[8] He indicted the Ukrainian intelligentsia for having betrayed its people and the national cause, and he initiated the slogan of a "single, united, indivisible, free and independent Ukraine from the Carpathians to the Caucasus." He reaffirmed the existence of the Ukrainian people despite their blindness, lack of resistance to duplicity, and the low state to which their culture had declined during the preceding two centuries.

Significantly, no mention of socialism was made in the brochure because Mikhnovsky was convinced that social liberation would naturally follow if precedence were given to the attainment of national independence by revolutionary means. His unwillingness to reverse this order soon prompted the socialists in the new Revolutionary Ukrainian party to conclude that it was a mistake to have adopted this "chauvinistic" brochure as a programmatic document. This dissatisfaction did not manifest itself within the party until 1903, but the gap which separated most of the youths from the Kharkiv lawyer was already evident in 1900 when the latter left the organization and established his own

"Pereiaslavski Dogovor" in *Sbornik Statei posviashchennykh Pavlu Nikolaevichu Miliukovu* (Prague, 1929), pp. 241ff. It is probably not incorrect to refer to the relationship as that of a protectorate of Muscovy over Ukraine.

[8] The second half of the seventeenth century saw Bohdan Khmelnitsky's successors to the Hetmanate dissatisfied with their status under the protectorate. New orientations and unsuccessful revolts were attempted in 1658 by Ivan Vyhovsky, who secretly placed himself under the protection of Poland, in 1660 by George Khmelnitsky, and in 1668 and 1671 by Ivan Briukhovetsky and Peter Doroshenko, who allied themselves with Turkey. In 1708-1709 Ivan Mazepa, although lacking the support of the peasantry because of his failure to champion its rights, cast his lot with Charles XII of Sweden and when defeated was compelled to seek refuge in Turkey together with his ally.

Ukrainian People's party (*Ukrainska Narodnia partiia*). Apparently the presence of so many socialists in the Revolutionary Ukrainian party had caused Mikhnovsky no small amount of discomfort.

His new party was, like the others, conspiratorial and was organized on a purely national basis demanding the separation of Ukraine from Russia in accordance with Mikhnovsky's conviction that "political independence is the primary condition of a nation's existence." It adopted a program which declared that all peoples were brothers of the Ukrainians except the Muscovites, Poles, Magyars, Rumanians, and Jews; these peoples were to be regarded as enemies so long as they continued to dominate Ukraine. Ukrainians were admonished by the party to employ their native tongue and were advised "not [to] select your wife from foreigners because your children will become your enemies; do not fraternize with the enemies of our people because you give them strength and courage."[9] Concern over the future political structure of Russia was regarded as a waste of energy because the championing of a Russian constitution would only lead to an exchange of chains rather than to a loosening of the bonds.

This small, weak party could offer little to the economically downtrodden, but the events of the 1905 Revolution compelled Mikhnovsky and his group to adopt an anticapitalist stand. They belatedly declared that an independent Ukraine could only be a socialist Ukraine and advocated the eight-hour working day as well as agrarian reform for the benefit of the landless peasants. Yet the continued dominance of the nationalist theme became ap-

[9] For the Ukrainian People's party see Panas Fedenko, *Ukrainski Hromadski Rukh u XX st.* (Poděbrady, ČSR., 1934), pp. 17f. Although Mikhnovsky did not die until 1924, his major contribution to the national movement was confined to the pre-1905 period. Following the revolution of that year he published a weekly, *Snip* (The Sheaf), in Kharkiv His life ended in suicide on May 3, 1924, probably as the result of a long period of melancholy brought on by his dissatisfaction with life under Soviet rule and the difficulties involved in becoming an émigré. Cf. the memorial written by Serhi Shemet and published in *Khliborobska Ukraina* (Vienna, 1925), v, pp. 3ff.

parent in the organization's 1907 congress when it recognized the need for the Ukrainian proletariat to struggle against capital but simultaneously expressed concern over the increasing competition which resulted from the influx of Russian workers into the area of the Left Bank, east of the Dnieper. The emulative and possibly hypocritical nature of its socialism was evident in its assertion that "the proletariat of the ruling nation and that of the subjugated nation are two different classes with dissimilar interests."

In contrast to Mikhnovsky's group, the Kiev committee of the Revolutionary Ukrainian party in 1903 adopted a program, later approved by the central committee, which was far more liberal, at least in its social and economic planks. At this early date it demanded the eight-hour working day, a program of social security, and the confiscation of large landholdings on the basis of the doctrine that only persons engaged in cultivation have a right to the land. Unlike the Ukrainian People's party, it believed that any effort to achieve national independence would be doomed to fail. As a result, it contented itself with a proposal for national-territorial autonomy which would permit the use of the Ukrainian language in schools, universities, courts, banks, and government offices as well as in books and publications.

The Revolutionary Ukrainian party developed its own underground press where it printed its illicit proclamations; brochures were published in East Galicia and Bukovina and were smuggled across the Austro-Russian frontier into Eastern Ukraine. The party's theoretical publication was *Haslo* (The Watchword) while its organ for revolutionary propaganda among the peasantry was *Selianin* (The Peasant). No periodical was designed especially for the industrial workers until the small Ukrainian Socialist party merged with the Revolutionary Ukrainian party in June of 1903 and utilized its organ, *Dobra Novina* (Good Tidings), to this end. This small separate socialist body had been founded in 1900 by Bohdan Iaroshevsky (1869-1914) and was composed largely of Ukrainians who were products of a Polish cultural milieu. The socialists had hoped to create national consciousness by developing in the masses an understanding of their class interests. However, the primacy of the Revolutionary Ukrainian party was illustrated by its absorption of the independent socialists although in January of 1904 the latter seceded only to wither away.

The Revolutionary Ukrainian party's strength began to decline in 1904 as a result of the development of a profound division among the membership. The cause for this schism was a disagreement over the national question which arose when some of the members, led by Marian Melenevsky, Victor Mazurenko, and Peter Kanivets, wished to become a part of the All-Russian Social Democratic party. This group emerged in 1904 and forced the issue at their party's December congress. It seceded and established the Ukrainian Social Democratic Union (*Spilka*) as an autonomous unit of the Russian Social Democratic Labor party. The secessionists, although Ukrainians, had come under the ideological influence of Lenin's newspaper, *Iskra* (The Spark), and many of them, while sitting in tsarist jails, had read *The Development of Capitalism in Russia* which Lenin had written under the pen-name of Ilin. They branded the majority of the Revolutionary Ukrainian party members, who did not follow them, as "bourgeois radicals." One of the secessionists, Dmitro Antonovich, the son of the prominent historian, regarded the national problem as "a non-existent question" and in January of 1905 wrote an article under that title in which he contended that the bourgeoisie had fabricated the national question in order to confuse and blind the proletariat.

Yet the men in the *Spilka* did not in any sense regard themselves as traitors to the national cause. Certainly Alexander Skoropis-Ioltukhovsky, in view of his later contributions to the Ukrainian state, could not be labeled as a renegade. He based his withdrawal from the Revolutionary Ukrainian party on the assumption that it was of primary importance to develop political and social consciousness among his people; to him it was inconceivable that they could be anything but Ukrainian.[10] Whatever rationalization the schismatics utilized, there could be no escaping the fact that the result of their action was short of being disastrous. The party, weak as it was to commence with, was further debilitated by this internal division which made it impossible for the Ukrainians to play any significant collective role in the critical period of the 1905 Revolution.

The split in the party over the national question was not in itself the cause of the insignificance of the Ukrainian political movement at that time. More important was the fact that the Revolutionary Ukrainian party was not a real political party in that it lacked a popular basis, a fully developed program, and a leadership trained in the theory underlying the organization. It was composed of a few small groups which contained mostly students and socialistically inclined intellectuals. This was not a proletarian party and could not become one so long as it insisted that membership was not open to non-Ukrainian workers.[11] Here was a dilemma: if an attempt were made to appeal to the Russified proletariat the party could lose much if not all of its national character; yet if it did not make such an attempt it would continue to be a negligible factor in the urban revolutionary milieu in Ukraine. This, together with the organization of the *Spilka* and the events of 1905, caused the Revolutionary Ukrainian party at its congress in December of that year to rename itself as the Ukrainian Social Democratic Labor party. The nationalism which distinguished it from the *Spilka* demanded no more than autonomy for Ukraine. The renaming of the party was undoubtedly indicative of the tenor of the time, but it did not enable the membership to rise above the three thousand

10 Fedenko, *op.cit.*, p. 32. The Revolutionary Ukrainian party was also weakened somewhat by a personal rivalry which arose between Volodimir Vinnichenko and Nicholas Porsh; the former advocated immediate and direct action while the latter favored detailed preparation.

11 Nicholas Halahan, *Z Moikh Spominiv* (Lviv, 1930), I, pp. 125ff.

mark by March of 1907 when the opportunity for substantial growth was rapidly drawing to a close.

In addition to the two socialist groups and the Ukrainian People's party, there was an organization of moderates which emerged in the spring of 1904 among the Kiev Ukrainians who prior to that time had formed a non-partisan and purely cultural body. Some of the older participants, including Volodimir Naumenko, the editor of *Kievskaia Starina*, were opposed to the formation of a party on the grounds that it would necessitate formulation of political, economic, and social objectives. Others, such as Boris Hrinchenko, Serhi Efremov, and Dr. Modest Levitsky, felt compelled to extend their range of activity beyond the cultural sphere and proceeded to organize the Ukrainian Democratic party, which in 1917 played an important role under the Socialist-Federalist label. The older and more reserved members entered the new organization, but an inevitable conflict soon occurred over the party's program.

A small majority of the Democrats adopted a platform which criticized centralism and which blamed autocracy for Russia's unfortunate condition and the interruption of the normal development of the various peoples in the country. It called for an end to political absolutism and the introduction of parliamentary government together with popular participation in public affairs on the basis of general, direct, equal, and secret suffrage and proportional representation. It advocated freedom of the individual person, the right of free speech, the separation of church and state, and the freedom to strike and assemble. Besides favoring the abolition of social distinctions it asked for the introduction of the language of the people in the schools and courts and in all phases of public administration. National-territorial autonomy was to be established in Ukraine and elsewhere and local parliaments were to enact the eight-hour working day and provide state pensions for aged and disabled persons. Public revenue was to be obtained from a progressive income tax. The Ukrainian parliament was also to establish a land norm by fixing the absolute minimum which a peasant required, and agrarian reform was then to be undertaken on that basis. Equal cultural, political, and economic rights were to be accorded to the Russians, Poles, and Jews in Ukraine.[12]

The older members could not accept this program in its entirety. The resultant distrust caused the authors and supporters of this document to secede early in 1905 and organize their own Radical party despite efforts made by moderates like Eugene Chikalenko to dissuade them. The most prominent leader of the new party, Boris Hrinchenko, was now able to enjoy the unchallenged position of primacy which had been denied him in the Democratic party. The new group's platform differed from that of the Democrats only in its more detailed nature and in its emphasis on social and economic issues. It declared flatly that the workers were crushed under capitalism and that only a socialist order could best serve the interests of the people; public ownership was demanded for mineral wealth, factories, electric utilities, railways, waters, and forests. Opposing all exploitation, whether by individual groups or by the state, the party advocated the eight-hour working day for adults and also stood in opposition to the employment of minors under sixteen years of age. Those who were younger than eighteen were to be allowed to work a six-hour day. Night employment was to be restricted to adult males and permitted only when technological circumstances made it necessary, and then on the condition of payment of a higher wage. Every worker employed continuously in one establishment for the period of a year was to receive an annual vacation of two weeks with pay. Pregnant women were to be granted leave with pay for a period of ten weeks. An extensive program of health insurance and workmen's compensation was also advocated. Large landholdings were to be sold under compulsion and redistributed. The civil liberties plank included the right of an individual to reside in any place of

[12] For the program and an excellent treatment of the Democratic party see Eugene Chikalenko, *Spohadi* (Lviv, 1926), III, pp. 9ff.

22

his choosing and also provided for the abolition of corporal and capital punishment and of life imprisonment.

With reference to the national question, the Radicals favored federalism with the component parts of the union bound by a parliament composed of salaried members elected by all persons over twenty-one on the basis of proportional representation. The division of powers was to allow the federal government to control foreign relations, finances for federal matters, external trade and tariffs, the armed forces, and questions of war and peace. The Russian army was to be reorganized and military service was to be performed on one's native territory; the period of such service was to be reduced gradually so that a people's militia could eventually replace the standing army. All residual powers were to be exercised by the territorial legislature (narodnia rada) which would be elected on the basis of general suffrage. The police were to be subordinated to organs of local government, churches were to be supported exclusively by their communicants, and primary education was to be free, compulsory, and secular, and Ukrainian was to be the language employed in government offices and in schools.[18]

The Radicals, despite their small membership, carried out an ambitious program of publication which, like their platform, was bold and unswerving. Numerous pamphlets were printed in Lviv during 1905 and smuggled across the Austro-Russian frontier for distribution in Eastern Ukraine. One of the brochures, written by S. Iaroshenko under the title How Can the Working People Free Themselves from Poverty? dealt with the disparity in income and general economic well-being by dividing the population into proletarians and capitalists. In a very simplified exposition of Marxist dogma, replete with the theory of surplus value, the author claimed that socialism would prevail but only after a struggle marked with blood and tears.

---

[18] The party's program was published in pamphlet form in Lviv in 1905 under the title of *Platforma Ukrainskoi Radikalnoi partii*; this was due largely to the efforts of Fedir Matushevsky.

To him socialism meant that there would be neither lord nor peasant, neither rich nor poor, neither master nor servant. All men would be free and equal, private ownership and payment of interest would be abolished, and crime and deception would automatically disappear.

Other Radical pamphlets indicted tsarism, complaining that the tsar and his family received sixteen million rubles annually while the bureaucracy obtained more than six times that amount. The contention was advanced that it was impossible to get the tsar's ear and as proof the bloodshed of January 9, 1905, was cited; in that instance Father Gapon had led a peaceful Sunday procession of Saint Petersburg workers into a death trap. The fact that only ministers, functionaries, and noblemen could obtain audiences demonstrated the need for representative government. The belief that the tsar was kind and would give the peasants land was dismissed as an old wives' tale. Strikes were advocated against unfair landowners in place of the useless burning of buildings.[14]

The Russo-Japanese War was attacked in other Radical publications on the grounds that Russia had no right to Chinese and Korean territory since it was not part of the "fatherland." The tsar, princes, landowners, industrialists, contractors, and merchants were said to benefit from the war while the peasant paid with his life. Japan's victories were attributed to her high literacy rate and to alleged freedom of speech and religion as well as equality before the law. It was denied that this was a war for the Orthodox faith because thousands of Japanese had already become converts. The Ukrainian Radicals advised the readers of their tracts to fight autocracy rather than the Japanese, and one wag commented that in the event of Russian acquisition of Manchuria the tsar could be titled as the Sovereign of Great, Little, White and Yellow Russia.

The over-riding nature of the anti-autocratic attitude of the Radicals was evident in their republication of Mi-

[14] Cf. M Dolenko, *Khto Narodovi Vorokh*; S. Iaroshenko, *Iak Liude Prav Sobi Dobuvaiut*; and Leonid Iavorenko, *Chomu u Nas Dosi Nema Dobroho Ladu?* all published in Lviv during 1905.

chael Drahomaniv's pamphlet on the Swiss federal union in which the Ukrainian exile expressed admiration for the elected officialdom of that country. The Radicals also published in translation Count Leo Tolstoy's open letter to Nicholas II in which the noted author addressed the tsar as "Dear Brother." Tolstoy, who did not wish to die without first expressing his views on Nicholas' regime, warned the tsar that autocracy was on its way out and that he should not be deceived by his entourage since police-managed demonstrations did not indicate that the people loved him. He criticized Nicholas for calling the Hague Conference and then simultaneously increasing his army for the illegal plundering of China. Tolstoy argued that the people had to be freed from economic servitude by means of state-ownership of all land, with the peasant being allowed to use as much as he could cultivate. The Ukrainian Radical party leaders accepted Tolstoy's desiderata but could not assume, as he did, that the tsar was listening to unwise advisers; the Radicals, in an addendum to the letter, commented that Nicholas was neither free nor wise nor good.

While the Radicals, the Democratic party, the Revolutionary Ukrainian party, the Social Democratic *Spilka*, and the Ukrainian People's party each pursued independent policies and undertook activities without reference to any common plan, the events of 1905 appeared to be cracking the foundation stones upon which the structure of Russia's autocratic government rested. The agrarian problem had been becoming more acute in Ukraine and the lack of land, accompanied by an increasing population, had compelled many peasants to embrace urban life and to be subjected to its denationalizing influence. During the twelve years preceding 1907 more than 600,000 Ukrainians had settled in Siberia. As early as 1902 peasant risings had occurred in Kharkiv and Poltava provinces, and in 1905 more serious agrarian disturbances broke out in Chernihiv and Katerinoslav provinces as well.[15]

The prevailing unrest also made itself felt among the

[15] See N. Mirza-Avakiants, *Selianski Rozrukhi na Ukraini, 1905-1907* (Kharkiv, 1925).

sailors of the Black Sea fleet, many of whom were Ukrainians. In June of 1905 a mutiny broke out aboard the Battleship *Potemkin* under the leadership of Panas (Athanasius) N. Matiushenko, a Ukrainian who had joined the Russian Social Democratic Labor party in 1903. The mutiny resulted from mistreatment which the men suffered under the officers and was precipitated by the bad meat which the crew members found in their *borshch*.[16] When the Admiralty sent a squadron of vessels after the *Potemkin*, the crew took the ship to Constanta in Rumania where it issued a proclamation "to the whole civilized world." Claiming to be fighting for "freedom and a better life," the mutineers denounced autocracy and demanded an end to the blood-letting in the Far East and convocation of a constituent assembly elected on the basis of general, direct, equal, and secret suffrage.[17] The sailors also issued a declaration to all European governments guaranteeing the inviolability of all foreign vessels in the Black Sea.

After failing to replenish the ship's supply of coal and provisions in Rumania, the crew sailed to the Russian port of Feodosiia in a vain effort to obtain stores. Finally after consulting with the Rumanian Social Democrat, Christian Rakovsky, the mutineers surrendered the vessel in that country. Matiushenko fled to Switzerland and later to Paris, where he joined the anarcho-syndicalist movement; when he returned to Ukraine in 1907 he was promptly hanged. One of his aides in the mutiny was Alexander Kovalenko, a member of the Revolutionary Ukrainian party, who also fled to France but remained in exile.

This unorganized and poorly led mutiny did not present the tsarist government with a serious threat. Such a situation developed only in September with the occurrence of numerous separate strikes which were economic in nature. The strikes commenced on a large scale in Moscow during the latter half of the month and included printers, tobacco

[16] A. P. Platonov, *Vosstanie Chernomorskogo Flota v 1905 godu* (Leningrad, 1925), pp. 44ff.
[17] *Ibid.*, pp. 108ff.

workers, trolley workers, and bakers. On September 29, in Moscow alone approximately fifteen thousand workers were on strike, and the wave of labor disturbances quickly spread to Saint Petersburg. Soon it swept up hundreds of thousands of the Empire's railroad workers and halted traffic on more than 26,000 miles of trackage. The employees in numerous industrial enterprises followed suit. The government was confronted with a general strike which had become political in character.[18] The demand for constitutional government was raised and was made effective by the totality of the strike which was participated in by more than one and one-half million workers. The provinces were cut off from the large cities, no one received mail or telegrams, and telephone service became sporadic.

In the face of such formidable opposition the government was helpless. Nicholas II, who less than a year before had termed the demand for a constitution as "an unthinkable illusion," was compelled to issue the Manifesto of October 17. In this document the tsar committed his government to fulfill three obligations. The first of these was the granting to the population of immutable fundamentals of civil liberty on the basis of the inviolability of the person and freedom of conscience, speech and press, assembly, and union. The second obliged the government not to postpone the scheduled elections to the Imperial Duma and to extend the suffrage, as soon as circumstances would permit, to those classes of the population which were deprived of the right to vote.[19] The third provision pledged the government to establish as a fundamental law the right of

18 See A Shestakov, "Vseobshchaia Oktiabrskaia Stachka 1905 goda," *1905*, ed. by M. N. Pokrovsky (Moscow, 1925), II, pp. 264ff.

19 On August 6, 1905, a manifesto had been issued providing for a consultative duma to be elected by the landowners, bourgeoisie, and the wealthier peasants. The regime had a special interest in the last-named group and was willing to allow it to participate in the government in the hope that it would develop into a strong source of support for the autocracy. This projected body, usually referred to as the Bulygin Duma (after the then minister of the interior, Alexander G. Bulygin) could render decisions on issues, but these would have had to be approved by the State Council before they could be submitted to the tsar.

the Duma to exercise an absolute veto over all legislation and to give that body an opportunity to participate in the examination of the legality of acts committed by authorities appointed by the emperor. Thus the autocrat, after prayer and meditation, legally shed the mantle of autocracy.

The Ukrainian nationalists accepted at face value the provision regarding freedom of the press and immediately set about planning the establishment of a daily newspaper to be published in Kiev. This was not to be the first Ukrainian daily; that distinction had already been accorded to *Dilo*, which had been published in Lviv as a daily since 1888. This Galician newspaper had been founded in 1880 and was issued as a semi-weekly for three years and was then published three times per week. The Kiev journalistic venture was to be the second Ukrainian daily and the first of its kind in Eastern or Russian Ukraine. The possibility of publishing such a newspaper on a legal basis and without interruption made it necessary to have adequate financial support. This was beyond the means of the Radical party and soon its leader, Boris Hrinchenko, expressed an interest in reuniting his group with the Ukrainian Democratic party. This was accomplished late in 1905 despite Hrinchenko's vain effort to obtain autonomous status and carry on an independent program of publication at the expense of the Democrats. The new party took the name of Democratic-Radical and adopted a program which was substantially that of the Radicals.

The reunion facilitated the publication of the new daily which was called *Hromadska Dumka* (Civic Thought) and which made its first appearance on the streets of Kiev late in 1905. The debut had been preceded by intense activity. The first application to publish such a newspaper was denied by the office of the provincial governor, and it was only when one of the wealthy publishers, Volodimir Leontovich, utilized his influence that permission was finally obtained. According to the original prospectus the newspaper was to defend the interests of the working class, support the demands of the peasantry for land, and prevent

28

the exploitation of hired workers. It was to be primarily for popular consumption while a monthly, *Nova Hromada* (The New Community), was to meet the needs of the Ukrainian intelligentsia.[20]

Neither of these enterprises could be self-supporting. Five thousand copies of the first issue of the newspaper were printed although there were only a thousand paid subscribers. The costs for the first year of publication were estimated at fifty thousand rubles while the annual subscription rate was fixed at four rubles. Other difficulties arose to plague the journalists and the three wealthy publishers. Shortly before the debut of the newspaper one of the most talented writers, Serhi Efremov, was arrested by the police, and when the great day finally arrived the first issue of *Hromadska Dumka* was confiscated by the authorities. However, the use of discretion on the part of the journalists enabled subsequent issues to be mailed to subscribers and purchased at kiosks. One of the fixed operating costs was a regular monthly expenditure of fifty rubles made for the purpose of ensuring a friendly attitude on the part of the censor, Sidorov; at Christmas and Easter this stipend was supplemented by a bonus of one hundred rubles.

The cost of maintaining the newspaper could not be met from subscription receipts. In August of 1906, after eight months of publication, there were only four thousand regular subscribers and only five hundred of these had paid for an entire year. In short, the staff realized that the first Ukrainian daily in Kiev was not having a tenth of its expected success.[21] Its existence was made possible by the generosity of three Ukrainian philanthropists: Volodimir M. Leontovich, Eugene Chikalenko, and Vasil F. Simirenko. The last-named of these, although the son of a serf, had acquired a fortune of more than ten million rubles in the sugar-refining industry and, being childless, could afford to defray half of the deficit of *Hromadska Dumka*.

[20] For an excellent treatment of Ukrainian journalism during 1906 see Chikalenko, *op cit.*, III, pp. 8off.
[21] *Ibid.*, III, p. 106.

He also met the annual deficit of *Kievskaia Starina* with unfailing regularity. Leontovich and Chikalenko were landowners but differed considerably in their social outlook.

Chikalenko regarded agrarian reform as inevitable and pursued an enlightened policy of selling immense amounts of land to his peasants on reasonable terms. He subsidized the Ukrainian belles-lettres which were published in *Kievskaia Starina* and promoted the career of the young socialist writer, Volodimir Vinnichenko. He gave the Revolutionary Ukrainian party the sum of one thousand rubles in order to enable it to publish its peasant organ *(Selianin)* outside of Russia. Prior to the 1905 Revolution, Ukrainian intellectuals and socialist students were able to gather in the Chikalenko parlor and meet Galicians who were visiting Kiev. Chikalenko, unlike most landowners, was not opposed to the socialists; he probably attributed their attitudes to youthful enthusiasm and, in any event, was especially pleased with their not having joined the Russian socialist parties.

The three philanthropists were able to solve the newspaper's financial problems, but other difficulties arose to plague the new enterprise. One of the first of these was the conflict among staff members over the orthography to be employed; honest differences of opinion were possible because of the novel character and lack of complete development of literary Ukrainian. Provincial barriers and dialectical differences had not as yet been liquidated, and the inhabitants of the province of Poltava were not yet prepared to accept words which were peculiar to the people of the Kiev province. Subscribers complained that the Galician language was being used and that "grammatical chaos" prevailed in the newspaper. Actually there was Galician linguistic influence; it resulted from the fact that Ukrainian literature had been developing rapidly under Austrian rule, and intellectuals in Eastern Ukraine, who read the works of Markian Shashkevich, Ivan Franko, and Vasil Stefanik, were unconsciously adopting Galician modes of expression. Hrushevsky, working in Galicia, finally transferred the publication of the *Literary and Scientific Herald* to Kiev late in 1906 because of his fear that two Ukrainian literatures and cultures would develop unless cultural activities were centralized. Chikalenko later concluded that the most important reason for the limited success of the newspaper was the inability of many readers to become accustomed to having abstract notions described in the language of the people; this made the journalistic language seem strange and incomprehensible at the time.[22]

In addition to the problems of diction and orthography there was, on occasion, lack of literary materials because of the relatively small number of writers. The public authorities were also not sympathetic with the newspaper because of the radical views which were often expressed on its pages. Many priests and teachers concurred with the authorities, and most of those who did not were afraid to subscribe or write. Ironically, the workers and peasants to whom the newspaper was directed constituted but a small portion of the total circulation. Soon the editorial policies caused Volodimir Leontovich to accuse Hrinchenko and others of inciting peasants to seize the land without compensation for the owners. This schism persisted until August 18, 1906, when the police raided the offices and found "incriminating" papers, including copies of the Viborg Manifesto which some of the members of the First Duma had signed in protest over the dissolution of that assembly.

The newspaper was closed and forbidden to reopen under the same name. This presented no particular difficulty because originally when the publishers had been seeking to obtain permission to issue the newspaper they had filed several applications. Hrinchenko had also submitted an application late in 1905 for publication of a newspaper

[22] *Ibid.*, III, p. 108. The linguistic problem caused Boris Hrinchenko, one of the leading staff members, to write a booklet entitled *By the Difficult Pathway* (*Tiazhkim Shliakhom*) published in Kiev in 1907. In it he recounted the criticisms of subscribers and appealed for patience and broadmindedness.

31

to be called *Rada*. His application was acted upon favorably, but the name was not used at the time because Leontovich had already succeeded in securing the right to publish *Hromadska Dumka*. Thus by mid-September the Ukrainian daily was able to resume publication as the *Rada*. But the raid had caused some of the subscribers to be arrested and the circulation was reduced to a new low of 1,500.

This decline placed an added burden on the philanthropists at a time when doubts were arising in their minds regarding the utility of the newspaper. Simirenko, who was seventy years old, was not aware of the schism which had rent the organization. He could contribute no more than five thousand rubles for the 1907 budget; the previous year had been unsatisfactory for him and he could not bear to draw on his capital if the rate of interest was not adequate. Leontovich reduced his contribution because of his feud with Hrinchenko over editorial policy on the agrarian question. The newspaper was faced with a rising deficit and a reduced income. Chikalenko altruistically sold 540 acres of his land in the Tiraspil region to German colonists and in that way raised ten thousand rubles. Additional income was obtained by increasing the annual rate of subscription from four rubles to six. At the time Hrushevsky consoled the editors by saying that *Dilo* in Lviv had a higher rate and was the most expensive newspaper in the world. Additional subscribers were found, and the total circulation rose to 2,000. Administration was improved and a more stringent control over the content of the newspaper was exercised by the publishers in order to prevent conflict with the staff.

The first Ukrainian daily in Kiev had temporarily weathered the storm, but the other more modest publishing ventures of the period had a less fortunate fate. A Ukrainian weekly, *Khliborob* (The Agriculturalist), had appeared in Lubni in November of 1905 and was edited by Volodimir Shemet and his two brothers, Serhi and Nicholas. It soon encountered difficulties; the fourth issue was confiscated, and the fifth was the last to appear. In Poltava during December 1905 the first and last issue of a supposed weekly, *Ridni Krai* (Native Land), was published. In Odessa Dr. Ivan Lutsenko was also able to publish only one issue of his *Narodnia Sprava* (The People's Cause). Any Ukrainian publication of this period was faced with a short life expectancy. A very profuse flowering had occurred in Ukrainian journalism during 1906, but, in the opinion of Hrinchenko, it bore little fruit.[23]

This opinion was arrived at too quickly following the event; it failed to take into account the necessity of passing through an embryonic period. It was only in 1905 that the Imperial Russian Academy of Sciences adopted a report, prepared by one of its commissions at the request of the government, in which it recognized the existence of a separate Ukrainian language. Two Russian philologists, Fedor E. Korsh and Alexei A. Shakhmatov, prepared the report regarding the "lifting of constraint on the Little Russian word" and were instrumental in obtaining its adoption. They concluded that:

"The commission has a basis for declaring that the circulation of books among the Little Russian [Ukrainian] population written in its native tongue would be much more successful than is the case with books written in Great Russian. For this there is much evidence and especially the fact of widespread circulation in Little Russia [Ukraine] of books published in Galicia despite restrictive measures which carry with them the threat of a jail sentence for the person found to be possessing the works of Shevchenko or Kotliarevsky in Lviv editions."

The philologists further observed that "the contemporary Great Russian language spoken in Moscow, Riazan, Iaroslavl, Arkhangelsk, and Novgorod cannot be termed

---

[23] Hrinchenko, who died in 1910, could not participate in the effort to establish a Ukrainian state at the time of the Russian Revolution. Yet his popular writings on Ukrainian history, folklore, and education and his poetry were of tremendous importance in furthering the development of the language. An excellent Ukrainian-Russian dictionary was published in 1909 under his editorship.

'conjoint-Russian' [*obshcherusski*] in contrast with the Little Russian language of Poltava, Kiev, and Lviv." They found it impossible to justify the existing prohibitions since neither the Ukrainian people nor its intelligentsia in any way threatened the unity of Russia. Indeed, positive harm resulted in that the peasant population was prevented from reading educational matter because of its inadequate knowledge of Russian. Inevitably the scholars recommended that the Ukrainians have the same right as the Russians to employ the native tongue in public speech and print.[24]

The tsarist government on March 24, 1906, lifted the restrictions of the preceding four decades and in that way provided an impetus for the Ukrainian journalism of the period. Encouraged by the new freedom, the publishers of *Kievskaia Starina* renamed their historical monthly *Ukraina*. During 1907 most of the articles published in the journal were written in Ukrainian and many current books were reviewed in the same language. Some of these reviews were written by Simon Petliura, who also prepared articles on literary subjects, on life in Austrian Ukraine, and on current events.

While some Ukrainians wrote, others engaged in political action and sought seats in the First Imperial Duma. The Revolutionary Ukrainian party refused to participate in the Russian parliament, and the Hrinchenko group in the Democratic-Radical party also wished to boycott the parliament because the suffrage was not general, equal, and direct.[25] However, the majority of the Democratic-Radicals desired to support candidates in the electoral contests.

[24] For lengthy excerpts from the commission's report see Lototsky, *op cit.*, ii, pp. 365ff. Cf. A. Chigirin, *Ukrainski Vopros* (Paris, 1937), pp. 19f.

[25] In 1905 Hrinchenko's Radical party published a pamphlet by S Iaroshenko entitled *How the Tsar Deceives the People*. The pamphleteer denied the possibility that Russia's heterogeneous masses could be ruled by an autocrat He was unable to equate the granting of the Duma with the former policies of the tsarist regime and doubted that the law could be regarded as a constitution. Iaroshenko claimed that a true parliament would have exclusive legislative power including the right to remove ministers and control of the purse-strings; he also regarded as anomalous the oath in support of autocracy which deputies would have to take.

Recognizing their weakness and not desiring to reveal it publicly, they decided to cooperate with progressive Russian and Jewish parties in electing deputies. Of the forty-four deputies of Ukrainian origin in the First Duma, only one, the Democratic-Radical Volodimir Shemet, was elected by a Ukrainian party; the others were sponsored by Russian parties. In Kiev the Democratic-Radicals united with the Constitutional Democrats and elected Baron Fedor Shteingel, who considered himself a Ukrainian although he did not speak the language.

The deputies were, for the most part, peasants who were not accustomed to the political life of the capital. Many of them regarded their salaries as an economic windfall and consequently lived in very modest quarters and ate herring in order to save as much as possible for the purchase of additional land. The small number of intellectuals among the Ukrainian delegation in the Duma made it necessary for some of the Ukrainian residents of Saint Petersburg to constitute an amateur legislative counseling and reference service. Alexander Lototsky and Peter Stebnitsky, employees of the Russian Government, were largely responsible for preparing drafts of bills which it was hoped the deputies would be able to introduce. The Duma was in existence for seventy-two days and met only thirty-eight times during that brief period. This doomed the Ukrainians to play an ineffectual although active role.

Understandably, the Ukrainian as well as the other deputies concerned themselves primarily with the agrarian question. Some of the Ukrainian peasant deputies did not hesitate to declare that their constituents required land as a child needs its mother's breast and that land was a gift from God to be held by those who cultivate it. Some of the leaders of the Ukrainian faction inserted the nationalist theme into the debates by insisting that the problem be dealt with on an autonomous basis. Volodimir Shemet on June 5, 1906, in addressing the Duma stressed his Ukrainian nationality and argued that "national particularisms" should be recognized. He pointed out that the Ukrainian people expected their deputies in the Duma to obtain not only land but freedom as well. Shemet revealed his national sentiments in the following terms: "In deciding such an important social question as the agrarian problem it is necessary to bear in mind that Ukraine is not only a part of a state but is a nation and is to a much greater degree a nation than a part of a state. The Ukrainian people will regard its demands as satisfied only when they will have the opportunity to determine their fate independently."[26] The leader of the Ukrainian faction, Elias Shrah, took a similar stand and went so far as to attribute anti-Jewish pogroms to political centralism on the grounds that the perpetrators were being protected by the authorities of the central government.

The Ukrainian deputies also published a weekly journal in Russian, *The Ukrainian Herald (Ukrainski Vestnik)*, but its life was as brief as that of the Duma and was confined to fourteen issues. Another extra-cameral activity was the faction's participation in the Union of Autonomists, which was composed of more than one hundred deputies representing the national minorities in the Empire. The Union, of which Elias Shrah was vice president, advocated equal rights for all nationalities, the decentralization of administration on a purely territorial or national-territorial basis, and the use of local languages in courts, schools, and political institutions. Yet it did not hesitate to reaffirm the indivisibility of the Russian State as a united whole.[27]

While the Ukrainian faction desired autonomy, Paul Chizhevsky, one of its members from the province of Poltava, realized that the agrarian problem was so urgent as to make impossible any postponement of it pending the reorganization of the state on an autonomous basis. This

[26] *Gosudarstvenaia Duma, Stenograficheskie Otchety, 1906 god, sessiia pervaia* (St Petersburg, 1906), II, pp. 994f. For a good general account of the Ukrainian hopes and frustrations of 1906 see Dmitro Doroshenko, "Ukraina v 1906 rotsi," *Ukraina*, I, Part Two (January, 1907)

[27] See Ali M. B. Topchibashi's article on the Union in *Spohadi* (Warsaw, 1932), pp. 133ff. (volume eight in the publications series of the Ukrainian Scientific Institute). Cf. Lototsky, *op.cit.*, III, pp. 33f.

was a recognition of the fact that the national question was of secondary importance and, accordingly, the Ukrainian deputies devoted most of their time to protesting arbitrary arrests and repressive measures which officials were taking against the peasantry. Eugene Sholp, from the Kiev province, proposed the abolition of the gendarmerie, which he regarded as antithetical to liberty. The deputies were profoundly aware of the importance of the Duma as a representative organ and as Russia's sole link with constitutionalism.

One of the most prominent figures in the struggle for constitutional and parliamentary government in Russia was Professor Maxim Kovalevsky (1851-1916), who, although not regarding himself as a Ukrainian, represented the Kharkiv province in the Duma. This noted historian and sociologist lived in Western Europe prior to the 1905 Revolution but returned to Russia in order to participate in the constitutional experiment. In several brilliant addresses he pleaded for the political responsibility of ministers and referred to the English model of parliamentary government with an apolitical titular executive. He contended that it was difficult for monarchy to exist in the twentieth century unless the king's ministers were politically responsible. This, he argued, would make the opposition party His Majesty's as in England rather than a group acting in opposition to the king. Thus monarchy, by adapting itself to a changed environment, could survive and make a significant contribution to modern government.

Kovalevsky's experience as a teacher and scholar in exile had enabled him to acquire considerable knowledge of comparative government. He had read Dicey on the English constitution and was especially impressed with the right of assembly as practiced in England and the United States; he cited to the Duma the instance of a pacifist demonstration which was held in Trafalgar Square during the Boer War under the protection of the police. Aware of the incompatibility between parliamentary government and a strong second chamber, Kovalevsky opposed the use of the Russian State Council in such a capacity. He also called on the Russian Government to protect all its subjects and prevent pogroms against the Jews. Such outspokenness earned for him the reputation of political unreliability and caused the government to confine him to the capital.[28]

The activities of Professor Kovalevsky and the other courageous deputies were suddenly terminated when the irked autocrat issued a manifesto on July 8, dissolving the Duma because its members had allegedly intervened in matters which did not concern them when they "investigated the activities of local authorities designated by Us." This, the tsar contended, caused the peasants to become agitated and engage in looting. In the manner of an annoyed parent the "Emperor and Autocrat of all Russia" admonished:

"Let Our subjects understand that it is only through peace and order that lasting improvements in the standard of living can be achieved. Let it be understood that We do not permit any insubordination or illegality and will with all of the force of the state cause all law-breakers to submit to Our Tsarist will. We call upon all well-intentioned Russian persons to unite in support of legal authority and the restoration of peace in Our dear Fatherland. . . .

"With firm faith in God's mercy and in the intelligence of the Russian people We shall await from the new composition of the Imperial Duma confirmation of Our expectations."

In response, almost two hundred of the members of the First Duma, under the leadership of the Constitutional Democrats, went across the Finnish frontier to Viborg and issued a manifesto calling on the people of Russia to cease paying taxes and to refuse to perform military service. This courageous but futile act did not receive any popular support, and the signers, including many Ukrainians, were prosecuted and deprived of their electoral rights.

The Second Duma met on February 20, 1907, and contained forty-seven Ukrainian deputies although none of

[28] For Kovalevsky's main addresses see *Gosudarstvenaia Duma, op.cit.,* I, pp. 158ff., pp. 172ff., and II, pp. 1458ff.

them had been a candidate of any of the Ukrainian parties. The separate faction which they organized early in March did not have its own platform on social and economic issues since it was an extra-party organization concerned solely with the national question. When the Ukrainians finally concluded that none of the existing Russian parties stood for national autonomy, they established their own parliamentary organization and advocated old-age pensions, workmen's compensation, and other social and economic measures. The faction published its own organ, *Ridna Sprava—Dumski Visti* (Our Cause—Duma News), which contained articles and texts of important addresses delivered in the chamber. Here as in the First Duma the Ukrainian membership was largely peasant and concerned itself primarily with the agrarian question.

During March the Ukrainian peasant deputies attacked the administration of famine and unemployment relief, and the Reverend Anthony Hrinevich from the province of Podolia proposed that a special supervisory commission be established. Vasil H. Sakhno, representing the Kiev province, addressed the Duma on April 2, and complained of landlessness, attributing to it the unrest and tension which pervaded the countryside. He criticized the priests who told the peasant to seek the kingdom of heaven rather than land and cited the instruction, in Leviticus 25:23, which the Lord gave to Moses: "The land shall not be sold for ever: for the land is mine; for ye are strangers and sojourners with me." For this he was applauded only by the left wing in the chamber. On April 12, Proctor S. Moroz from the Podolia province singled out the landowning clergy for attack and quoted Christ (from Matthew 7:7 and Luke 11:9): "Ask, and it shall be given you; seek, and ye shall find; knock, and it shall be opened unto you." He asked if the door would not have to be broken down and the request fulfilled by seizure and appealed to the landed interests to give up the land voluntarily and make freedom possible.[29]

[29] For these addresses see *Vtoraia Gosudarstvenaia Duma, stenograficheskie otchety* (St. Petersburg, 1907), I, cols. 322ff., 1482ff., 1954f.

Later in the session when an opportunity occurred to deal with other matters the Ukrainians pressed their demand for educational facilities. On May 15, Efim A. Saiko, representing the Poltava province, protested a report of the education minister to the Duma in which no mention was made of the Ukrainian nation. He informed the Duma that the Ukrainians had had their own schools till the end of the eighteenth century and had been able to export clergymen and teachers to Muscovy. The enlightened peasant deputy complained of political centralism and claimed that the regime collected 520 million rubles annually in taxes from Ukraine but spent only 280 million there. He cited the Ukrainian literacy rate of thirteen per cent and compared it with that of the Russians, which he placed at thirty-six per cent. Saiko then demanded a free national Ukrainian school system with the native language as the medium of instruction and Russian as one of the subjects in the curriculum, the preparation of the necessary textbooks, the organization of an adequate teacher training program to meet immediate and long-range needs, and the establishment of chairs in Ukrainian language, history, ethnography, and literature in the Russian universities of Kiev, Kharkiv, and Odessa.[80]

While these demands were being made, the government decided to dissolve the Duma and the tsar accordingly issued an order of dissolution on June 3. The pretext for the dissolution was the alleged implication of some of the Social Democratic deputies in subversive activities. The tsar referred to the composition of the Duma as "unsatisfactory" and declared that his hopes regarding it had not been justified. In order to prevent a recurrence of this legislative pattern in the Third Duma the tsar indicated that the electoral law would be changed and in doing so reaffirmed his exclusive right to modify it in the following

[80] *Ibid.*, cols. 542ff. Saiko was supported by Vasil Khvist from the province of Chernihiv who argued that education was as vital a matter as the solution of the agrarian problem. He contended that it was the general lack of education which enabled Stolypin to declare to the Duma that the ministers were the state.

terms: "Only the Authority which granted the initial electoral law, the historic Authority of the Russian Tsar, enjoys the right to change that and substitute a new act. The
Tsar's Authority over Our people has been committed to
Us by the Lord. We shall answer for the fate of the Russian
State before His Throne." The unconstitutional restric-
tion of the suffrage which occurred in 1907 decreased the
size of the peasant vote and thus reduced the Ukrainian
representation in the Third Duma to an inconsequential
level.

The Ukrainians who sat in the new Duma lacked the
determination and sense of nationality which characterized
so many of their predecessors. The change in political
circumstances which enabled them to enter the chamber
also crippled the small segmental Ukrainian political
parties which were inherently weak because of their re-
markable propensity to splinter and wither as a result of
conflicting social attitudes and personalities. The Ukrainian Social Democratic party lapsed into a state of desuetude
from which it was jolted only by the shock of the March
Revolution of 1917. The Social Democrats who organized
the *Spilka* as an autonomous unit of the all-Russian party
fared well for a period of five years. They were able to
elect fourteen members to the Second Duma and maintained a "passport bureau" which contained sixty-three
varieties of government rubber stamps and was even capable of producing a forged Austrian passport. However,
the Stolypin reaction caused many of the *Spilka* members
to be arrested and compelled the organization to curtail
its activities; within a few years much of the rank and
file was absorbed into the Russian Social Democratic party
at the expense of denying its Ukrainian nationality.

The other major Ukrainian political group, the Democratic-Radical party, had been numerically weak since its
inception and was not strengthened by its failure to submit its own slate of candidates to the electorate in the Duma
elections. Many of its members were drawn into the Russian
Constitutional Democratic party, and in 1908 those who

remained reorganized the defunct party as the Society of Ukrainian Progressives (*Tovaristvo Ukrainskikh Postupovtsiv*). This illegal but non-revolutionary organization favored federalism together with constitutional and parliamentary government but was far removed from the peasant village and its immediate needs. In general, its program was not in contradiction with the editorial policies of the *Rada* after 1907.

The conditions which had stunted the growth of the Ukrainian parties also placed additional burdens on the harassed publishers of the *Rada*. The editorial offices were raided on innumerable occasions, and the editor was jailed. The Ukrainian daily, which was in existence for eight years, never succeeded in becoming economically self-supporting, and it was only the efforts of Eugene Chikalenko which prevented its becoming a weekly in 1910. Decline rather than growth seemed to characterize the Ukrainian national movement during the post-1907 stabilization of autocracy in Russia.

Under these trying circumstances the Ukrainians were alone in their struggle for recognition except for the sympathy which was occasionally expressed by some of the Russian liberals. The latter were unwilling to support the demand for federalism but saw no reason for refusing to grant the Ukrainians a separate educational system and cultural autonomy. Yet they were in the minority, and when Bishop Nikon Bezsonov of Volynia introduced an education bill in the Fourth Duma he was rewarded for his efforts by being transferred to the diocese of Krasnoiarsk in Siberia on orders from the Holy Synod. When the government forbade public celebrations in February 1914 commemorating the centenary of Shevchenko's birth, the Constitutional Democrats rose in the Duma to defend the Ukrainians, and Paul Miliukov protested in the following terms:

"The movement exists, and you can neither suppress it nor alter its significance; the sole question is whether you wish to see this movement as inimical or friendly. That will depend upon whether the movement will regard you as friends or enemies. There is as yet no separatist movement in Ukraine, and if the beginnings of one exist they are very weak. But such a movement can be developed and those who are actually developing it, the true 'separatists,' those who are really working on behalf of Austria are Mr. [A. I.] Savenko [leader of the Ukrainophobes in the Duma] and his political friends."[31]

Thus on the eve of World War I, the Ukrainian nationalists had little reason to be anxious to die for the preservation of the Russian Empire although the peasant masses were ready and willing to do so.

The advent of the war was both a curse and a blessing for the nationalists. It enabled the enemies of the national movement to close the *Rada* and the cultural and educational *Prosvita* societies and arrest numerous Galician intellectuals during the occupation of that region. The Russian authorities were especially apprehensive regarding the establishment of the League for the Liberation of Ukraine (*Soiuz Vizvolennia Ukraini*), an organization founded in Lviv early in the war by a group of political émigrés from East Ukraine which included Marian Melenevsky, Alexander Skoropis-Ioltukhovsky, and Dmitro Dontsov. When the Russians occupied Lviv the League moved to Vienna where it carried on an information program publishing numerous brochures as well as periodicals in Ukrainian and German. The Society of Ukrainian Progressives in Kiev denied that the League had the right to engage in political activity in the name of the Ukrainians of Russia, but this declaration did not deter the Russian government from its anti-Ukrainian policy.

The war, when viewed in its historical context, can be said to have provided the prelude to the collapse of the Russian Empire. Shortly after the 1905 Revolution Hrushevsky had warned the Russians that the Ukrainian problem revolved about what would be done to correct the terrible harm done to his people by the policy of sup-

[31] Lototsky, *op.cit.*, II, pp. 422f.

pression which had left them in a torpor. He contended that the mere lifting of restrictions could not solve the problem and that any attempt to retain the Ukrainian nationality in a subordinate position by depriving it of the means of cultural advancement would be a "terrible, unpardonable sin against those principles which contemporary Great Russian society has placed on its banner in the struggle for the liberation and renewal of Russia." The eminent historian turned oracle and informed the Russian intelligentsia that "such sins do not go unpunished."[32] The "sins" of the rulers of the Russian Empire were manifold, and unquestionably one of them was the denial of autonomy to Ukraine and other territories; yet the collapse which eventually enabled the Ukrainians to proclaim their independence was caused and precipitated by non-national factors.

[32] Hrushevsky, *Ukrainski Vopros* (St Petersburg, 1907), p. 32.

CHAPTER II
The Rise of the Central Rada

The Rada had to exist because the nation as such, like all nations, like a true organism, had to have a single means of expression, a single organ through which to manifest itself.—VOLOD-IMIR VINNICHENKO, *The Rebirth of the Nation*

A revolution is a period of illusions and disillusions, a period during which the mob dominates, and the mob is essentially an unstable element, infinitely changing.—ALEXANDER SHULGIN,
L'Ukraine contre Moscou

A GENUINE revolution renders improbable a restoration of the status quo and at the same time creates many opportunities for the reorganization of political life since it brings into being a state of flux which is terminated only by the consolidation of power in the hands of one group. The group which ultimately emerges as the dominant force is that which succeeds in persuading its active opponents and the vast but politically inept and inarticulate neutral remainder of the population to acknowledge its right to monopolize legality. During the transitional period of instability there are numerous contenders for the public authority which can exact obedience.

In the course of the Russian Revolution of 1917 and the ensuing civil war there developed a struggle between nations which temporarily transcended conflict between personalities, classes, or parties. Young nations which had been subject peoples of Tsar Nicholas II arose, and those who purported to be their spokesmen fought to terminate Russian domination. Ukraine, because of its size and location, was the most important of these suppressed nationalities. If a distinction is made between nationality and nation on the basis that a desire for independent statehood is a particular attribute of the latter, it can be said that Ukraine ceased to be a mere ethnic and cultural mass and commenced its emergence as a nation at this time. For it was only after the November Revolution that a significant number of Ukrainians began to demand political independence rather than a cultural and political autonomy.

The first and most honorable stage in this transformation began with the establishment of the Rada Government, which led a somewhat precarious existence between March 1917 and April 1918. This first Ukrainian government in modern times took its name from the *Ukrainska Tsentralna Rada* (Ukrainian Central Council), an initial representative and temporary constituent body which sat in Kiev. The noun "rada" is the Ukrainian equivalent of the Russian word "soviet" but is employed in this study to refer specifically to the Central Rada.

Immediately after the March Revolution, leadership in the Ukrainian national movement was assumed by the democratically inclined petite bourgeoisie, the intelligentsia with nationalist sympathies, and the middle strata of the peasantry which supported the cooperative movement.[1] The peasant masses, the soldiers, and the urban proletariat were not participants at this early period, and it cannot be said that the national movement permeated their ranks to any significant extent in the months that followed since it was competing with more urgent social and economic issues.

The Rada was first organized on March 17 by the Society of Ukrainian Progressives (*Tovaristvo Ukrainskikh Postupovtsiv*), which was led by Professor Michael Hrushevsky. This group of petit bourgeois intellectuals issued a statement of objectives on March 22,[2] in which it announced that the Provisional Government would soon call a constituent assembly; it also asked the Ukrainian people in the interim to obtain by peaceful means the rights which belonged to them. These objectives were national-cultural in nature and included the establishment of Ukrainian schools and cultural-educational societies and the wider dissemination of Ukrainian books and newspapers; this was to be accomplished not at the cost of the Provisional Government but by popular Ukrainian subscription. By April 8, however, the Society had held a congress in which it plunged from national-cultural objectives to purely political matters by declaring that the role of the All-Russian Constituent Assembly should be confined to a simple ratification of Ukrainian autonomy. At this time the Society also changed its name to the Union of Ukrainian Autonomists-Federalists; shortly after it adopted the name Socialist-Federalist. The very small Rada which the Society organized included

[1] Paul Khristiuk, *Zamitki i Materiali do Istorii Ukrainskoi Revoliutsii 1917-1920* (Vienna, 1921), I, p. 13.

[2] All dates which refer to events occurring after the February Revolution are according to the Gregorian calendar. Previous events are dated according to the Julian calendar.

teachers, clergymen, students, and representatives from newly re-organized *Prosvita* (Enlightenment) societies.

The Rada, in order to make itself more representative, called an All-Ukrainian National Congress which met in Kiev April 17-21, 1917. Nine hundred delegates with mandates attended and another six hundred participated in the proceedings. The delegates who held mandates had received them from peasant cooperatives, professional and cultural-educational organizations, municipalities, and *zemstvos* (local bodies of self-government which were given authority to deal with education, roads, and public health). Hrushevsky presided, and the Provisional Government's ranking official in the Kiev province, Michael A. Sukovkin, who represented the Hetman Government in 1918 in Constantinople, addressed the Congress in Russian since he was unable to speak Ukrainian.

The Congress dealt with two issues in its deliberations: the question of Ukraine's political status and the necessity of broadening the Rada's membership. After hearing addresses on autonomy and federalism by Dmitro Doroshenko and Alexander Shulgin, the Congress adopted a resolution which declared that only national-territorial autonomy would meet the needs of the Ukrainian people and other nationalities living in Ukraine. It was willing to guarantee the rights of the national minorities and constitute a component part of a federated Russia. Although recognizing the right of the All-Russian Constituent Assembly to sanction the new autonomous and federal order, the advocates of autonomy, declaring that they could not remain passive, directed the Rada to assume the initiative in organizing a strong union of all peoples of Russia who were striving for national-territorial autonomy within a democratic Russian republic. The Congress also demanded that frontiers between states be demarcated in accordance with the will of the border population and asked that Ukraine be granted a seat at the coming peace conference for the purpose of claiming the ethnically Ukrainian region of Eastern Galicia.[8]

The Rada which emerged from the National Congress contained approximately one hundred and fifty bourgeois professional and intellectual members, one-third of whom were to represent the Kiev province, including the delegates from the central organs of the political parties and cooperatives which had headquarters in the Ukrainian capital. The balding, bearded, and bespectacled Hrushevsky was unanimously re-elected to the presidency of the Rada on a secret ballot. The Congress did not deal with social and economic problems except to urge the Rada to obtain from the government prohibition of the sale, mortgaging, or leasing of lands, forests, natural resources, and factories.

The atmosphere in which the National Congress convened was one of hopeful enthusiasm if not euphoria. Ukrainian newspapers appeared, among them the democratic daily *Nova Rada* (New Council), the Social Democratic daily *Robitnicha Gazeta* (The Workers' Newspaper), and the non-party socialist daily *Narodna Volia* (Popular Will). The Social Revolutionaries commenced publication of the weekly *Borotba* (The Struggle). Numerous diverse congresses were held in Kiev during the spring. These included a Congress of the Cooperatives of the Kiev region which met on March 27, the First All-Ukrainian Pedagogical Congress held during the third week in April, the First Ukrainian Military Congress (May 18-21), the First Ukrainian Peasants' Congress (June), the congresses of the Social Democratic and Social Revolutionary parties (April 17 and 18), and the First Ukrainian Workers' Congress (July 24-27).

The resolutions adopted at these meetings followed a relatively consistent pattern. In general, the desiderata were a democratic federal Russian republic with national-territorial autonomy for Ukraine (although little effort was made to define these terms); the protection of the rights of national minorities residing in Ukraine; introduction

8 Khristiuk, *op.cit.*, 1, pp. 39ff.

of the Ukrainian language in the schools, courts, political institutions, and the Church; the establishment of Ukrainian military units within the Russian army; and the release of Galician Ukrainians, citizens of Austria, who had been interned during the course of the war. The leadership in these congresses remained substantially the same despite diversity in the membership. Thus the Rada's spokesmen, the leaders of the Social Democratic and Social Revolutionary parties, were able to obtain resolutions of confidence in each of these meetings.

At this time there were three principal Ukrainian political parties. The largest of these numerically was the Social Revolutionary party, which emerged as a unified entity only in 1917 and which enjoyed considerable peasant support. It regarded the agrarian problem as being of primary importance and advocated the expropriation of large estates without compensation for the owners. While the leadership of this party was extremely youthful and contained many hotheads, that of the Social Democrats had a higher proportion of intellectuals and professional men. This fact, when combined with its program and organization, enabled the Social Revolutionary party to assume leadership of the Ukrainian movement. The Social Democrats were Marxists and were more concerned with the fate of the urban worker, although at the same time they regarded Marxism as a means by which national independence could be achieved.

If the importance of a party were to be determined on the basis of the level of education and sense of political moderation prevailing in it, that of the Socialist Federalists would undoubtedly be regarded as having been pre-eminent at this time. This numerically small but influential liberal bourgeois democratic group emerged from the Society of Ukrainian Progressives and disapproved of revolutionary experiments or any intensification of the class struggle; it advocated compensation to landowners as an essential part of any program of agrarian reform, but was not opposed to evolutionary socialism. The party derived its name from the stand which it took on the national question: it advocated federal ties with Russia as long as that was possible. Among its leaders were such outstanding intellectuals as Dmitro Doroshenko, Alexander Shulgin, and Alexander Lototsky. Hrushevsky originally led the Society, but shortly after the March Revolution he became convinced that the future lay with the Social Revolutionaries. He deserted his old friends by surrounding himself with a devoted circle of radical youths from that party. Instead of attempting to play the role of mediator, this bourgeois historian mistakenly believed that he could take these young men under his wing. His refusal or inability to personify the nation by remaining above all partisanship is indicative of the political turmoil which surrounded the would-be Ukrainian provisional parliament.

The Rada's Ukrainian membership increased from one hundred and fifty to approximately six hundred as a result of its acceptance of representatives from each of the functional national congresses. The Peasants' Congress provided more than two hundred delegates while the Soldiers' and Workers' Congresses sent approximately one hundred and fifty and a hundred, respectively. On May 6, when the Rada adopted its rules of procedure it defined itself as "the representative organ of the whole organized Ukrainian population."[4] The criteria of representation which are employed in governments are manifold and include election, appointment, and inheritance. However, no method is in itself proof that representativeness will be obtained, and the members of the Rada, although not elected by direct popular suffrage, considered themselves to be the representatives of the Ukrainian nation.

The Rada did not meet in continuous session since its membership as such was non-salaried. It met in the auditorium of the Pedagogical Museum on Volodimirska Street under the ubiquitous portrait of Shevchenko; the Ukrain-

---

[4] *Ibid*, I, p. 134, n. 26. A plenary session of the Rada constituted a veritable sea of military uniforms; these were worn in order to prevent one's being regarded as "bourgeois."

ian flag·which was displayed in the chamber was decorated with the slogan "Long live autonomous Ukraine in a federated Russia." The Rada's rules of procedure provided for a regular plenary session to be held at least once every month and extraordinary sessions whenever necessary. These rarely commenced on time. An interim committee, usually referred to as the *Mala Rada* (Little Rada), composed of the presidium and over twenty other members, sat in continuous session. It made a number of important decisions while the Rada was not in plenary session.

These men did not, however, constitute a sovereign government during the greater part of the period between the March and November revolutions, and they were not recognized as such by the Provisional Government in Petrograd. Initially they did not manifest any serious desire for national independence. The Ukrainian Social Democratic party in its April Congress almost unanimously rejected a proposal to secede from Russia because such a course "would weaken the revolutionary forces of all Russia." At the same time the party adopted a resolution which expressed its acceptance of "the federal order of the Russian state, as a union of autonomous national-territorial or purely territorial units."[5] The party's leader who became the head of the Rada Government, Volodimir Vinnichenko, in writing of this period concluded:

"Here is the root of separatism. We all desired to separate from oppression, from the autocratic hand, from a shameful death in the slip-knot of the all-Russian gallows. . . . Ukrainian separatism died with its *raison d'être* [tsarism]. Ukrainism oriented itself solely on the all-Russian Revolution, on the triumph of justice. . . . We became a part—an organic, active, live, willing part of a united whole. All separatism, all self-exclusion from revolutionary Russia appeared to be laughable, absurd and foolish. . . . Where in the world was there such a broad, democratic, all-embracing order? Where was there such unlimited freedom of speech,

[5] Volodimir Kirilovich Vinnichenko, *Vidrodzhennia Natsii* (Vienna, 1920), 1, pp. 45f.

53

of assembly, of organization as in the new great revolutionary state?"[6]

The modest requests which the Rada presented to the Provisional Government were largely political and cultural in nature. Yet the Rada, which was not representative of the landowners and the *haute bourgeoisie*, also advocated and ultimately enacted, but never implemented, such social legislation as the eight-hour day for all factories and workshops, the abolition of the existing rights of ownership to land not directly tilled by the owners, and the establishment of "state control over production."[7] These social and economic desiderata indicate the existence of a significant petit bourgeois socialist influence in the Rada represented by such Social Democrats as Vinnichenko, an author and son of impoverished peasants; Ivan Steshenko, a teacher; Valentine Sadovsky, the son of a priest; and Boris Martos, who was born of an impoverished noble family. Thus the national revolution was bound up with a social and economic revolution. Agreement with the Provisional Government was possible in the latter, but ultimately the Rada and Petrograd clashed over the political form which the national movement was to assume.

Few Ukrainians were willing to advocate national independence during 1917, and yet Hrushevsky threatened the leaders of the Russian State with the unfurling of the flag of independent Ukraine if the "Russian centralists" attempted to tear from the hands of the Ukrainians the banner of a broad autonomy within a federated and democratic Russian republic.[8] However, this was an exception

---

[6] *Ibid.*, p. 37 and pp. 42f.

[7] These measures together with the abolition of the death penalty, a full amnesty, and guarantee of the rights of freedom of press, speech, religion, assembly, strikes, and inviolability of person and domicile were enacted with the promulgation of the Rada's Third Universal on November 20, 1917.

[8] In the April 12 issue of *Nova Rada*, quoted in Khristiuk, *op.cit.*, 1, p. 124, n. 7. At the Ukrainian National Congress held in Kiev later in April, Hrushevsky is said to have unsuccessfully advocated the immediate convocation of a Ukrainian Constituent Assembly for the purpose of enacting autonomy without the consent of the Provisional Government. Cf.

to the general practice of expressing confidence in the Provisional Government during this initial period of ebullient optimism. On April 1, Hrushevsky had led a large demonstration on behalf of the new democratic order and the Ukrainian national objectives. This was followed by a mass meeting on St. Sophia Square at which a resolution was adopted in support of the Provisional Government and an autonomous order in Ukraine. This huge gathering empowered the Rada to come to an understanding with the Provisional Government and demand the convocation of the All-Russian Constituent Assembly for the purpose of ratifying the autonomy.

By the end of May a ten-man delegation headed by Volodimir Vinnichenko arrived in Petrograd for the purpose of presenting a declaration of the Rada to the government as well as to the Petrograd Soviet which shared authority with the government in the capital. The declaration stated that "the voice of the Central Rada is the voice of the organized people" and denied that the Ukrainian movement, the support of which was illustrated by the numerous congresses held in Kiev, was either counter-revolutionary or separatist. It contended with considerable validity that the Ukrainians were being exploited by the

---

Alexander Shulgin, *L'Ukraine contre Moscou (1917)* (Paris, 1935), pp. 108f. Hrushevsky's position at this time is stated in his brochure *Iakoi Mi Khochemo Avtonomii i Federatsii* (The Kind of Autonomy and Federation Which We Want) published in Kiev in 1917. He defined autonomy as "the right to live according to your own laws, to make your own laws and not under foreign laws and government" (p. 3) but insisted that in the case of Ukraine it must be very broad and "more or less approach state independence." Such autonomy would be secure only if Russia were converted from a unitary state to a federal republic with equal, secret, direct universal suffrage for men and women over twenty years of age. The competence of the federal government was to include questions of war and peace (to be decided in consultation with the republics), the conclusion of international treaties, the command of military forces, uniformity in currency and weights and measures, tariffs and customs, post and telegraph and railways, and the establishment of uniformity in criminal and civil law. Ukrainian troops were to be supported by Ukraine and were to leave the territory of the Republic only in the event of war. In this discussion Hrushevsky admitted that the All-Russian Constituent Assembly was to have the right to ratify the statute for Ukrainian autonomy.

non-Ukrainian ruling classes. It declared that a people of thirty-five million had awakened and that this was not, as the tsarist government had claimed, the voice of a handful of intellectuals. The Ukrainian was no longer to be a *khokhol*—a derogatory term, which Russians sometimes employed in referring to Ukrainians, derived from the name for the long lock of hair which adorned the shaved heads of the Zaporozhian Cossacks of the Dnieper. The Ukrainians had ceased being slaves; they were now human beings.

This hortatory introduction was followed by the Rada's requests. These were: acceptance of autonomy for Ukraine *in principle*, participation of Ukrainian representatives in the peace conference in connection with the disposition of Eastern Galicia, the establishment of a post in the Provisional Government for the purpose of keeping it informed of the consensus of opinion and needs of the Ukrainian people, the appointment of a special commissioner for Ukraine with whom the Rada could deal, the establishment of separate Ukrainian military units in the rear and at the front wherever possible, the Ukrainization of primary schools and the broadening of Ukrainian studies in secondary and higher schools, the appointment of persons to responsible civil and ecclesiastical positions who are acquainted with the Ukrainian language and customs and who enjoy public confidence, the placing at the disposal of the Rada for "national-cultural needs" necessary funds from the state treasury, and the release of unjustly interned Ukrainians and Galician Ukrainian prisoners of war.[9]

All of the Russian socialist newspapers in Petrograd refused to print the text of the declaration of the Rada delegation. According to Vinnichenko, the Petrograd Soviet, which was not under Bolshevik control at the time, compelled the Ukrainians to cool their heels for three days

[9] The full text of the declaration is to be found in Khristiuk, *op.cit.*, I, pp. 55ff. Also see "Iz Istorii Natsional'noi Politiki Vremenogo Pravitel'stva," *Krasnyi Arkhiv*, xxx (1928), pp. 46-55.

before it heard their case. Later he referred to the Soviet as Pilate since it refused to take a definite stand on the Ukrainian question but instead figuratively engaged in a hand-washing ceremony and sent the Ukrainians to Caiaphas, the Provisional Government, where they were also accorded a cold reception.[10]

Early in April the Provisional Government established a special commission of juridical and legal experts to which it deferred on constitutional questions. It was this professorial body, headed by Fedor F. Kokoshkin of the University of Moscow law faculty, which finally heard the demands of the Rada's delegation. The Ukrainians regarded this commission as supercilious in its attitude. While the delegation was in the Russian capital, the enemies of the Ukrainian movement in Kiev bombarded the Provisional Government with protests, stating that the Rada was nothing more than a hotbed of treason. The South Russian Democratic Union declared that the Rada did not enjoy the support of all of the population of "south Russia" or even of the majority of "Little Russians." The delegation returned to Kiev empty-handed, and the Provisional Government issued a statement based on the commission's findings, in which it repeated in much milder form some of the assertions of the South Russian Democratic Union.

The members of the commission unanimously agreed that the Provisional Government lacked authority to grant autonomy to any portion of the Russian State. It observed that the resolution containing the Rada's demands was "the expression of will of an organization which, because of the manner of its establishment, cannot claim the right to represent all of the population of Ukraine." It noted that the Rada had not been elected by popular suffrage. The theme of the rejection, however, was the contention that the Provisional Government, if it accepted the demands, would be prejudging a matter on which only the All-Russian Constituent Assembly was empowered to pass. The law professors informed the Ukrainians that only repre-

[10] Vinnichenko, *op cit.*, I, pp. 157ff.

sentatives of states can have a voice at international conferences; if the Provisional Government were to allow the
Rada to send a delegation to the general peace conference
it would be granting illegally to Ukraine the right to exist
as a state and would be subjecting an internal Russian
matter to international scrutiny. In rejecting the demand
for the appointment of a Ukrainian commissioner in Petrograd, the commission expressed the belief that it would be
better for the Provisional Government to learn of the
desires and needs of the Ukrainian people from the "democratic organs of local self-government" rather than from
an individual. The Rada's delegation had also requested
that an official be appointed by Petrograd to co-ordinate
its measures in all provinces having Ukrainian population;
the commission rejected this proposal on the grounds that
the creation of such a post would necessitate a delimitation
of the Ukrainian frontier for the purpose of establishing
the official's jurisdiction, and this could not be done legally
by the Provisional Government. The Ukrainization of the
army was regarded as a military matter.

In the sensitive sphere of education the commission contended that Ukrainization had already been achieved on the
primary level; it refused to commit itself on the question of
secondary schools since Ukrainization on this level presented
a complex problem because of the significant number of
city children for whom Ukrainian was not the native
language. The commission recognized that full freedom
must be had for the development of Ukrainian secondary
schools, and at the same time pointed out that further
study of the problem was required before a just solution
could be reached. No objection was raised to the demand
for officials who would enjoy public confidence and know
the Ukrainian language. However, acceptance of this demand was followed by the assertion that local national-
cultural needs would have to be financed by local organs of
self-government; joint action with the central government
would have to be based on an over-all plan of financial
relations between the state and local institutions.

The Provisional Government attempted to placate the Ukrainians and demonstrate its good faith by pointing to its achievement of granting to all citizens, irrespective of nationality or religious faith, equality before the law. It asserted its adherence to the right of all nationalities to enjoy national-cultural self-determination and recognized the national individuality of the Ukrainians, but this failed to assuage their ruffled feelings.

During the spring, conversations of a semi-official nature were also held. Participants were the Ukrainian nationalists in Petrograd; these included the ethnographer Fedir Vovk, Peter Stebnitsky, Alexander Lototsky, and Alexander Shulgin. The Russian point of view was presented by the philologist Shakhmatov, a long-time friend of the Ukrainian cause; the eminent historian and leader of the Constitutional Democrats, Paul Miliukov; and the Kadet jurist, Kokoshkin, who was later brutally murdered in his hospital bed in January of 1918. It was argued here by Kokoshkin that federalism on a national basis was impossible since the component parts of the all-Russian federation would not be equal (presumably in influence), and as an alternative he proposed the granting of autonomy to individual provinces (*gubernii*).[11] The Ukrainians then approached the moderate socialists Miakotin, the noted Russian historian of Ukraine, and Peshekhonov; they were informed that only a constituent assembly representing all of the former Russian Empire could rule on the question of federation.[12]

This dilatory legalistic approach, which was characteristic of the moderate Provisional Government and its adherents, was regarded by many Ukrainian leaders in the Rada as a smoke screen for Great Russian chauvinism and imperialism. Hrushevsky informed the First Ukrainian Peasants' Congress, being held in Kiev when the Rada's proposals were rejected by the government, that "the holiday of the

---

[11] Alexander Shulgin, *Vers l'indépendance de l'Ukraine* (Paris, n.d) p. 14. Cf. Lototsky, *op.cit.*, III, pp. 363ff.
[12] Alexander Shulgin, *L'Ukraine contre Moscou*, pp. 111ff.

revolution has come to an end. We are approaching a dire period. Ukraine must be organized. Only the Ukrainian people must decide their fate."[13] His words were greeted by the peasant delegates with the nationalist slogan *Nekhai zhive vilna Ukraina* (Let free Ukraine live). At the same time a large number of Ukrainian soldier-delegates to the Second All-Ukrainian Military Congress gathered at St. Sophia Square and vowed not to return to their units until Ukrainian autonomy was proclaimed.

As the men in Kiev and Petrograd came to distrust each other with growing intensity an impasse developed. This impasse was broken on June 16 by the Rada's adoption of a resolution which was strongly supported by the two hundred new members who had recently entered the Rada as representatives of the Ukrainian Peasants' Congress. This resolution, based on a proposal made by Vinnichenko, stated that the Provisional Government "deliberately acted against the interests of the toiling people of Ukraine and contrary to the principle of self-determination of nations." It also provided for the issuance of a Universal in the manner of the seventeenth century Cossack hetmans for the purpose of informing the Ukrainian people of "the reality of the demands of Ukrainian democracy . . . and the problems which lie ahead [of the Rada] in the establishment of an autonomous order in Ukraine in collaboration with the other nationalities living in Ukraine."[14]

The First Universal, which was issued on June 23, and addressed to the "peasants, workers and toiling people" of Ukraine, recapitulated all of the requests of the Rada and declared that the Provisional Government had rejected them and had ignored the extended hand of the Ukrainian people. The Rada declared that it could not allow Ukraine to fall into a state of disorder and decline. It solemnly announced:

[13] Khristiuk, *op.cit.*, I, p. 68.
[14] For the full text of the resolution see Khristiuk, *op.cit*, I, p. 69. Cf. Dmitro Doroshenko, *Istoriia Ukraini* (Uzhorod, 1932), I, pp. 88f.

"Let Ukraine be free. Without separating themselves entirely from Russia, without severing connections with the Russian state, let the Ukrainian people in their own land have the right to order their own lives. Let law and order in Ukraine be given by the all-national Ukrainian Parliament elected by universal, equal, direct, and secret suffrage. . . . From this day forth we shall direct our own lives."

Yet the Rada also recognized that "laws which are to establish order in the entire Russian state should be enacted by the all-Russian Parliament."

Since the Ukrainian national movement had a considerable number of enemies within Ukraine the members of the Rada called upon their countrymen to "carry out the organization and education of the people for the purpose of taking over the administration" in those areas "where for some reason or other administrative authority has remained in the hands of people who are inimical to the Ukrainian movement." At the same time it promised, when agreement had been reached between Ukrainians and non-Ukrainians, to "call together representatives from all of the peoples of the Ukrainian land for the purpose of making laws for it. These laws and the whole order which we are preparing will have to be confirmed by the All-Russian Constituent Assembly."[15] The Rada's lack of funds caused

15 *Ibid.*, I, pp. 72ff. The text of the First Universal is also to be found in Vinnichenko, *op.cit.*, I, pp. 219ff. The First Ukrainian Peasants' Congress and the Second Military Congress which met at this time undoubtedly exercised considerable influence upon the Rada since the advocates of autonomy were predominant in both of these meetings The 2,300 delegates to the military congress adopted a resolution calling upon the Rada to cease negotiating with the Provisional Government and to turn, instead, to the organization of the autonomous Ukrainian territory in agreement with the national minorities. This step may have been prompted by Kerensky's order forbidding the convocation of the Congress on the grounds that it was "untimely" Antagonism between Russians and Ukrainians in Kiev at this time resulted in angry exchanges of opinion on the streets; the sessions of the Congress were held under Ukrainian guard because of the anti-Ukrainian crowds which gathered outside the meeting hall to taunt the delegates. This tension did not, however, prevent the Rada from having a moderating effect at this time as is evident in the text of the Universal.

it to include a passage in which various Ukrainian organizations were requested to levy a special voluntary "tax" for the work of the Rada and to send such funds regularly to the treasury of that body. Although the Universal contained statements that Ukraine must be free to determine its fate, it did not proclaim autonomy but merely stated that it would be established in collaboration with the non-Ukrainian population residing in Ukraine and would be ratified by the All-Russian Constituent Assembly. Thus it is difficult to conclude that the Rada's First Universal was radical or subversive in nature.

Shortly after the proclamation of the Universal a General Secretariat was established with the Social Democrat Vinnichenko as general secretary of internal affairs and head of the Secretariat. This action was prompted by the opinion in the Rada that the provincial governors were being left by Petrograd to rely upon their own devices. Besides the secretaryship of internal affairs the Secretariat contained eight portfolios: agricultural affairs, Boris Martos; military affairs, Simon Petliura; judicial affairs, Valentine Sadovsky; education, Ivan Steshenko; supply, Nicholas Stasiuk; nationalities, Serhi Efremov; financial affairs, Christopher Baranovsky; and a general secretaryship held by Paul Khristiuk. This was a coalition secretariat in which the Social Democrats predominated, as they did in later secretariats and ministries, largely because of the higher proportion of intellectuals in that party in contrast with the overwhelmingly peasant composition of the Social Revolutionary party. This "cabinet" had hardly any of the authority which is customarily associated with a government. Ironically, this twentieth-century effort to govern lacked the power to tax and had "no officials or clerks or even a janitor."[16] It was located in very confined quarters in the Pedagogical Museum, where the Rada also met, and was compelled to share the building with the air arm of the Russian army.

Despite this unpretentious beginning much of the Great

16 Vinnichenko, *op.cit.*, I, p. 259.

Russian press regarded the issuance of the Universal and the establishment of the Secretariat as a crime against the state and as a product of German intrigue although there was no tangible evidence to corroborate such conclusions. From some of the more radical supporters of the Provisional Government there arose cries of "bourgeois nationalism." Yet calmer counsels also asserted themselves. Early in July the All-Russian Congress of Soviets of Workers' and Soldiers' Deputies resolved to "give full support to revolutionary democracy in Ukraine in its efforts to obtain democratic autonomy with protection of the rights of national minorities."[17] It urged the Provisional Government to come to an understanding with the organs of Ukrainian revolutionary democracy for the purpose of meeting the national needs of the Ukrainian people and organizing a general provisional territorial organ for Ukraine. However, the national minorities in Ukraine were apprehensive and believed that decisions affecting their future would be made without their participation. The Southern Bureau of the Jewish Social Democratic "Bund," for instance, resolved that the Universal "places the Ukrainian national movement on the road to a break with revolutionary democracy and establishes the conditions for the intensification of internal friction among the population of Ukraine."[18]

The Provisional Government was taken aback by the proclamation of the First Universal, but soon developed an untenable policy of silence. Then on June 29, the Minister-President, Prince George Lvov, antagonized the Rada by appealing over its head to the Ukrainian people "in the name of all of free Russia" and pointing out that the

[17] Khristiuk, op.cit., I, p. 84. The Bolshevik minority at the congress protested the policy of the government and announced that so far as it was concerned Ukraine had the right to enjoy full self-determination. Yet the issuance of the First Universal several weeks before had prompted George Piatakov, leader of the Kiev bolsheviks, to label the Ukrainian movement as nonproletarian and "chauvinist."

[18] A. Zolotarev, Iz Istorii Tsentral'noi Ukrainskoi Rady (1917 god) (Kharkiv, 1922), pp. 9ff., n. 1.

revolution was in danger. He reassured the Ukrainians that they were part of free Russia, and stated that the task of the Provisional Government was to preserve the country from all dangers and to ensure the election of the Constituent Assembly. The government, said the Prince, was endeavoring to remove all traces of the oppression which the Ukrainians had suffered under the tsars, and it was aware of the need for an agreement with the democratic organizations of Ukraine. He promised local self-government and the Ukrainization of schools and courts but cautioned that complete reconstruction of the state organism was impossible while Russia was being threatened by external and internal enemies. "Brother Ukrainians! Do not embark upon the heedless path of destroying the strength of liberated Russia. Do not separate yourselves from the common Fatherland!" He pleaded with the Ukrainians not to provoke fratricidal quarrels and "deliver a fatal blow to the state" in their "impatient desire to strengthen the form of political order in Ukraine"; he prophetically warned them that "the destruction of Russia will also be the ruin of your endeavor."[19] The Minister-President concluded his appeal by calling upon the peoples of Russia to unite and to leave the final solution of all fundamental questions to the not too distant Constituent Assembly.

This plea fell upon deaf ears and failed to cause the dissolution of the Rada or the cessation of its activities. Yet the status of that body was beclouded. The Rada recognized this when it adopted a declaration which had been issued by the General Secretariat on July 9. While it regarded itself as "the supreme executive and legislative organ of the whole of the organized Ukrainian people," it also acknowledged that its authority lay in a twilight zone between that of a purely moral character and a public-legal authority.[20] It further expressed doubt as to precisely which of these forms of authority predominated. This uncertainty did not prevent some of the men in the Provisional Govern-

[19] Khristiuk, *op.cit.*, I, p. 90.   [20] *Ibid.*, I, pp. 78ff.

ment from coming to their senses and recognizing the need for an agreement with the Rada.

On July 12, the war minister, Alexander Kerensky; the foreign minister, Kievan landholder, and millionaire sugar-producer, Michael Tereshchenko; and the interior minister, Irakli G. Tseretelli, arrived in Kiev for the purpose of negotiating with the Rada's General Secretariat. The result of these conversations was the Second Universal issued by the Rada on July 16, and acceded to by the three representatives of the Provisional Government. It was addressed to the "citizens of the Ukrainian land" and declared that the Provisional Government recognized the right of the Ukrainian people to self-determination. However, here again as in the First Universal, there was an expression of "opposition to the separation of Ukraine from Russia" and support for "the unity of all of Russia's democratic forces." The Universal also provided for the broadening of the Rada by the inclusion of representatives of the non-Ukrainian nationalities living in Ukraine and thus made the Rada "the sole supreme organ of revolutionary democracy in Ukraine." This provision increased the number of seats in the Rada to more than eight hundred, giving to non-Ukrainians over twenty-five per cent of the seats as well as a number of posts in the Secretariat.[21] This distribution of seats was arrived at only after considerable negotiation. The Rada had originally adopted a resolution in which it favored proportional representation allowing each minority the percentage which it enjoyed in the total population of Ukraine. However, many non-Ukrainian groups,

[21] Data regarding the total membership of the Rada is contradictory even when presented by members of that body. Hrushevsky has stated, in his *La lutte sociale et politique en Ukraine (1917-1919)*, that there were 702 mandates in the Rada (p. 9, n. 1). N. Hryhoriyiv, in his *Ukrainska Borot'ba za Derzhavu v rokakh 1917-1920* (Scranton, 1934), has placed the total membership at 689 (p. 8); while according to A. Zolotarev, a member of the Jewish Social Democratic "Bund," the total number of deputies was 820 (*op.cit.*, pp. 7f., n. 1). These discrepancies probably occurred as a result of the many changes in the Rada's membership during 1917 and also may be attributed to the fact that plenary sessions could never be attended by all of the members.

especially the Jewish Social Democratic "Bund," had unsuccessfully advocated the election of an entirely new territorial representative body which would also contain the Rada. The minorities, as is usually the case, were compelled to submit to the will of the national majority and enter the Rada.

Kerensky and his two colleagues, in order to protect their status in Petrograd, did not wish to grant what they were of the opinion they had no authority to concede. Consequently, they insisted upon the inclusion of the following passage in the Second Universal: "Recognizing that . . . the fate of all of the peoples of Russia is closely tied to the general advantages of the revolution, we resolutely reject any attempt to implement independently the autonomy of Ukraine prior to the All-Russian Constituent Assembly."[22] Vinnichenko, in his memoirs, later contended that *de facto* autonomy actually existed in July 1917 and that this passage was included in the Universal solely to placate the three visiting ministers who had adopted an infantile, ostrich-like attitude towards autonomy.[23] Opinions concerning the atmosphere surrounding these conversations have differed. Vinnichenko concluded that the talks were devoid of "true warm sincerity." Another member of the Secretariat, Paul Khristiuk, attributed the agreement to Tseretelli's sympathy with the Ukrainian movement. In any event, the mission to Kiev was an unprecedented conciliatory step although it probably was prompted in large part by the failure of Kerensky's July military offensive. The issuance of the Universal precipitated a crisis in the government and caused four of the Kadet (Constitutional Democratic) ministers, including Prince Dmitri I. Shakhovskoi and Andrew Shingarev, to resign from the cabinet. N. V. Nekrasov, the Kadet minister of communications, voted to support the Universal and remained in the cabinet. Shortly after this crisis Prince Lvov resigned in protest over Victor Chernov's agrarian policy, and Kerensky assumed the premiership.

[22] Khristiuk, *op.cit.*, I, pp. 92f.   [23] Vinnichenko, *op.cit.*, I, pp. 284f.

The Universal, because of its ambiguity, was not the grant of autonomy which Hrushevky and the resigning Kadet ministers interpreted it to be. It failed to define even in general terms the territory over which the Rada and its Secretariat were to exercise jurisdiction. Nor was an effort made to define the administrative competence of the Secretariat. These serious omissions were probably not due to chicanery but resulted instead from lack of time and a superfluity of mutual confidence which was based on the naïve assumption that several prominent men seated for a few days at a conference table can provide permanent and binding solutions. The mere fact that a delegation arrived in Kiev from Petrograd and participated in cordial conversations served to create an unwarranted optimism.[24]

However, all Ukrainians in Kiev were not so optimistic in their appraisal of the Universal and the conversations which led to its promulgation. The focal point for dissatisfaction with the Rada's moderation lay in the Paul Polubotok Regiment, a Ukrainian national military unit, which had been organized in April without the consent of the Russian military authorities. A similar body, the Bohdan Khmelnitsky Regiment, had also been seeking recognition as a regular army unit; the Rada had especially supported the claim of the latter group. The Polubotok Regiment, in which Nicholas Mikhnovsky played a prominent role, had within its ranks many who disliked Vinnichenko and others in the Rada for their socialism and especially for their "pacifism" in dealing with Petrograd. Signs of an approaching rebellion among the soldiers caused Petliura and

[24] Khristiuk, *op.cit.*, I, p. 94. Kerensky informed the present writer that the Universal was based on a tacit agreement resulting from the discussions and that no other joint document was drawn up at that time. However, Khristiuk (I, pp. 93f) quotes the text of a vague declaration issued simultaneously by the Provisional Government and signed by Kerensky, Tseretelli, and Tereshchenko. According to this document the government recognized the Secretariat as the supreme organ for the administration of territorial affairs but insisted that it determine the composition of that body in consultation with the Rada. It also reiterated the need for maintaining the unity of the army and not infringing upon the exclusive right of the All-Russian Constituent Assembly to decide on the agrarian question and the national-political order in Ukraine.

Vinnichenko to go to the barracks in a vain effort to persuade them to remain quiet. The regiment finally did surround the Rada's building, probably for the purpose of establishing a military dictatorship. However, the unorganized attempt at a coup was liquidated on July 19 by the Khmelnitsky Regiment which, after some hesitation, remained loyal to the Rada.

The Rada's leaders took seriously the reference in the Second Universal to "the creation of a new life in Ukraine" and assumed that they had been given the "go" signal. The inclusion of the national minorities in the Rada was completed by July 25, when the newly-enlarged Committee (*Mala Rada*) first met. Within four days it drafted a statute for the administration of Ukraine in accordance with that provision of the Universal which empowered the Rada to prepare, in collaboration with the national minorities, the draft of a statute for the autonomous order. This statute was to be approved by the All-Russian Constituent Assembly. The Universal also contained a provision which provided for the reorganization of the General Secretariat, subject to confirmation by the government. The Committee proceeded to add five new portfolios to the nine which already comprised the Secretariat: trade and industry, labor, post and telegraph, transportation, and controller-general. The first three positions were allotted to the Russian Social Democrats in Ukraine, but they refused to accept them until a final agreement with the Provisional Government was arrived at and the competence of the Secretariat defined. Vsevolod Holubovich, a Ukrainian Social Revolutionary who became the second head of the Rada Government, was given the secretariat of transportation while M. Rafes was appointed controller-general. Professor Alexander Shulgin replaced Professor Serhi Efremov as secretary of nationalities and was given three under-secretaries for Jewish, Polish, and Russian affairs. These under-secretaries were to have the right to report to the General Secretariat at its meetings and could vote on matters which directly concerned them. Meanwhile, with the inclusion of more than one hundred representatives from the Ukrainian Workers' Congress, the Rada reached its full theoretical membership of more than eight hundred delegates.

The statute was taken to Petrograd by the head of the Secretariat Vinnichenko, secretary of finance Christopher Baranovsky, and controller-general M. Rafes, the last-named of whom represented the Jewish Social Democratic "Bund." The Provisional Government was in the process of recovering from the abortive, unorganized Bolshevik July coup, and Kerensky managed to avoid the Ukrainian delegation. The reception accorded the men from Kiev was, in their estimation, far from cordial, and an inevitable difference of opinion arose over the exact division of powers which was to prevail between the autonomous government and the Central Government in Petrograd. The proposed statute declared the Rada to be "the organ of revolutionary democracy of all of the nationalities of Ukraine, having for its purpose the preparation of Ukraine for the definitive establishment of its autonomy and the governing of Ukraine until the convocation of the Constituent Assembly of Ukraine and the All-Russian Constituent Assembly." All nominations to the new fourteen-member General Secretariat were to be confirmed by the Provisional Government and were to be made by the Rada's Committee and approved by the Rada in plenary session. The statute contained a passage which was designed to clarify the position of the Secretariat by stating that it was "the highest territorial administrative organ in Ukraine . . . which is formed by the Ukrainian Central Rada, is responsible to it and is confirmed by the Provisional Government." The Secretariat was to be empowered to "exercise its authority through all existing administrative organs in Ukraine. . . . All administration in Ukraine is subordinated to the General Secretariat."[25] All non-elective posts were to be filled by it or by its subordinate organs. A secretary of state for Ukrainian affairs was to be included in the Provisional

[25] For the texts of the statute see Shulgin, *L'Ukraine contre Moscou* (*1917*), pp. 125ff. and Khristiuk, *op.cit.*, I, pp. 96f.

Government and was to be appointed by Petrograd with the consent of the Rada; this official was to defend the interests of Ukraine before the Central Government and, if he deemed it necessary, send draft statutes to the Rada for its examination. The General Secretariat was to submit to the Provisional Government for its approval all laws and budgetary estimates enacted by the Rada. Funds placed at the disposal of the Rada were to be disbursed by the General Secretariat in accordance with the Ukrainian budget. The Secretariat was to be responsible to the Rada and subject to the interpellations of that body and to submit to it all matters which it deemed to be of primary importance. While the Rada was not in session the Secretariat was to be responsible to the Rada's Committee (the *Mala Rada*), and if differences between these two bodies were to arise the Rada was to be convened immediately for the purpose of resolving them. The Rada was to be empowered to ask for the resignation of the General Secretariat. All laws, administrative orders, and decisions were to be published in the Ukrainian, Russian, and Yiddish languages, and no law of the Provisional Government was to be applicable to Ukraine prior to its publication in the official organ of the Rada.

The Provisional Government, which was not seeking a definitive settlement but desired only a modus vivendi, regarded these proposals as going beyond the agreement of July 16, which found expression in the Second Universal. The Ukrainians have since argued that the statute was not a violation of the Universal since the national minorities, habitual supporters of the Provisional Government, voted for the draft statute. On August 7, the Ukrainian delegation met the finance minister, N. Nekrasov, who was acting Minister-President in the absence of Kerensky, in the presence of several advisers, including Baron Nolde and the lawyer Halperin, the authors of the counter-proposal ("Instruction") which the government issued later. The Ukrainians, much to their chagrin, were subjected to a discussion of the administrative competence and territorial

70

jurisdiction of the Secretariat which the government could afford to embark upon in view of its strengthened position resulting from the suppression of the July Bolshevik demonstrations. On August 8, the Ukrainian majority in the Rada's Committee voted to instruct the three delegates to be firm and not to permit any modifications without the Committee's consent; this action deprived the delegates of all discretion. The national minorities in the Committee opposed this resolution since, in their opinion, it constituted an ultimatum to the government.[26]

A similar difference of opinion between the Ukrainians and the minorities arose one week later when Alexander Shulgin, secretary of nationalities, stated that the Secretariat had resolved to continue its work irrespective of its confirmation by the Provisional Government. M. Balabanov, speaking for the Russian Social Democrats, argued that such a resolution was inopportune in view of the fact that negotiations had not been completed; he added that the national minorities desired a settlement with the Provisional Government. The Ukrainians claimed that they were not usurping authority but merely exercising it until confirmed by the government. The Ukrainian majority in the Committee finally approved this stand over the opposition of the Russian Social Democrats, the Jewish "Bund," and the Russian Constitutional Democrats.

On the same day, August 15, the counter-proposal made by the government, in the form of a "Provisional Instruction to the General Secretariat," was introduced into the Petrograd conversations. Two days later it was formally approved by the government and sent to the Rada over the signatures of Kerensky and the justice minister Zarudny. The "Instruction," instead of recognizing the Secretariat as the supreme organ of the Rada, defined it as "the supreme organ of the Provisional Government in Ukraine" until such time as the All-Russian Constituent Assembly would determine what the nature of future local administration would be. The Provisional Government was un-

[26] Khristiuk, *op.cit.*, I, p. 113, n. 1.

doubtedly justified in maintaining this definition since the Rada in its Second Universal referred to the Secretariat as "operating in matters of state government as an organ of the Provisional Government," and defined the Rada as "the organ of revolutionary democracy in Ukraine." According to the "Instruction" the Secretariat was to be appointed by Petrograd on the basis of proposals made by the Rada. Its authority was to be confined to the provinces (*gubernii*) of Kiev, Poltava, Volynia, Podolia, and Chernihiv and could be extended to Kharkiv, Katerinoslav, Kherson, and Taurida only upon the request of local *zemstvos*. The number of portfolios in the Secretariat was to be reduced to the following nine (instead of the existing fourteen): interior, financial affairs, agriculture, the general secretaryship, education, commerce and industry, labor, nationalities, and the controller-generalship. At least four of the nine secretaryships were to be held by non-Ukrainians and the three under-secretaries for nationalities were to represent the leading national minorities. The General Secretariat was to enact laws for Ukraine but only with the approval of the Provisional Government; the Rada could discuss such proposed laws. The Provisional Government was to treat with local officials only through the Secretariat, but in the event of urgency Petrograd was to retain the right to transmit orders directly to local authorities in Ukraine rather than by means of the Secretariat, although Kiev was to be informed at the time that such directives were to be issued.[27] A Ukrainian commissioner was to be appointed by the government for the purpose of serving in a liaison capacity in Petrograd.

The Ukrainians interpreted the "Instruction" as an attempt to undermine the Rada by placing its authority in the General Secretariat and then transforming the latter into an organ of the Provisional Government by reducing it to a mere clearing-house for the transmission of directives from Petrograd to local officials in Ukraine. The compe-

[27] For the full text of the "Instruction" see Khristiuk, *op.cit.*, I, pp. 114f. and Shulgin, *L'Ukraine contre Moscou (1917)*, pp. 129ff.

tence of the Secretariat was restricted by the abolition of the secretaryships for military affairs, post and telegraph, transportation, supply, and judicial affairs. Petrograd rejected the Rada's proposal that it be allowed to ratify all laws enacted by the government prior to their enforcement in Ukraine. Ukrainian ire was further aroused by the exclusion of the Rada from the ethnically mixed provinces of Kharkiv, Katerinoslav, Kherson, Taurida, and Bessarabia.

Two of the Rada's delegates, Vinnichenko and Rafes, returned to Kiev and were superseded by two substitute negotiators, Alexander Zarubin, a Russian Social Revolutionary who had accepted the dubious secretaryship of post and telegraph, and M. Mickiewicz, under-secretary of nationalities for Polish affairs. These men were selected for the purpose of attempting at the last moment, as members of national minority groups, to persuade the government to accept the larger fourteen-member Secretariat.

The Rada, having convened for its sixth regular plenary session on August 18, and charged with determining what the Ukrainian attitude towards the "Instruction" was to be, met under circumstances which were not conducive to the development of amicable Russian-Ukrainian relations. During the spring and early summer, both of the Ukrainian regiments in Kiev had hesitated to depart for the front since many of the men sincerely believed that in doing so they would leave the Rada defenseless. This attitude enabled enemies of the Ukrainian movement as well as those who wished to continue Russian participation in the war to accuse the soldiers of shirking their duty. The issuance of the Second Universal and the suppression of the abortive Polubotok coup strengthened the hand of the Rada and empowered it to compel the Khmelnitsky Regiment to go to the front. As the troops left Kiev on August 8, an unfortunate shooting incident occurred with some Don Cossacks who were under the jurisdiction of the Russian military commander of the Kiev region, Colonel Constantine M. Oberuchev. The exchange of shots took place when the

Ukrainian regiment apparently fired a farewell salvo upon leaving the railroad station and caused or enabled the Russian troops, which had been conveniently deployed along the railroad trackage, to return the fire. A number of Ukrainians were killed and wounded, and the Rada claimed that the Russians shouted at the time that this mêlée was their reply to the Ukrainian request for autonomy. An official investigation was never made, and it is impossible to determine whether or not the Russians actually mistook the farewell salute for a salvo fired at them.

In the light of this event as well as the failure of the Petrograd talks, the stormy debates in the Rada were understandable if not fully justifiable. In the Committee meeting of August 19, Nicholas Kovalevsky, a Ukrainian Social Revolutionary, branded the "Instruction" as "the child of the illicit cohabitation of the Russian Social Revolutionaries with the Kadets." Nicholas Liubinsky, the impetuous leader of the national revolutionary faction, called upon the Rada's members either to manifest their solidarity or to prove that the Rada contained mice who were deserting the burning vessel. Reverend Mateiuk, a nonpartisan delegate from the Kholm region, defined the "Instruction" as "the stillborn child of the recently wed democratic Petrograd and bourgeois Moscow."[28] References were made to the "Instruction" as "that unsightly scrap of paper" and "this unnecessary paper."

Vinnichenko, however, adopted a moderate attitude based on the overly-sophisticated assumption that Petrograd's rudeness, as he termed it, was shrewdly calculated to provoke the Ukrainians to sever relations with the Russian capital.[29] In the debate he posed three alternatives which the Rada could follow: it could choose to reject, ignore, or accept the "Instruction." Favoring acceptance, the popular author criticized those who drew analogies

[28] Khristiuk, *op.cit.*, I, pp. 145ff., n. 40.

[29] Vinnichenko, *op cit.*, I, pp. 313f. While Vinnichenko was in Petrograd the Ukrainian provincial commissars, including Dmitro Doroshenko, met and adopted a resolution urging the Rada to accept the "Instruction."

with the Finnish independence movement; he stated that the Finns were at a higher stage of political development than the Ukrainians. He contended that the document embodied the achievements of the Rada which were won at great effort and recognized by the Provisional Government with great reluctance; rejection of it would mean commencing anew with empty hands and would leave the Secretariat with great responsibilities but with no legal authority. Rejection would indicate that the Ukrainians had allowed themselves to be provoked and would only satisfy the enemies of Ukraine by revealing the political immaturity of the Rada. Acceptance would consolidate previous gains; the "Instruction" would serve as a basis for further efforts.

Vinnichenko was supported by his Social Democrats and by the national minorities. Zolotarev of the Jewish Social Democratic "Bund" pointed out that rejection would endanger the revolution; the fears which became real in September when General Kornilov attempted his coup to make himself dictator were already present in August. It was also generally believed that rejection would bring about a break with the national minorities in Ukraine and divide all "revolutionary democracy" as well as endanger the military front and possibly facilitate German occupation of Ukraine. On August 21, as the would-be parliamentarians began to tire, Christopher Baranovsky, the finance secretary, returned from Petrograd and urged the Rada not to sever its ties with the Provisional Government.

For three days the debate raged and finally, on August 22, resulted in the adoption of a resolution embodying a reluctant and qualified acceptance of the "Instruction." Declaring that the Provisional Government was prompted by distrust for the objectives of Ukrainian democracy and manifested the imperialist tendencies of the Great Russian bourgeoisie towards Ukraine, the resolution stated that the "Instruction" failed to meet the needs and desires of the Ukrainians and the national minorities. It charged that the stipulation which required the four secretaries to be non-Ukrainians had as its purpose "the destruction of the unity of Ukrainian and non-Ukrainian democracy."[30] In a face-saving manner the Rada "informed" the Provisional Government that it was necessary to take steps to implement the agreement of July 16. Thus the Rada deemed it necessary to take the first step by submitting the enumerated nine of its fourteen secretaryships for confirmation. The resolution also directed the Committee and Secretariat to prepare a statute which would define the relations between the Secretariat and the Rada and charged the Secretariat alone with the drafting of a series of laws dealing with labor problems, the agrarian question, supplies, and education. It further urged that preparatory work preliminary to the convocation of the Ukrainian and All-Russian Constituent Assemblies be embarked upon. The resolution was adopted by a vote of 247 to 36 with 70 Social Revolutionaries abstaining; the support came largely from the Social Democrats and Kadets. The total number of votes cast in the balloting was less than half of the Rada's total membership; this is understandable in view of the fact that the actual number of mandates in the Rada never equaled the theoretical membership of 822.[31]

Vinnichenko wished to resign because of Social Revolutionary criticism, and the *Mala Rada* gave the task of forming a new Secretariat under the "Instruction" to Dmitro Doroshenko, a Socialist Federalist who had been the Provisional Government's commissar for Galicia and Bukovina. Doroshenko failed to obtain the confidence of the Social Democrats and Social Revolutionaries, and Vinnichenko, who had already packed his valises and was prepared to leave Kiev for the country, had to be prevailed upon to return to the head of the Secretariat. Doroshenko, who

[30] For the full text of the resolution see Khristiuk, *op cit*, I, pp. 118f. The Provisional Government is said to have given a verbal promise to Zarubin and Mickiewicz to reduce the number of non-Ukrainian positions in the Secretariat from four to three and to have agreed not to issue orders directly to local officials except in time of war and to appoint the Ukrainian commissar in Petrograd only after consulting with the General Secretariat.
[31] *Ibid.*, I, p. 137, n. 31.

was not an enemy of the Provisional Government, later concluded that his relations with Hrushevsky had cooled as a result of this moderation and that he had been asked to form a Secretariat only because he was *persona grata* in Petrograd and would be able to obtain its confirmation.[32] The new Secretariat, headed by Vinnichenko, was formally organized on September 3, and was reluctantly confirmed by the Provisional Government on September 14. This Ukrainian government was composed largely of Social Democrats and Socialist Federalists, the latter of whom were socialist in name rather than in fact. The Social Revolutionaries and the left Social Democrats refused to participate in this Secretariat although the secretary of agriculture, Savchenko-Bilsky, was an S. R. sympathizer.

On the surface it appeared that an agreement had been concluded between the Rada and the Provisional Government. The Ukrainian desire to have a representative accredited to Petrograd was mutually acceptable and soon Peter Stebnitsky was appointed to the post. However, the development of amicable relations between Ukraine and Russia did not continue. The weakened position of Kerensky's government, as a result of his reliance upon the Bolsheviks and the Soviet for support in crushing the Kornilov coup, caused the Secretariat to reassert its previous claims.

On October 12 the Secretariat informed the *Mala Rada* that it stood for the political rights of the Ukrainian people within an equally federated Russian republic; termination of the artificial and painful division of the Ukrainian nation caused by the "Instruction" (a reference to the ethnically mixed provinces of Kherson, Kharkiv, Katerinoslav, and Taurida which had been excluded from the Rada's jurisdiction); and inclusion of the following portfolios in the Secretariat: supply, post and telegraph, transportation, justice, and military affairs. It also advocated the extension of the Secretariat's competence as a fully authorized au-

[32] Dmitro Doroshenko, *Moi Spomini pro Nedavne-Minule (1914-1918)* (Lviv, 1923), II, p. 10.

tonomous state government and preparation for the early convocation of the Ukrainian Constituent Assembly for the purpose of bringing the national-liberating struggle of the Ukrainian people to a culmination.[33] In dealing with such issues as the termination of the war, the agrarian question, the grievances of labor and state control over banking, commerce, and industry, the Secretariat was very circumspect not only because these were, in the eyes of some, secondary to the national-political issue but also because the Rada lacked authority to deal with such matters.

The members of the Secretariat were irked by the Provisional Government's consistent practice of sending administrative directives directly to its own personnel in Ukraine rather than through the Rada Government. In Vinnichenko's terms, the "Instruction" was a truce rather than a peace settlement. During the early part of the autumn the Ukrainians spoke of convoking their own constituent assembly, but a dispute with the national minorities in the Rada's Committee did not arise until the last week in October when the latter questioned the probable nature of such a gathering. Alexander Sevriuk, who later negotiated for Ukraine with the Central Powers at Brest-Litovsk, in referring to the proposed assembly foolishly injected the term "sovereignty" into the debate. The Russian Social Democrats and Social Revolutionaries as well as the Jewish "Bund" protested the use of this term

[33] Khristiuk, *op cit.*, II, p. 12. These same national-political demands were made as early as mid-September at the Second All-Ukrainian Congress of Railroad Workers (who advocated the inclusion of the Kuban region within the Rada's jurisdiction) and the second session of the All-Ukrainian Council of Peasants' Deputies which met on September 15-18. Continued lip service was paid to the social and economic objectives as at the general assembly of the Kiev organization of the Social Democratic party (September 23, 1917) where the following measures were favored: introduction of the eight-hour day; workers' control over production and distribution; nationalization of all important branches of production (coal, metals, and petroleum); merciless taxation of the interests of large capital and property; confiscation of war profits; the immediate proposal of a general democratic peace to all peoples engaged in the war; purging the army of all counter-revolutionary influences; and the confiscation of landowners' estates for the land fund (Khristiuk, II, p. 27).

as being counter-revolutionary since it meant a break with the All-Russian Constituent Assembly and the proclamation of *de facto* Ukrainian independence. Vinnichenko hastened to add to the confusion by declaring himself to be in favor of Ukrainian sovereignty; he defined the term, in a non-legal and highly literary manner, as "full expression of the will" but denied that it involved separatism. Vinnichenko explained that his Social Democrats were not raising the banner of independence, but he threatened that they could not promise to maintain this position since they had never committed themselves not to secede from the Russian State. The fire-eating young Social Revolutionary, Mikita Shapoval, who in the Rada had opposed the acceptance of the "Instruction," protested that it was not permissible for Ukrainians to allow Buriats and other non-Ukrainian peoples to discuss the question of Ukrainian autonomy at the All-Russian Constituent Assembly. He attacked "Russian centralism" and stated that he did not fear civil war.

This heated debate ended in a compromise resolution which satisfied the national minorities by eliminating the term "sovereignty." It recognized the Ukrainian Constituent Assembly as the sole means of expressing the will of the peoples of Ukraine for self-determination and voiced the hope that this right would be ensured in the All-Russian Assembly. Despite this apparent agreement, rumors of separatism persisted, and Vinnichenko endeavored to clarify the Ukrainian position in a letter to the editor of the newspaper, *Kievskaia Mysl* (Kievan Thought). He reiterated the ideal of a federated Russian republic with Ukrainian participation as an equal member of the body politic and repeated his contention that the sovereignty of the local constituent assembly did not necessarily imply independence. Observing that a state structure can be firmly established only when it is based on the mutually expressed good will of its component parts rather than on force, the noted literateur argued that only the enemies of a federated Russia were attacking the Secretariat and the Rada's Committee.[34]

This letter failed to improve relations since the march of events was making the demise of the Provisional Government more inevitable with each passing day. The Ukrainians have contended that Kerensky's government in its last days was considering prosecuting the members of the Secretariat for their allegedly separatist stand and was contemplating the dispersal of the Rada with armed force. Apparently the Secretariat was being called to Petrograd for an explanation, and a previous financial credit extended by the Provisional Government to the Rada was withdrawn.

This break between the Russians and Ukrainians also revealed itself in Ukrainian dissatisfaction with Kerensky's coalition government and its policy regarding social and economic issues. The Petrograd government was termed "coalition" because, in the eyes of the Ukrainian Social Democrats, it included a bourgeois element which was becoming more dominant. The Ukrainian Social Democrats at their fourth party congress held in Kiev on October 13-17, 1917, adopted a resolution demanding a non-coalition (socialist) revolutionary democratic government of organized proletariat, peasantry, and soldiery. At this party congress Vinnichenko found himself in the minority despite his position as titular leader of the party. However, his address, delivered less than a month before the November Revolution, was of importance since it contained a passage[35] which revealed how advanced his separatism had become:

"For Russia a socialist [non-coalition] ministry would be ruinous and would only serve to discredit socialism. The sole problem of socialist ministers must be the question of peace. Such a ministry could not govern the country and reorganize the economic apparatus. The current coalition ministry is pursuing the old policy. Therefore it is im-

[34] *Ibid.*, II, pp. 18ff. For the text of Vinnichenko's letter see pp 188ff, n. 5.
[35] *Ibid.*, II, p. 31.

possible to place our hopes in it. In Petrograd there is eternal anarchy, complete ruin, hungering masses, and the absence of an actual government which would satisfy the masses. Because of this, authority must be transferred to the locale in the form of self-government and the self-determination of nationality. Our problem then is the organization of government and its transfer to the locale."

While the Provisional Government was attempting to call the Ukrainians to account on the eve of the November Revolution, the Third All-Ukrainian Military Congress met in Kiev (November 2-12) with approximately three thousand delegates in attendance. The hostility which Ukrainian nationalists manifested towards Petrograd made itself felt at the congress when Vinnichenko, in addressing one of the sessions, sounded the call for a Ukrainian People's Republic. He promised that the Secretariat would not enter into relations with Kerensky's government over the convocation of the Ukrainian Constituent Assembly and would only discuss the matter of a delineation of functions.

"The secretaries general must declare categorically that they are not officials of the Provisional Government, that the General Secretariat was not established by it, but is the organ of Ukrainian democracy. Because of this the General Secretariat is in no way responsible for its acts before the Provisional Government; the Secretariat is responsible only to that authority which led it out onto the stage of life. The secretaries general must further declare that the full unrestricted will of a given people can be manifested only at its own constituent assembly. And if that is sovereignty, then we welcome it. The General Secretariat shall insist that all authority in Ukraine pass into its hands. . . . When revolutionary Ukrainian democracy recognizes the General Secretariat, the latter has authority. The Provisional Government has become disconcerted because it does not sense support beneath itself. It does not believe that there can be another government which enjoys firm ground. And

I can frankly state that the General Secretariat has this basis. (Applause.) We shall inform the Provisional Government of this."

Vinnichenko concluded by confidently stating that the federation of free republics would soon be confirmed, and the Provisional Government would be unable to preserve a centralist Russia.[86]

This fine dream was rudely interrupted by the November Revolution, which plunged Russia into the greatest political maelstrom it had experienced since the sorrowful "Time of Troubles" which preceded the establishment of the House of Romanov in 1613. In the initial confusion which surrounded the coup, the Rada's Committee joined with the Kiev Bolsheviks on November 8 in organizing a Territorial Committee for the Defense of the Revolution in Ukraine for the purpose of "struggling with the enemies of the revolution, preserving order in the territory, and defending all of the achievements of the revolution." There was fear in Ukraine that the enemies of the Revolution would attempt to profit from the struggle between the Provisional Government and the Petrograd Soviet for the purpose of restoring the tsarist order. This new body was composed of representatives from the Rada, the various Ukrainian parties, the Jewish "Bund," the Kiev Soviet, the United Jewish Socialists, the All-Ukrainian Council of

[86] *Ibid.*, ɪɪ, p. 41. Ukrainian leadership of the new nationalities of the former Russian Empire had resulted in the "Congress of Nationalities" which was held in Kiev during the week of September 21-28, and was attended by representatives from the Latvian, Tartar, Georgian, Lithuanian, Esthonian, Bielorussian, Jewish, and Buriat nationalities as well as by some Don Cossacks. The Provisional Government sent the Ukrainian writer Maxim Slavinsky as its delegate. The theme of the congress was democratic federalism, and the basic fault of the Russian Empire was found to lie in an excessive centralization of legislative and executive authority. It also declared itself in favor of territorial constituent assemblies to be held for the purpose of determining the form of government for each autonomous territory and the norms for relations between the territories and the central organs of the federation. The purpose of the congress was the transformation of Russia from a "jailhouse of nationalities" into a "temple of peoples' freedom," but no concrete results emerged from the meeting. (Khristiuk, ɪɪ, pp. 21f.)

Soldiers' Deputies, and other revolutionary organizations; its membership included two Bolsheviks, Zatonsky and L. Piatakov, as well as Simon Petliura, Alexander Sevriuk, and M. Rafes. A revolutionary staff committee was established for the purpose of organizing a military force and was headed by General Victor Pavlenko.

The Committee for the Defense of the Revolution vowed to employ armed force against all counter-revolutionary activity and demanded that its orders be obeyed by all civil and military authorities (in the rear) in all nine Ukrainian provinces: Kiev, Podolia, Volynia, Poltava, Chernihiv, Kharkiv, Kherson, Katerinoslav, and Taurıda. It forbade all rallies and open-air mass meetings and promised to prevent all disorders. This was the "non-coalition" revolutionary socialist "government" which the majority of Social Democrats had favored at their recent congress.

The Committee was not without its critics. The Russian Mensheviks, the Kadets, and the Russian Social Revolutionaries, meeting on November 8 at a special session of the Kiev city council, defended the record of Kerensky's government and severely criticized the Bolshevik uprising. In the Rada's Committee (*Mala Rada*) the Russian Social Revolutionaries and Mensheviks joined with the Jewish Social Democratic "Bund" in attacking the Revolutionary Committee and obtained the passage of a resolution[37] censuring the Bolshevik coup.

"Recognizing that authority in the whole state, as in each individual territory, should be placed in the hands of the whole of revolutionary democracy; and regarding as impermissible the transfer of all authority exclusively into the hands of the soviet of workers' and soldiers' deputies which is but a segment of organized revolutionary democracy, the Ukrainian Central Rada hereby expresses its disapproval of the Petrograd uprising."

This resolution caused the death of the newborn Revolutionary Committee and precipitated civil strife in Ukraine.

[37] *Ibid.*, II, p. 44. Cf. M. Rafes, *Dva Goda Revoliutsıı na Ukraıne* (Moscow, 1920), p. 48.

The Bolshevik George Piatakov resigned from the *Mala Rada*, and the party withdrew its representatives from the Revolutionary Committee.[88] The new Russian military commander of the Kiev region, Kvetsinsky, who supported the Provisional Government, attacked the former tsar's palace in Kiev which was the headquarters of the local soviet of workers' and soldiers' deputies. The Rada intervened and caused the troops to lift their siege of the palace. This action brought about a short and uneasy truce which was broken on November 11, when violent street fighting broke out between the adherents and enemies of the Kerensky government. Barricades arose, a workers' strike was called, and the delegates to the Third Military Congress adjourned in order to participate in the fighting even though only a fifth of the delegates had firearms. Instead of remaining neutral as it had done previously, the Rada, which held the balance, threw its limited military forces on the side of the enemies of the Provisional Government and forced the allegedly counter-revolutionary forces to withdraw from Kiev.

The ill-fated and brief marriage between the Rada and the Bolsheviks was terminated when the Military Congress reconvened and called upon the Rada and the General Secretariat to assume full civil and military authority in Ukraine and to oppose the efforts of the Bolsheviks to transfer power to the Kiev Soviet. Yet the Congress did not censure the Petrograd uprising nor did it favor Ukrainian separatism when it repeated the formula regarding the transformation of Russia into "a federation of sovereign equal democratic republics with protection of the rights of

[88] Eugenia Bosh, a prominent Kiev Bolshevik, admitted that she and her comrades had a low opinion of the Rada but were willing to participate in it in order to obtain information and dispense propaganda. In August they stated their position in a resolution: "Having entered the Central Ukrainian Rada we shall wage a relentless struggle against the bourgeoisie and against bourgeois nationalism, and we shall call the workers and peasants of Ukraine, under the red banner of the International, to the complete victory of the proletarian revolution." (Bosh, *God Bor'by* [Moscow, 1925], pp. 240f.)

minorities."[89] Acting on the basis of the blank check granted it by the Congress, the Rada on November 12 decided to expand the General Secretariat to include the following portfolios: supply, Nicholas Kovalevsky; trade and industry, Vsevolod Holubovich; labor, Nicholas Porsh; justice, Michael Tkachenko; military affairs, Simon Petliura; transport; and post and telegraph. These six secretaryships were divided equally between the Ukrainian Social Democrats and the Social Revolutionaries although one of the latter, secretary of post and telegraph Zarubin, was a Russian Social Revolutionary. The fall of the Kerensky government and the disintegration of the united revolutionary front had temporarily restored the Rada's freedom of action.

[89] Khristiuk, *op.cit.*, II, p. 194, n. 12. The Military Congress also favored the convocation of a sovereign Ukrainian Constituent Assembly on the basis of popular, secret, equal, direct, and proportional electoral law within the ethnographic limits of Ukraine; it was to ratify the republican-democratic form of governing Ukraine and introduce agrarian reform. A resolution providing for the immediate secession of Ukraine from Russia obtained only twenty-one votes.

CHAPTER III
The Demise of the Rada

By your strength, will, and word there has arisen in the Ukrainian land a free Ukrainian People's Republic. Realized is the age-old dream of your forefathers, champions of the freedom and rights of the toiling masses.

The Rada's Fourth Universal

My Fatherland cannot become the ground for socialistic experiments.

Hetman Paul Skoropadsky

As THE conflict between the Bolsheviks and their opponents spread in the north the isolated Rada issued the Third Universal on November 20, 1917, for the purpose of clarifying its position. This document, which was addressed to the "Ukrainian people and all peoples of Ukraine," pointed out that in the course of the "internecine and sanguinary strife" which prevailed in the north "the Central Government has disappeared and anarchy, disorder, and ruin are spreading throughout the country." The Rada, for the purpose of preserving order in Ukraine, proclaimed the Ukrainian People's Republic but with the following qualification: "Without separating ourselves from the Russian Republic and respecting its unity, we shall firmly establish ourselves in our land for the purpose of aiding with all our strength Russia as a whole so that all of the Russian Republic shall become a federation of equal and free peoples."[1] The Rada declared itself to be the repository of all authority until the convocation of the Constituent Assembly of Ukraine on January 22, 1918. Its jurisdiction was to embrace the nine Ukrainian provinces (*gubernii*), excluding the Crimea, and portions of the ethnically mixed regions of Kholm, Voronezh, and Kursk, although in the case of the latter group the Rada was willing to await manifestations of "organized popular will." The Kuban was not included because of its desire to constitute a separate republic.

Under the influence of the prevailing social and economic trend, the Rada announced that lands belonging to

[1] These passages are quoted from the text of the Universal which is to be found in Vinnichenko, II, pp 74ff. and in Khristiuk, II, pp. 51ff. It should be noted that the Rada in this Universal neither recognized nor rejected the government of Bolshevik commissars in Petrograd. It was willing to accept that government as a purely Russian government for the north but not for all of Russia. A similar position was taken by the Third Ukrainian Military Congress which did not specifically censure the Bolshevik seizure of power but did express disapproval of efforts to impose the soviet system upon Ukraine. It was at this time that the Rada's provincial officials replaced Kerensky's portrait in their offices with that of Vinnichenko.

the Church, to the Crown, to monasteries, and private landowners and not worked directly by the proprietors were to become "the property of all of the toiling people" without compensation being made to the former owners. The eight-hour day for all factories was proclaimed, together with "state control over production in the interests of Ukraine as well as of all Russia." A complete amnesty was granted to all persons who had been judged guilty of or who were being tried for political activities; capital punishment was abolished; and the secretary general of internal affairs was directed to strengthen and broaden the rights of local self-government. Freedom of speech, press, religion, assembly, association, strikes, person and domicile, and the right to employ local dialects and languages were declared to be achievements of the revolution which must be safeguarded. The principle of "national-personal autonomy"[2] was also proclaimed for all national minorities living in Ukraine.

While the Rada's economic and social objectives, as enunciated in the Third Universal, were in some respects similar to those of Lenin's government, there were marked divergencies in outlook which made it impossible for Kiev and Petrograd even to attempt to arrive at an agreement regarding the political status of Ukraine. The general in-

---

[2] The Third Universal declared that "the Ukrainian people, having struggled for many years for its national liberty and now having obtained it, will firmly defend the freedom of national development of all nationalities living in Ukraine." It directed the secretary general for nationalities, Alexander Shulgin, to prepare a draft of a statute embodying the principle of "national-personal autonomy" which granted personal rights to the individuals of each nationality but presumably denied the collective right of a national minority to secede from Ukraine. Shulgin states that this autonomy was not territorial and was based on the plan of the Austrian socialist, Karl Renner. In general, the Rada pursued a sound and enlightened national minorities policy, although it delayed the enactment of its national minorities law until January 22, 1918, when it was on the verge of collapsing. The representatives of the minorities usually spoke in the Russian language and were never silent in the Rada. However, Shulgin admits that on certain issues, especially in the field of foreign policy, the Ukrainian parties did not take the minorities into their confidence. (Shulgin, L'Ukraine contre Moscou [1917], pp. 155f. and p. 167.)

stability and the seemingly transient nature of the Bolshevik regime were factors which when combined with the Bolshevik abhorrence of the Rada and its despicable "bourgeois" spokesmen made the two governments incompatible from the outset.

This basic incongruity was accentuated when the Rada Government sent its general secretary, Alexander Lototsky, and its commissar for Chernihiv province, Dmitro Doroshenko, to the general staff headquarters (*Stavka*) at Mogilev for the purpose of obtaining a merger of the separate Rumanian and southwestern military fronts into a single Ukrainian front. The presence at headquarters of such prominent anti-Bolshevik figures as Chernov, Dan, and Gots caused the Ukrainians by their presence at the *Stavka* to be associated, in the eyes of the Petrograd Government, with counter-revolutionary forces. On November 21, in the building which Nicholas II had occupied on his visits to the *Stavka*, the Ukrainians concluded a convention with General Dukhonin, who was brutally murdered by Bolshevik armed units a few days later. In this agreement the *Stavka* did not obligate itself to Ukrainize the army but merely recognized the desirability of having the army organized on a territorial basis and promised to support this measure before the government. The Ukrainian Secretariat for Military Affairs was to have its own representative attached to the *Stavka*, but the existence of such a post was to be made public by the supreme commander only after the announcement of the appointment. The obligation on the part of general headquarters to concentrade Ukrainian units from other fronts on the Rumanian and southwestern fronts was not binding since it was to be carried out only if it did not interfere with operational matters.[3]

3 Doroshenko, *Moi Spomini pro Nedavne-Minule*, II, pp 36ff. For the text of the agreement see *Razlozhenie Armii v 1917 godu* (Moscow, 1925), pp 83f., document no 71. The agreement also provided that the appointment of the commandants of the Kiev and Odessa military districts was to be made with the concurrence of the General Secretariat. The Ukrainian

The Rada also antagonized the Bolsheviks when it questioned their right to constitute an all-Russian government; on December 6, it sent a note to the Council of People's Commissars in Petrograd and to the various new territorial "governments" proposing the establishment of a central Russian government for the purpose of obtaining a general democratic peace. The "governments" which were invited were the Southeastern Union of Cossacks in the Don region; the governments of the Caucasus and Siberia; the autonomous administrations of Moldavia, Crimea, and Bashkiria; and the Petrograd Bolshevik government. The proposed talks were to be held in Kiev with the Rada participating, and the basis for discussion was to be the acceptance of the principle of a general democratic peace and the convocation in due time of the All-Russian Constituent Assembly. Only the government of the army of the Don responded favorably to this invitation, and, as a result, no conference was held. Agreement was impossible because the "governments" were too diverse and, as in the case of the Don Cossacks and the Bolsheviks, were antithetically opposed to each other.[4] The Bolsheviks, in a manner which became increasingly familiar to a later generation, insisted upon an agreement based solely on their own terms. The Rada had been attempting in vain to unite mutually incompatible elements.

The tension between the north and the south mounted as Petliura, the Rada's war minister, ordered all Ukrainian

Secretary for Military Affairs was empowered to call officers and officials to his staff for assignment there in agreement with the general staff and the staffs within its jurisdiction.

[4] On November 15, 1917, Lenin and Stalin, the latter as commissar for nationalities, issued a Declaration of Rights of Peoples which contained four essential principles: all peoples of Russia are equal and sovereign; all peoples of Russia enjoy free self-determination even to exercise the right of secession and establish an independent state; all national and national-religious privileges and restrictions are abolished; all national minorities and ethnographic groups living on the territory of Russia are to enjoy free development. For the text of this declaration see M. D. Orakhelashvili and V. G. Sorin, *Dekrety Oktiabrskoi Revoliutsii* (Moscow, 1933), pp. 28ff.

troops not to obey the orders of the Bolshevik Government and censured the Petrograd commissars for arbitrarily entering into peace negotiations with Germany in the name of the whole of Russia. On December 13, the Secretariat issued a notice denying that the Council of People's Commissars represented all of Russia. Further complications developed on December 17, when the Council of People's Commissars sent the Rada an ultimatum in which it recognized, with tongue in cheek, Ukraine's right to self-determination even to the point of complete secession but at the same time leveled three accusations at the Ukrainians. It charged them with disorganizing the front by recalling Ukrainian troops, disarming Bolshevik forces in Ukraine, and shielding General Alexei M. Kaledin's counter-revolutionary rising in the Don region by preventing the passage of Bolshevik troops sent to crush that movement and by allowing Don Cossacks who were joining Kaledin to cross Ukraine. If the Ukrainians failed to cease these practices within forty-eight hours and did not return the arms seized from the Bolshevik forces, a state of war was to follow between the Rada and the Soviet Government in Russia and in Ukraine.[5]

Simultaneously the Bolsheviks in the Kiev Soviet, who were too weak to stage a coup, called an All-Ukrainian Congress of Workers', Soldiers', and Peasants' Soviets on December 17, in an effort to circumvent the Rada. The attempt failed when only eighty of the 2,500 delegates proved to be controlled by the Bolsheviks. Instead of censuring the Rada, the Congress protested the ultimatum and refused to listen to the Bolshevik Zatonsky. His comrade,

[5] At this time the Rada was disarming Bolshevik-dominated Russian troops in Ukraine who had left the front; Vinnichenko contended quite correctly that they were undisciplined and anarchistic. During December the Secretariat also made an unsuccessful effort to establish federal ties with the Don and the Kuban regions; one of the reasons for the failure was the refusal of the Don Government to accept the Bolsheviks as the government of Great Russia, i.e. of northern Russia. Cf. Halahan, op.cit., III, pp. 63ff. For the text of the Soviet ultimatum to the Rada see William H. Chamberlin, *The Russian Revolution* (New York, 1935), I, pp. 486ff.

Vasili Shakhrai, who later appeared at Brest-Litovsk as spokesman for the Ukrainian Soviet Republic, asked that the Bolshevik delegates be regarded as Ukrainians but that nationalist emotionalism be dispensed with. He pledged continued opposition by his party to the bourgeois politicians of the Rada whom he accused of being aligned with the landowners and capitalists rather than with the workers and peasants. Terming the ultimatum a "misunderstanding," he expressed the hope that peace would prevail. When it became obvious that the Congress was overwhelmingly in favor of the Rada, the Bolsheviks, together with a few sympathizers, withdrew and proceeded to Kharkiv, where they called a new Ukrainian Congress of Soviets that is referred to in official Communist histories as the first such meeting. This body, which had few peasants, proclaimed the Rada dissolved on December 26, and proceeded to organize the Ukrainian Soviet Republic.

On December 19, the Kiev Congress almost unanimously adopted a resolution which termed the ultimatum an attempt against the Rada and a violation of the right of the Ukrainian people to self-determination. It appealed to the peoples of Russia:

"Brethren! For more than three years the sons of all the peoples living in Russia have fought side by side in the trenches. For many years we struggled together against the odious autocratic order, and with our common forces we achieved the victories of the revolution. The first task of the great revolution was the promulgation of the right of all peoples to self-determination. The Ukrainian people utilized their right and proclaimed the Ukrainian People's Republic. The Council of People's Commissars declares war on this People's Republic. The Council of People's Commissars is negotiating peace with General Hindenburg and threatens the democracy of all peoples of Ukraine by issuing an ultimatum and threatening war."[6]

[6] Khristiuk, *op.cit.*, II, pp. 73f. Conflict between the Bolsheviks and Rada had persisted since March despite the presence of Bolshevik members in

It sardonically accused the commissars of permitting self-determination only to their own party and "wish[ing] to keep all other groups and peoples under their yoke by armed force in the manner of the tsarist government." The Congress denied that the Rada was bourgeois, defended its record by citing its "achievements" as embodied in the Third Universal, and expressed the hope that all democratic forces in Ukraine would support the Rada until the convocation of the Ukrainian Constituent Assembly.

"What do we desire? We wish to create an all-Russian federative authority based on the organized will of peoples and territories. This authority must be uniformly socialist including the bolsheviks and popular socialists. We demand an immediate general democratic settlement. This is a program of our activities and of our demands. Would you conspire to undercut us with cannons and bayonets because of this program? Brethren and comrades, do not allow a single hand of a peasant, worker or soldier to be raised against a brother! Let not a single drop of blood be shed in fratricidal war! There has been enough bloodshed!"

But events were to prove that enough blood had not been shed.

The General Secretariat replied to the ultimatum on December 20, and stated that a peaceful settlement between the Russian Republic and Ukraine had to be based on four conditions: recognition of the right of the Ukrainian people to self-determination and no intervention in the internal affairs of the Ukrainian Republic; the transfer of Ukrain-

---

the Rada until November 8 Shortly after the overthrow of the monarchy, the central committee of the party had sent Klimenti Voroshilov to Lugansk (since appropriately renamed Voroshilovgrad) for the purpose of combatting the Rada's influence. Eugenia Bosh, interior commissar in the first Ukrainian Soviet Government, admitted that the Bolsheviks had no interest in the national movement itself since their lives had been geared to a totally different revolutionary struggle; to them the Rada was but a temporary nuisance and the right of national self-determination nothing more than a "bare slogan" (Bosh, *op.cit.*, pp. 45f.).

ian troops from other fronts to Ukrainian territory; a financial agreement regarding Ukraine's share of state treasury funds; and no intervention on the part of the Council of People's Commissars or the supreme headquarters in the administration of the Ukrainian military front. Petrograd replied by accusing the Rada of remaining silent on the real subject of conflict—the support which it was allegedly giving the counter-revolutionary bourgeoisie, the Kadets, and Kaledin. Attempts to obtain an agreement continued but in the end proved to be futile. The Ukrainians believed that Bolshevik forces, if allowed to remain armed in Ukraine or if permitted to pass through, would succeed in overthrowing the Rada.

Such suspicion was well-founded. As early as December 7, Stalin, the Commissar for nationalities, had demanded in *Pravda* that a congress of representatives of workers', soldiers', and peasants' deputies be held in Ukraine with or without the consent of the Rada. On December 26, when threats had failed, he accused the Rada of desiring to retain the landowners and capitalists and informed the Ukrainian people:

"There is not and cannot be any conflict between the Ukrainian and Russian peoples. The Ukrainian and Russian peoples, like all the other peoples of Russia, are composed of workers and peasants, of soldiers and sailors. They all fought together against tsarism and the Kerensky regime, against the landowners and capitalists, against war and imperialism. . . . Conflict has arisen not between the peoples of Russia and Ukraine but between the Council of People's Commissars and the General Secretariat of the Rada."[7]

Stalin denied that the conflict was one between self-determination and centralism. He attributed it rather to three concrete issues.

The first of these issues had arisen as a result of Petliura's

[7] Josef Stalın, *Stat'ı ı Rechi ob Ukraine* (Kiev, 1936), pp. 2ff.

alleged order calling all Ukrainian troops home from the front; this, Stalin claimed, threatened the front with complete disorganization. The second source of conflict was the disarming of Soviet forces in Kiev, Kharkiv, and Odessa by units which were loyal to the Rada. Stalin made this action appear to be criminal and declared the Soviets to be the stronghold and hope of the revolution.

"Who disarms the soviets is disarming the revolution, harming the cause of peace and freedom and is betraying the cause of the workers and peasants. The soviets saved Russia from the yoke of Kornilov. The soviets saved Russia from the infamy of the Kerensky regime. The soviets obtained land and an armistice for the peoples of Russia. Only the soviets are capable of bringing the people's revolution to a complete victory. Because of this, he who raises his arm against the soviets is aiding the landowners and capitalists. . . ."

The third counter-revolutionary act was the Secretariat's refusal to allow "revolutionary forces" to proceed against Kaledin; Stalin could not understand how Russian troops could be "foreign" to the Ukrainians. The uncompromising form in which these allegations were stated made it evident that an impasse had been reached in the relations between the northern and southern capitals.

Soon it became increasingly obvious that the new Ukrainian state, like other newly-established small states in recent times, could not hope to survive unless it relied upon some greater power for support. Alexander Shulgin, the 29-year-old acting Ukrainian foreign minister at the time, later stated that by November he had realized that French aid was indispensable to Ukraine and that if such assistance were not forthcoming the new state would inevitably come under the political and economic influence of Germany.[8]

8 Shulgin, *L'Ukraine contre Moscou*, p. 161. Shulgin was also secretary of nationalities and became a *de facto* foreign secretary as early as July, when the Rada instructed him to endeavor to coordinate the efforts of all nationalities within Russia who were striving for a federal order.

Meanwhile the Bolshevik coup had removed the Provisional Government upon which the Entente Powers had been relying to continue the war and necessitated a reorientation of Allied policy. As Russia's fighting capacity withered, the Entente, and notably France, attempted to encourage new centers of resistance to the German military advance. In mid-November General Tabouis of the French military mission in Kiev and a British Major Fitzwilliams called on Shulgin and, according to the Ukrainian record, offered the aid of their governments in the establishment of the new republic. Shulgin states that, acting upon the direction of the cabinet, he did not specifically reply to the Allied offer of aid but instead demanded that the powers recognize Ukraine and exchange diplomatic missions with it as a prerequisite to any conversations concerning aid.[9]

The British and French did not press the matter for a month, but by December 18, General Tabouis assumed the initiative stating that he had been directed to consult the Ukrainians regarding their financial and technical needs. At this time he informed the Ukrainians that he had been instructed to transmit to the Rada Allied sympathy "for the effort made by the Ukrainian government to re-establish order and to reorganize the forces of resistance and remain faithful to the Allies."[10] A letter of appointment

[9] Alexander Shulgin, *L'Ukraine, la Russie et les Puissances de l'Entente* (Berne, 1918), pp. 32f. Prior to this, France had ignored the Rada. Albert Thomas, the French socialist minister of munitions and later director of the International Labor Office, when sent to Russia in 1917 with Arthur Henderson for the purpose of buoying up Russian resistance, did not deem it necessary to visit the Rada or its president, Hrushevsky, while in Kiev in June. By August, however, the French ambassador to Petrograd, M. Joseph Noulens, successor to Maurice Paléologue, had lunched with Shulgin; this meeting was arranged by the Ukrainophile French journalist Jean Pélissier. The French envoy enquired concerning events in Ukraine but was unwilling to intervene in what he regarded at that time as a Russian internal affair. During September General Niessel, chief of the French military mission in Russia, and General Tabouis while visiting Kiev paid a social call on some of the members of the General Secretariat.

[10] *Ibid.*, p. 53. Texts of these diplomatic documents are to be found in Arnold Margolin, *From a Political Diary* (New York, 1946), pp. 182f.; also see Khristiuk, II, pp. 198f., n. 20. The United States in December of 1917 was as desperate as Britain and France to sustain Russian participation in

authorizing Tabouis to employ the title "Commissioner of the French Republic" in Ukraine was issued on December 29, 1917, by Saint-Aulaire, the French envoy to Rumania. Alexander Shulgin was not fully satisfied and blandly informed Tabouis that an ambassador would have been preferable.[11]

The British Government pursued a similar policy and appointed Mr. (later Sir) John Picton Bagge, former consul-general in Odessa, to the post of "British Representative in Ukraine." Bagge declared that his government would "support to the utmost of its ability the Ukrainian Government in the task which it has undertaken of introducing good government, maintaining order, and combatting the Central Powers who are enemies of democracy and humanity."[12]

Some of the leaders of the Rada, notably Vinnichenko and Shulgin, as well as Arnold Margolin, have insisted in their memoirs that Britain and France "recognized" the Ukrainian Republic and were morally as well as legally obligated to support it. However, French Ambassador Noulens later dissociated himself and General Niessel, chief of the French military mission in Russia, from the appointment of a French representative to Ukraine in the person

---

the war. Although Secretary of State Robert Lansing distrusted the Bolsheviks as much as the other Allies did, Washington did not support the Rada but instead placed its concealed confidence in the counter-revolutionary Kaledin movement among the Don Cossacks. See *Papers Relating to the Foreign Relations of the United States (The Lansing Papers)* (Washington, 1940), II, pp. 343ff.

[11] General Tabouis, "Comment je devins Commissaire de la République Française en Ukraine," *Spohadi* (Warsaw, 1932), p. 154. This is volume eight in the publications of the Ukrainian Scientific Society.

[12] Vinnichenko, *op.cit.*, II, p. 242. This sentiment was in marked contrast to the statement made on October 24, 1917, by foreign secretary A. J. Balfour in the House of Commons when asked about the Provisional Government's recognition of the Rada: "Nothing would be gained by answering a question which deals with the internal arrangements of Allied countries." *Parliamentary Debates* (Vol. 98, col. 803.) *The Foreign Office List and Diplomatic and Consular Year Book for 1919* contains an admission that Bagge was "employed on special service at Kiev from January 17 to February 22, 1918, when he left for England, owing to the approach of enemy forces" (p. 248).

of General Tabouis, stating that neither of them was consulted in the matter. Noulens explained this appointment in terms of the presence of several officers, within the French military mission in Kiev, who desired to improve their positions and who planned to profit from Ukraine's natural wealth. By means of personal influence within the French Government this clique of officers was able to obtain the designation of Tabouis as official French representative. Noulens concluded that the winter of 1917-1918 was an inopportune time to accredit a representative since the Rada lacked the effective authority which legal recognition implies.[18]

In claiming recognition the Ukrainian spokesmen ignored the fact that in diplomatic practice the sending of a special representative to a newly established state does not necessarily imply even *de facto* recognition. Such an emissary must send a letter to the chief of the new state or to its foreign minister in order to establish the contact and carry on oral negotiations. Such a note is not a letter of credence and is not signed by the chief of state or foreign minister of the nation which is sending the special representative. Neither Tabouis nor Bagge had such letters of credence since the British and French, as a result of their pre-World War I policy of rapprochement with Russia, found it difficult during the revolutionary period to conceive of a dismembered Russian state.

Prior to the emergence of the Ukrainian national movement in 1917, the Allies, as a result of their preoccupation with Germany, shut their eyes to any application of the principle of self-determination of nations which would have weakened Russia's ability to continue the war. Yet once the Ukrainian movement had demonstrated that it was not merely the product of German and Austrian intrigue, the

---

[18] Joseph Noulens, *Mon Ambassade en Russie soviétique (1917-1919)* (Paris, 1933), I, p. 241. Yet Noulens, despite his dissociation from the Tabouis fiasco, stated that "the reorganization of Ukraine presented for the development, be it intellectual or economic, of France an interest which I was not able to disregard" (I, p. 239).

British and French deemed it expedient to come to terms with this new government if it were to manifest signs of stability. Thus the Entente Powers, in sending Tabouis and Bagge to Kiev, were following a policy of exploratory opportunism prompted by military considerations. What was granted here was not recognition but a qualified acknowledgment which was later withdrawn. This policy of diplomatic flirtation was doomed to fail because the Rada could not keep pace with the promises of the masters of demagogy who were leading the Bolshevik party.

The French offer of aid to Ukraine, whether made in good faith or not, placed an added strain on Russo-Ukrainian relations because it aroused suspicion in Petrograd regarding French motives. On December 18 Foreign Commissar Trotsky called upon the French ambassador in person—a diplomatic practice which was unusual but understandable in the light of the initial Bolshevik obsession with the casting off of tradition's chains. Trotsky, who impressed the French envoy as being an "oriental despot," expressed his disapproval of the presence in Kiev of the French military mission which had formerly been attached to the Russian army on the southwestern front. He also protested the disarming of Bolshevik forces in Kiev and expressed the opinion that the Rada was organizing an army to be used against the Soviet Government. Noulens stated that since the Soviet Government recognized the principle of self-determination of nations it was proper and possible for his government to aid the Rada in the organization of its armed forces. When asked by Trotsky what the disposition of the French mission in Kiev would be in the event of war between Ukraine and Russia, Noulens replied that General Niessel's officers in Petrograd and those with Tabouis in Kiev would be on the soil of two different belligerents. However, this would not prejudice French neutrality since the Soviet Government had to accept the consequences of its having allowed Ukraine to become an independent nation when it issued the decree on self-determination on November 15.[14]

Apparently this explanation did not satisfy the Soviet Government for on December 28 an article by Stalin appeared in *Pravda* under the title "What Is the Rada?" The commissar for nationalities accused the Rada of being allied with Kaledin and of aiding the latter under the flag of "neutrality." He attacked it for opposing the "intervention" of the Soviet Government and countenancing actual French intervention. Stalin accused the French military mission in Ukraine of conducting itself as though it were in Central Africa. Branding the leaders of the Rada as "bourgeois" and a "government of betrayers of socialism, calling themselves socialists in order to deceive the masses,"[15] Stalin called for a new Rada—one which would represent the pro-Bolshevik Soviets in Ukraine.

The French hoped that the Ukrainians would continue the war against the Central Powers even though the Soviet Government were to conclude a separate peace. However, no Ukrainian army was available for this purpose since the Ukrainian soldiers in the Russian army, although numerous, were serving in all sectors of the front and were no less susceptible to the general demoralization than were the troops of other nationalities. The Ukrainian inability to continue to resist the Central Powers was obvious to the authors of the Third Universal who, in mid-November, called for an immediate general peace but at the same time appealed to the Ukrainians and to all peoples of the Russian Republic to "stand firmly in their positions at the front and in the rear" until the general peace conference would meet.[16]

---

[14] *Ibid.*, I, pp. 173f.   [15] Stalin, *op.cit.*, p. 31.

[16] The desire for peace was not novel at the time of the Bolshevik coup. The First All-Ukrainian Military Congress meeting in Kiev on May 18-21, 1917, adopted a resolution which declared that war was carried on in the interests of the imperialist politics of the ruling classes. It called for a Ukrainian people's militia to replace the army since it was believed that the former would not protect the interests of the ruling classes whatever their nationality might be (Khristiuk, *op.cit.*, I, p. 54). The First Ukrainian

This policy did not call for a separate Ukrainian peace concluded independently of Petrograd, but such a peace was advocated by the Third Ukrainian Military Congress, which met in Kiev at the time of the November Revolution, on the grounds that "prolongation of the war causes hunger and anarchy in the territory and destroys all of the achievements of the revolution." The moderate Social Democrats who were in power in the Secretariat hesitated to conclude a separate Ukrainian peace, but the utter impossibility of continuing the war prompted them to send official delegates to Brest-Litovsk "for the purpose of controlling and influencing the acts of the Bolsheviks."[17]

The Ukrainians found themselves in an unpleasant and difficult situation; the Bolsheviks had concluded an armistice with the Central Powers on December 15 in the name of the whole of Russia, including Ukraine. In addition they were confronted with a dilemma: if they refused to conclude a peace with the Central Powers the armies of the latter would invade Ukraine; if they did conclude a separate peace they would antagonize the Entente Powers who, although not in a position to render any effective aid, were insistent upon continued Ukrainian participation in the war. This led the Rada to attempt to clarify its position regarding the Brest-Litovsk peace talks. On December 24, it addressed a note to all belligerent and neutral states, drafted largely by Alexander Shulgin, informing them that the Ukrainian Government was adopting a policy of independence in international relations pending the establishment of a federation of republics which would embrace the territory of the former Russian Empire. The Rada complained bitterly that the Council of People's Com-

---

Peasant Congress meeting in June called upon the army to defend the native land but declared that war is necessary only for landowners, industrialists, and other wealthy persons. It appealed to the toiling peoples of all belligerent states to work for a peace without annexation of foreign territory and without indemnities (Khristiuk, I, pp. 101f).

[17] Vinnichenko described the objective of the delegation in these terms to the *Mala Rada*.

missars had signed an armistice agreement without first having consulted it. The peace program which the Ukrainians outlined in their note contained four primary desiderata: a general and democratic peace which would guarantee to each nation within each state the right to determine its own future; no annexations except by and with the consent of the inhabitants of the territory under consideration; no indemnities since they were "contrary to the interests of the working class the world over"; and compensation for "the little peoples and states," whose lands had been devastated by the war, on the basis of rules and procedures to be developed for this purpose by the peace conference. The Rada declared that it "must be regarded as an independent unit in international affairs and participate with other states in all peace negotiations, congresses, and conferences." It warned that any enemies of Russia making a peace with the Council of People's Commissars could not regard such a treaty as automatically binding upon the Ukrainian Republic. The appointment of a Ukrainian delegation to attend the Brest conference was rationalized by interpreting that meeting as a preliminary step to the conclusion of a general peace at an international congress. The Rada concluded its note by extending an invitation to all belligerents to attend such a general international peace conference.[18]

The delegates of the Central Powers at Brest responded to this note on December 26 with an invitation to the Rada to participate in the deliberations. When one of the Ukrainian observers at Brest, Nicholas Liubinsky, returned to Kiev on December 28, he informed the Rada of the need for sending representatives with full authority to negotiate. The Rada then resolved that "continuation of the war reduces the class consciousness of the toiling masses and threatens the achievements of the revolution in Russia and Ukraine." While recognizing that a peace treaty for all of

[18] For the text of this note see Khristiuk, op.cit., II, pp. 95f. Cf. Alexander Shulgin, L'Ukraine, la Russie et les Puissances de l'Entente, pp. 44ff.

Russia should be concluded by a federal government, it declared that such an authority was not existent. This fact made it necessary for the Ukrainian Republic to send its own delegation and empower it to negotiate a peace.

The Rada's delegation at Brest contained four representatives: Alexander Sevriuk, the gymnasium teacher Nicholas Liubinsky, Nicholas Levitsky, and Vsevolod Holubovich, the last-named of whom was minister of trade and industry and head of the peace delegation in the beginning. They had left Kiev on December 30, and arrived at Brest on January 1, with instructions from the Rada to "protect our interests." Trotsky did not protest the presence of these young nationalists who refused to speak in any language other than Ukrainian; he reiterated Lenin's stand that the Ukrainians had the right to secede from Russia. Despite this apparent Bolshevik cordiality, which was probably based on the assumption that the Rada would submit to Soviet leadership, the young Ukrainians at Brest remained aloof from the motley Soviet delegation.

The factor which finally caused Major General Max Hoffmann, German chief of staff on the Eastern front, to open formal negotiations with the Ukrainians on January 6, 1918, was Trotsky's propensity to harangue as well as his flippant attitude which prevented the theoretically victorious Central Powers from dictating a quick peace. Trotsky, whom the Germans referred to as Mephistopheles, did not conceal his belief that the "peace" was but a brief respite prior to the final struggle against world reaction of which the German and Austrian generals and negotiators were a part. The Soviet delegation did not turn against the Ukrainians at Brest until it became obvious that a separate Ukrainian peace was in the making.[19] Then on January

19 In December the Rada Government had been divided on the question of whether or not it would accept French aid. Vinnichenko did not oppose such support but was fearful that it would endanger the peace which was so indispensable to Ukraine. These deliberations were purely theoretical since a separate peace was becoming more inevitable with each passing December day. Tabouis then vainly advised the Ukrainians neither to fight nor to sign a peace treaty and cited the glorious examples of Belgium and

23, Adolf Joffe, acting head of the Soviet delegation during Trotsky's absence from Brest in connection with the dissolution of the All-Russian Constituent Assembly, informed the Central Powers that "the workers' and peasants' government of the Ukrainian Republic has decided to send two of its own delegates to Brest for participation in the peace negotiations as representatives of the Central Executive Committee of the All-Ukrainian Soviet of Workers', Soldiers', and Peasants' Deputies, but as a supplementary part of the Russian delegation."[20] The two new delegates were Medvedev, head of the Executive Committee, and Vasili Shakhrai, the commissar for military affairs. Trotsky pressed Joffe's claim on January 30, arguing that a change in circumstances necessitated the recognition of these two men rather than the Rada's delegates, as spokesmen for Ukraine.

The change in circumstances to which Trotsky referred was the launching of a full-scale drive by Bolshevik forces to seize Kiev from the Rada. Meanwhile the Rada's delegation had returned to Brest from Kiev on February 1, after narrowly escaping arrest by Bolshevik forces. Liubinsky and Sevriuk succeeded in obtaining their release by proving to their captors that they were empowered to negotiate with Medvedev of the Kharkiv Soviet Government. When

---

Serbia who had allowed the enemy to overrun them but who remained on the side of civilization, right, and justice. When it became obvious that the Ukrainians could not be prevented from going to Brest-Litovsk he recommended that Shulgin adopt dilatory methods in the negotiations. Shulgin promised Tabouis that he would not take any conclusive action without informing him and would definitely not conclude a separate peace while serving as foreign minister. This heroic commitment became worthless when Shulgin adroitly refused to head the Ukrainian peace delegation since his acceptance of that post would have made it difficult for him to remain personally faithful to Tabouis. Shulgin states that after the Brest treaty had been signed on February 9, 1918, he was asked by Hrushevsky and Holubovich, the new premier, to continue as foreign minister for the purpose of reassuring the Entente that Ukraine was still oriented in its favor. Shulgin, realizing the impossibility of such a dual policy, promptly resigned. See Shulgin's *L'Ukraine contre Moscou* (*1917*) for a vivid account of the diplomacy of this period.
20 Khristiuk, *op.cit.*, II, p. 102.

they were free and able to cross the front lines on January 31, they found the Russian trenches completely empty. The delegation was reorganized during its stay in Kiev as a result of the resignation of Vinnichenko and the appointment of a thirty-three-year-old engineer, Vsevolod Holubovich, as his successor to the premiership following the issuance of the Fourth Universal on January 22. Holubovich was replaced as head of the peace delegation by twenty-five-year-old Alexander Sevriuk; this appointment was not an error but probably was prompted by the fact that Hrushevsky envisaged the youth as the husband of his only daughter, Katherine, who had a romantic interest in him. At Brest Sevriuk gave the Soviet delegation a severe tongue-lashing; he questioned its representativeness by pointing out that it did not include delegates from Moldavia, Siberia, the Crimean Tartars, the Don Cossacks, and other regions and peoples which did not recognize the authority of the Council of People's Commissars. He stated that there had been street-fighting in Petrograd at the time of the brutal dissolution of the Constituent Assembly on January 18, yet he added that Ukraine was not prepared to follow Trotsky's example of intervention by challenging the right of the Bolsheviks to govern the Russians.

Medvedev answered Sevriuk by attacking the Rada and stating that the Ukrainian people could not accept a peace treaty concluded by it. Trotsky charged the Ukrainians with being opposed to participating in the federal Russian republic. Liubinsky then delivered a tirade[21] in response to the charges made by Trotsky and Medvedev and indicted the whole Soviet regime for demagogically preaching self-determination because of its fear of national revolutionary development:

"The Bolsheviks in order to prevent the fulfillment of this principle [of self-determination of nations] have not only employed bands of mercenary red guards but are . . .

---

[21] *Ibid.*, II, pp. 110f. contains excerpts from the address. Cf. Ivan Rudnitsky (or Ivan Kedrin) (ed), *Beresteiski Mir* (Lviv, 1928), pp. 108ff.

stifling the press and are dispersing political meetings, ar-
resting and shooting political leaders and are finally attempting with totally falsely interpreted information to
undermine the authority of the governments of various
of the young republics. Prominent socialists and old revolutionaries are being accused of being bourgeois and counter-
revolutionary. . . . In this way the Bolshevik government
gives life not to the right of self-determination but to the
principle of anarchy and decomposition because it knows
that it is easier to destroy than to create anew. . . . The
struggle of the Petrograd government against the government of the Ukrainian People's Republic and its obvious
insincerity in recognizing our delegation aroused in us
previously a not unfounded suspicion. We were convinced
that Mr. Trotsky would soon attempt to free himself from
the very lucid and definite words with which he accepted
our delegation as the legally constituted representative organ of our republic. That which we awaited has come true.
On the day on which we left for Kiev to receive final instructions there arrived in Brest, via Petrograd and Dvinsk
with the encouragement and aid of the Bolsheviks, a new
[only nominally Ukrainian] delegation which had as its
purpose the undermining of our authority in the eyes of
the toiling masses of Europe."

Liubinsky also stressed the lack of support for the Bolsheviks in the Kiev Congress of Soviets which had occurred
in December and pointed out that in the free elections for
the All-Russian Constituent Assembly held in 1917 under
the Provisional Government the Ukrainian parties had
obtained seventy-five per cent of the seats allotted to
Ukraine while the Bolsheviks had received less than ten
per cent.

Trotsky replied by stating that Liubinsky's rhetoric had
not caused him to be persuaded to modify his position and
warned the Central Powers that they would have difficulty
in defining the geographic frontiers of the newly recognized
republic. This did not disturb the Germans since they were
in a position to underwrite that Ukrainian government

which would best serve their purpose—the procurement of badly needed food and raw materials with which to continue the war in the West. The Bolshevik movement was regarded by the Germans as a temporary political aberration, and its Ukrainian delegation was not recognized by the Central Powers. Vinnichenko later admitted that the Rada regime was accorded continued recognition by the Central Powers at Brest only "because such recognition was both profitable and necessary for them."[22]

The Ukrainian delegates knew that their government was not able to withstand the Bolshevik onslaught. Pessimism had manifested itself as early as the beginning of the new year when the Red Guards seized Chernihiv, Poltava, Kharkiv, and Katerinoslav. This seizure caused Mikita Shapoval, the dramatic secretary of post and telegraph, while attending a gathering of Ukrainian leaders, to greet the year 1918 with the words *morituri te salutant*. Nevertheless the General Secretariat continued its attempt to maintain itself. On January 2, 1918, it issued a statement to the Russian people in which it expressed its willingness to provide grain for the North but protested the Bolshevik invasion which had cut off Kiev from its coal supply; it referred to the Bolsheviks as "gross violators, plunderers and counter-revolutionary red guards" and promised to drive them out of Ukraine.

Compromise between the Bolsheviks and the Rada was impossible because of the obstinacy of the former. A Soviet historian has observed that the Bolsheviks pursued a policy of opportunism while sitting in the Rada during the period from July to November: "they uncovered everywhere the petit bourgeois character of the Central Rada but did not attack it since it was first necessary to finish with the Kadet-Menshevik S. R. coalition in Russia."[23] They remained aloof from the conflict which prevailed between the Ukrainian and Russian nationalists but did employ the tactic of

[22] Vinnichenko, *op.cit.*, II, p. 211.

[23] M. Iavorsky, *Revoliutsiia na Vkraini v ii Holovnishikh etapakh* (n p., 1923), p. 38.

condemning Russian imperialism. A Jewish Social Democrat, who sat in the Rada and later became a Bolshevik, has stated that the alliance between the Bolsheviks and the Rada in November was based on expediency and the fact that the former "were not sufficiently strong in all of the south to seize authority immediately and consequently they temporarily came to terms with the fact of the Secretariat's triumph."[24] Another explanation of their motive in entering the Committee for the Defense of the Revolution in Ukraine was their fear that "reactionary units" stationed on the Rumanian and southwestern fronts would be sent to Petrograd to overthrow Lenin; to this end they obtained a promise from the Rada not to allow any reactionary troops to be sent to the North.[25] Thus it is clearly established that after the November Revolution there was no willingness on the part of the Bolsheviks to share power with other parties on any terms but their own. Instead, they became more firmly convinced that a struggle with the Rada was inevitable.[26]

The inability of the Rada to come to terms with the Bolsheviks and obtain a financial agreement from them compelled it to issue its own quadrilingual currency with the gold *karbovanets* being on a par with one Russian ruble. This act was followed by the issuance on January 22, 1918, of the Fourth Universal which was addressed to the "People of Ukraine" and which appeared at this time because the Rada in its Third Universal had committed itself to convene the Ukrainian Constituent Assembly on this day. Elections for the Assembly were to have been held on January 9, but the Bolshevik attack and the resultant chaos had made voting impossible in the eastern provinces. This document accurately described conditions

[24] Zolotarev, *op cit.*, p. 24. Cf. Rafes, *op cit.*, p. 55.

[25] Iavorsky, *op.cit.*, p. 41.

[26] The Soviet historian of this period sees the November Revolution as the turning point between two phases; the first of these is that of the national revolution while the second has been referred to as the struggle against the national counter-revolution. With the occurrence of the November Revolution the Rada and anyone who disagreed with the Bolsheviks became, ipso facto, counter-revolutionary. Cf. Iavorsky, p. 31.

in Ukraine: "factories are not producing goods . . . the railroad lines are severed, the value of the currency is declining. Bread is becoming scarce. Hunger is approaching."[27] Censuring the Petrograd commissars for waging war on Ukraine "in order to gain control over the free Ukrainian Republic," the Rada declared them guilty of "spreading anarchy, murder, and crime."

The Rada's reply to the Bolshevik invasion was the proclamation of Ukrainian independence contained in this Universal: "On this day the Ukrainian People's Republic becomes independent, dependent upon no one, a free sovereign state of the Ukrainian people." Although expressing its desire to have friendly relations with all neighboring states, including Russia, the Rada warned that "none must intervene in the life of the independent Ukrainian Republic." While this was a declaration of independence, in the opinion of many Ukrainians, including Vinnichenko and Shulgin, it merely confirmed an already existing *de facto* independence which resulted from the maintenance of separate Ukrainian armed forces (combatting the Bolsheviks for one month prior to January 22) and the establishment of diplomatic relations with the Entente Powers. Yet the Rada was not prepared, on the surface at least, to sever all ties with Russia since the Universal stated that the Ukrainian Constituent Assembly was to "determine the nature of the federal ties with the people's republics of the former Russian Empire." It is probable, however, that this provision was included for the purpose of placating the national minorities, most of whom looked askance at a complete separation.

The Rada, in an effort to persuade the peasantry to rally to its support, paid lip service to agrarian reform[28] and also declared all "forests, waters, and all subterranean wealth

---

[27] The text of the Fourth Universal is to be found in Khristiuk, *op.cit.*, II, pp. 103ff. and in Vinnichenko, *op.cit.*, II, pp. 244ff.

[28] Vinnichenko, *op cit.*, II, p. 230. The impact of the class struggle on the Universal is also evident in that passage which called for the replacement of what remained of the standing army by a people's militia "so that our armed forces shall serve to defend the working people and not to carry out the wishes of the ruling strata."

[to be] . . . placed at the disposal of the Ukrainian People's Republic." The Republic was also to assume "control over the most important segments of commerce and . . . employ all income derived from this source for the public welfare." The Rada directed the administration to "establish state-popular control over all banks which in granting credit to the leisure classes aided in the exploitation of the toiling masses," and it reaffirmed all democratic liberties initially promulgated in the preceding Universal but with the proviso that all who advocated the overthrow of the independent Ukrainian People's Republic or the re-establishment of the old order were to be regarded as traitors. In a burst of irresponsible optimism or in a futile attempt to obtain support, the Rada promised that all of the provisions in the Fourth Universal would be carried out in the ensuing several weeks either by the Rada or by the Ukrainian Constituent Assembly which it was hoped would meet shortly.

In the Universal the Rada also referred to the World War as having been "begun by bourgeois governments," voiced its desire for peace, and directed the cabinet to proceed with completely independent negotiations at Brest-Litovsk irrespective of any obstruction by former parts of the defunct Russian Empire. The national minorities, however, were not in complete agreement with the Rada regarding its peace policy. In January Zolotarev, who had recently replaced Rafes as the "Bund's" representative in the General Secretariat, contended that a separate peace of the kind advocated by the Rada would only subject Ukraine to German and Austro-Hungarian imperialist domination. He favored the Bolshevik proposal to transfer the negotiations from Brest to Stockholm in order to promote the demand of the whole European proletariat for a general peace. The "Bund" also opposed the issuance of the Fourth Universal and ordered Zolotarev to resign from the cabinet. It adopted a resolution censuring the Rada for "making it possible for German imperialism to dictate the conditions of a separate peace." Independence under such conditions was declared to be fictional and detrimental to the revolution since it would mean that the ties between Russian and Ukrainian democracy would be severed at the expense of international democracy.[29]

The determination of the Rada to make a separate peace, despite this minority opposition, accelerated the Soviet invasion since such a treaty would have deprived Russia of badly needed grain by diverting it to the Central Powers. At the same time it was becoming more obvious to the Rada's peace delegation that the only hope for the salvation of the tottering regime which they represented lay in obtaining German and Austrian support.[30] The only other alternative was to have Trotsky act as their spokesman. The Ukrainians were desperate and readily gave up their prior claim to Eastern Galicia and Northern Bukovina on the condition that the Ukrainians who remained in Austria-Hungary were to be granted their own province.

The new Social Revolutionary cabinet which replaced Vinnichenko's Social Democratic government after the issuance of the Fourth Universal had but one immediate task: the defense of Kiev against the Bolshevik offensive. Inside Kiev street-fighting broke out between the Rada's limited forces and the pro-Bolshevik non-Ukrainian proletariat. The Russian Mensheviks and the right Russian Social Revolutionaries refused to aid in the defense of Kiev. Many of the Ukrainian military units in Kiev at the time remained neutral, not only because the Rada had failed to fulfill their expectations but also as a result of

[29] Rafes, op.cit., pp. 70ff.

[30] The internal weakness of the Rada Government is well illustrated by the plot which was uncovered in January. The pro-Bolshevik left wing of the Social Revolutionary party, led by Liubchenko, Shumsky, and Polozov, had planned to overthrow the Rada, introduce the soviet form of government, and make peace with the Russian commissars. Kovenko, the Ukrainian military commander in Kiev, acted swiftly and arrested most of the conspirators in the building in which the Rada met, thus violating whatever legislative immunity they may have had. The center and right-wing Social Revolutionaries together with some left-wing Social Democrats set about organizing a new predominantly Social Revolutionary cabinet while at the same time attempting to avoid Bolshevik shrapnel.

the general fatigue brought on by the three and one-half years of seemingly interminable warfare. Disorder and confusion reigned within the city. Dmitro Doroshenko, an official of the Rada government, had his automobile requisitioned and was compelled to attend to his business on foot. Alexander Shulgin, when summoned to the telegraph office for the purpose of communicating with the delegation at Brest, found it necessary to go on foot and carry a revolver. Upon arrival at the office, he informed the negotiators at Brest that he no longer was foreign minister, and refused to advise them. Thus the government and its peace delegation were no longer in touch with each other.

As the main Bolshevik force approached Kiev at the end of January along the rail line from Kursk, the Rada was able to muster only a hastily organized and utterly inexperienced students' "military" unit. After a hopelessly one-sided engagement at the town of Kruti (directly east of Nizhin), in which most of the Ukrainian students fell, the road to Kiev lay open to the Bolsheviks. Soon the great city was under enemy artillery fire. A strike of workers at the waterworks and the electric station threw the city into darkness and deprived it of water; a Bolshevik armored train shelled and ruined Hrushevsky's six-story apartment house, destroying his valuable library in the process. Fires raged in many sections and civilian casualties were high as a result of the twelve-day shelling to which the Bolsheviks subjected the city.[81] The Ukrainian cabinet literally disappeared; meetings held in war minister Nemolovsky's office were attended only by Prime Minister Holubovich, Khristiuk (interior), Tkachenko (justice), and the former secretary for military affairs, Porsh. The other seven cabinet members had vanished.

The Rada was in dire straits, and the Entente could not send aid even if it had wished to do so—which was not the case since the Ukrainians had gone to Brest. The impossi-

---

[81] For a vivid eyewitness account of the Bolshevik siege of Kiev in January and February of 1918 see S. Sumsky, "Odinnadsat' Perevorotov," *Letopis' Revoliutsii* (Berlin, 1923), I, pp. 228ff.

bility of defending Kiev necessitated the Rada's fleeing secretly to Zhitomir on February 7, with two thousand disorganized troops. During the flight the few ministers who still constituted the Ukrainian government found it necessary to carry firearms on their persons.[32] Prior to leaving the city, the Rada, as if in a final gesture of heroic futility, enacted an agrarian law which abolished the right of private ownership of lands, subterranean wealth, and waters and made these public property. In the course of the flight the eight-hour day was also promulgated, but no law was enacted providing for the promised state control over banks, commerce, and industry.

The fatigued peace delegation at Brest, isolated from its fleeing government and realizing that only a peace treaty could salvage what little remained, signed the first Treaty of Brest-Litovsk at two o'clock on the morning of February 9. Within ten hours a courier arrived at the Brest fortress and informed the Ukrainians that Kiev had fallen. This peace, which the editors of the *New York Times* on the following day indignantly termed "secret diplomacy of the worst sort," gave to Ukraine the Kholm region which was also claimed by the Poles. In accordance with a secret appendix, Eastern Galicia and Northern Bukovina were to remain within Austria, subject to the establishment of a separate Ukrainian province. Austria's consent to the cession of Kholm, although reluctant, was motivated by foreign minister Count Ottokar Czernin's desperation. He hoped a Ukrainian peace would alleviate the serious food shortages. Czernin knew that the Ukrainian delegates, whose ability he respected, were aware of the internal difficulties which the Dual Empire was experiencing. Indeed, the Ukrainians were responsible for the detail in the treaty.

[32] Khristiuk, *op.cit.*, II, p. 128. The members of the national minorities in the Rada did not flee with what remained of the cabinet. According to Dmitro Doroshenko, few prominent Ukrainians suffered at the hands of the Bolsheviks during the three-week occupation of Kiev; this was probably due to the inadequacy of their intelligence service. Only the non-Ukrainian bourgeoisie, which predominated in the capital, was punished in any large degree. Michael A. Muraviev, the local Bolshevik commander in Kiev, levied a ten million ruble contribution on the bourgeoisie.

Had Czernin's will prevailed, the document would have done no more than terminate hostilities, provide for the establishment of diplomatic and consular relations, and obligate the Ukrainians to deliver one million tons of grain and supplies.

However, the detail was of little use. The Ukrainian annexation of Kholm was not realized because of strong opposition from the Poles in the Austrian parliament. In order to dispel Polish doubts and fears with respect to the new frontier, a special protocol was signed at Brest-Litovsk on March 4 by the four Central Powers and Ukraine. This agreement provided for the establishment of a mixed commission to determine the new Polish-Ukrainian frontier. It was expressly stated that this body was not to be bound by the frontier north of Galicia outlined in the original treaty of February 9, by which Kholm was ceded to Ukraine. Instead, the commission, which was to contain representatives from the Poles as well as from the five signatories, was empowered to move the frontier to the east.

Although the Rada lost Kholm for all practical purposes, it did obtain legal recognition from Germany, Austria-Hungary, Bulgaria, and Turkey or, in Vinnichenko's words, the treaty gave to Ukraine "the opportunity to strengthen and legalize our statehood on the international plane."[33] The price paid for this recognition was high; it required forfeiture of the "recognition" which had been accorded the Rada by the Entente, and it made Ukraine a German satellite. In return for this the Rada obtained a new lease on life. The Germans repaid the Ukrainians for what Chancellor von Hertling praised as their "practical attitude," by compelling Trotsky, in the March 3 treaty with Russia, to recognize the independence of Ukraine, withdraw all Bolshevik troops, and cease attempting to establish a Soviet Ukrainian government.[34]

[33] Vinnichenko, *op.cit.*, II, p. 197.

[34] On February 3, and again four days later, Trotsky maintained that the Rada was no longer in Kiev. When the Ukrainians signed their peace he became incensed and on February 10 walked out of the conference after accusing Germany of desiring a peace with annexations. He astonished the

While the Bolsheviks held Kiev for three weeks the Rada Government was without a capital. Upon arriving in Zhitomir the remnants of the Rada's cabinet were greeted with a city council resolution which instructed them to go elsewhere. This was impossible since the Rada was being pursued by Bolshevik forces from the east, and the route westward was blocked by pro-Bolshevik troops on the front in Volynia and Podolia. The Ukrainian peace delegation at Brest frantically appealed to the Central Powers for the use of Galician Ukrainian military forces and Ukrainian prisoners of war in Austria in order to facilitate the expulsion of the Bolsheviks from Ukraine. This appeal was rejected on the grounds that transportation was not available, but the use of German troops was promised as a substitute. The Rada was willing to agree to this on the condition that the German forces confine themselves to the Russo-Ukrainian frontier and not enter the central provinces. When this proviso, which illustrates the naiveté of the Ukrainian political novices, was rejected by the Germans the Rada had no alternative but to accept the latter's proposal of unconditional military aid. The Bolsheviks captured Berdichiv and the Ukrainian Government ordered its railroad cars pulled to Sarni in Volynia where it met, with surprise as well as with some relief, the advancing troops of the Central Powers. Hrushevsky, however, wept in his railroad car because his enemies had always accused him of being a Germanophile, and now denials would be useless.

The Germans had based their advance on an appeal made to them on February 12 by the Ukrainian delegates in Brest. This plea, addressed to the German people, was for aid against "the enemy of our liberty who has invaded our native land in order to subjugate the Ukrainian people

---

delegates of the Central Powers by declaring: "We are going out of the war but we feel ourselves compelled to refuse to sign the peace treaty." However, the resumption of military operations by the Germans compelled Trotsky to accept a peace treaty. Cf. John W. Wheeler-Bennett, *The Forgotten Peace: Brest Litovsk* (New York, 1939), p. 227.

with fire and sword."[35] Denying that the Rada was bourgeois and reaffirming its socialist nature and representativeness, the desperate delegates supplicated: "In this difficult struggle for our very existence we seek aid. We are
deeply convinced that the German people, who appreciate
peace and order, will not remain indifferent when it learns
of our need. The German troops which stand on the flank
of our northern enemy have the strength to aid us and . . .
protect our northern frontier." The peripatetic Rada was
in no position to stipulate any conditions regarding aid.
At the time the cabinet foolishly assumed that the Germans
would not intervene in Ukrainian internal affairs and that
troop requirements in the West would necessitate the
speedy withdrawal of occupation forces.

On February 23, the cabinet issued a statement in which
it referred to the German troops and the returning prisoners of war as harbingers of "peace and order in our land
so as to make it possible for the Council of People's Ministers to . . . establish an independent Ukrainian People's
Republic."[36] The Rada Government returned to Zhitomir
from Sarni and, while awaiting the capture of Kiev, made
the Gregorian calendar official as of March 1, established
the *hrivnia* as a medium of exchange, and decreed the
trizub (a trident found on the coins of Kievan Rus) to be
the coat of arms of the Ukrainian Republic.

Accompanying the Rada on its return to Kiev early in
March were the Sich Sharpshooters (*Sichovi Striltsi*), a
Ukrainian military unit composed of Galician prisoners
of war in Russia and organized in the late winter by Eugene
Konovalets and Andrew Melnyk. The opening of the western frontier enabled many Galician Ukrainian political leaders and émigrés from East Ukraine, including Dr. Dmitro
Dontsov and Dr. Vasil Paneyko, to come to Kiev. The
Rada's cabinet was enlarged to include minor Social Democrats and five Socialist Federalists, including Serhi Shelukhin, who was made minister of justice, but the Social

---

[35] For the full text of the appeal see Khristiuk, *op.cit.*, II, pp. 139f.
[36] *Ibid.*, II, p. 142. Cf. Doroshenko, *Istoriia Ukraini (1917-1923)* (Uzhorod, 1930), II, pp. 14f.

Revolutionaries held seven of the fifteen portfolios and were the largest single group in the cabinet.

The Rada's reliance upon Germany made a rapprochement with Russia's Bolshevik Government all but impossible. Hrushevsky gave expression to the prevailing sentiment when he returned to Kiev:

"German political circles have long desired Ukraine's secession and development into an independent strong state. They regarded this as profitable for Germany. During the war the German government employed instructors to teach captured Ukrainians, acquainting them with the Ukrainian point of view and organizing them into Ukrainian regiments which could defend Ukraine after the war. This was done without the understanding and consent of Ukrainian political leaders since they favored a peaceful settlement of the Ukrainian question within Russia. But the Germans believed that agreement was impossible, and their expectations proved to be correct."[37]

He also assured the Ukrainians that the German troops would "remain only so long as they will be needed by our government for the liberation of Ukraine." Premier Holubovich informed the Ukrainians that the Germans would punish only those who attacked them and aided the Bolsheviks. The Rada had issued an unbelievable statement on February 25, declaring that Ukrainian sovereignty would not be limited or its laws and customs modified. According to the premier, the delivery of supplies to the Central Powers would not place a strain upon the Ukrainian economy. Vinnichenko later frankly stated that the Rada had returned to Kiev on "heavy German artillery" and recalled that the Ukrainians had forgotten their old proverb which warns that "you must sing the tune of the person on whose wagon you ride." Soon they had occasion to end their self-delusion and learn of their presence on the high-powered vehicle of German imperialism.

[37] Khristiuk, op.cit., II, p. 143. Doroshenko, who witnessed the entry of the Germans into Kiev, maintains that the Rada was not enthusiastic about the Germans and regarded them as occupation forces rather than as allies (Moi Spomini pro Nedavne-Minule, II, p. 75).

The German military was concerned solely with obtaining a government which could guarantee the delivery of supplies. No realist could have expected it to serve as a neutral police and defense force, willing to accept all orders issued by the Rada. Because of Germany's social outlook it could hardly be in sympathy with the agrarian reform which was being sponsored by the nominally socialist cabinet. The weak ties which prevailed between the Rada and the provinces, and the complete breakdown of local government resulting from the Bolshevik invasion, made it impossible to prevent local landlords from organizing punitive expeditions to deal with those peasants who had accepted the Rada's new agrarian legislation at face value and had seized landed estates.

Opposition to the Rada arose not only among the landowners but also among the wealthier peasants. This dissatisfaction on the part of the latter had commenced in June 1917 when the Ukrainian Democratic-Agrarian party (*Ukrainska Demokratichno-Khliborobska partiia*) held its founding congress at Lubni. This meeting was attended by approximately 1,500 peasants despite several rude interruptions by soldiers who disagreed with the purpose of the gathering. The leading ideologist of this movement was Viacheslav Lipinsky who later defined *khliborobi* as:

"a group of families which sows its own land and with its own labor produces agricultural products. The quantity and the form of labor do not play a decisive role in the class consciousness of the *khliborob*; the decisive fact in this consciousness is the individual mastery of the land and individual tilling of it. Whether he has one *desiatina* [2.7 acres] or a hundred he is, in either case, interested in preserving his holding. Whether he plows this land himself or hires someone to do this and himself organizes this plowing he is nevertheless interested in cultivating this land in the best manner producing as much as possible at the greatest realizable profit."[38]

[38] V. Lipinsky, "Listi do Brativ Khliborobiv," *Khliborobska Ukraina*, II, pp. 10f.

120

The party in its initial program advocated the sovereignty of the Ukrainian people, the preservation of private ownership, and the division of the large landed estates with compensation for the owners so that the holdings of peasants could be increased in an orderly manner by purchase.

This genuinely nationalist movement was not strong outside the Lubni district and met with considerable opposition during 1917. However, it emerged as a stronger force in the political vacuum which prevailed after the Bolshevik retreat from Ukraine in March. On April 7, 1918, over 2,000 wealthy peasants from the six northern districts of Poltava province met in Lubni for the purpose of expressing their views on the "agrarian anarchy" which prevailed at the time. Popular opposition to the movement caused the peasants to arm their sons for the purpose of protecting the gathering. The party charged that the Rada's agrarian policy was ruinous; it demanded the recognition of private ownership, restoration of seized property to former owners, retention of a minimum of land by these owners and leasing of the remainder to those who were in need of it. It also advocated the establishment of a legal order to which socialists and non-socialists would be equally subject and the admission of *khliborob* representatives into the Rada.[39] On the following day a 200-man delegation, headed by the engineer Serhi Shemet, arrived in Kiev to press its demands. Hrushevsky refused to allow it to appear before a plenary session of the Rada. The delegates did, however, confer with party leaders and with Premier Holubovich and agriculture minister Kovalevsky. When their demands were rejected they decided to call a congress of all *khliborob* organizations in Kiev on April 28.

The dissatisfaction which the wealthier peasants had with the Rada was also beginning to manifest itself among the German military. As early as March 9, Colonel von

[39] Serhi Shemet, "Do istorii Ukrainskoi Demokratichno-khliborobskoi Partii," *Khliborobska Ukraina* (Vienna, 1920), I, pp. 67f. In Kiev the party demanded that the Ukrainian Constituent Assembly not meet in such "abnormal times" since that predominantly Social Revolutionary body would probably have approved of the Rada's economic program

Stolzenberg in Kiev telegraphed the German commander of the Eastern front: "It is very doubtful whether this government, composed as it is exclusively of left opportunists, will be able to establish a firm authority."[40] He doubted the ability of the Rada to ensure grain deliveries and advocated strong action in dealing with the Ukrainians since the outcome of decisive battles in the West would depend upon what was done in Ukraine. He was not, however, expressing official policy since at the time it was largely in the hands of the German ambassador (*Botschafter*) in Kiev, Baron Adolf Mumm von Schwarzenstein, who preferred to conduct relations with the Ukrainians in a manner befitting a diplomat.

German toleration of the ineffective Rada Government was due not only to Mumm's hesitancy to overthrow it but also to the lack of a definite policy. General Wilhelm Groener, chief of staff to the German commander in Ukraine and later minister of transport and war under the Weimar Republic, appealed to Ludendorff as late as March 21 for instructions.[41] On March 26, the foreign ministry sent Mumm a note directing him to inform the Rada that, in return for German aid, it must ensure and protect grain exports.[42] This note contained an indication of a possible shift in German support to a new regime: "We are far from the thought of intervening in Ukrainian internal affairs, but nevertheless we must see to it that the cultivation of the land is carried on to the fullest extent even if this means sacrifice of principles." By April 5, Mumm, who had previously served in Tokyo, was referring to the Rada as a "pseudo-government" and was considering a reorientation towards the right, but wanted the necessary contacts to be made by the Ukrainophile Baltic German journalist, Paul Rohrbach, rather than by officials.

This change in Mumm's attitude was caused by increas-

[40] I. I. Mints, and E. N. Gorodetsky (eds.), *Dokumenty o Razgrome Germanskikh okkupantov na Ukraine v 1918 godu* (Moscow, 1942), p. 16.
[41] *Ibid.*, pp. 20f.
[42] I. I. Mints, and R. Eideman (eds.), *Krakh Germanskoi Okkupatsii na Ukraine* (Moscow, 1936), p. 30.

ing difficulties which the Germans were having with the Rada. On March 23 the minister of justice had issued a circular to all procurators attached to regional courts, stating that German and Austrian military courts had no authority to try Ukrainian citizens. As the spring planting season approached, apprehensiveness among occupation authorities mounted. The most serious act of intervention occurred on April 6, when the supreme commander of the German forces in Ukraine, Field Marshal von Eichhorn, issued an order to his subordinates in which he stated that the peasants, under the leadership of the local land committees, were failing to sow the fields. The accusation was true; the peasantry, in the face of intense reaction on the part of the landowners, was uncertain of the future disposition of the harvest. Eichhorn commanded that the fields be sowed either by means of an understanding with the land committees or "by the initiative of the military authorities themselves." Completely ignoring the Rada's agrarian law, he declared that the harvest was the possession of the person who sowed it and would be purchased by the Germans at "suitable prices"; peasants holding more land than they could cultivate were to be severely punished. The reactionary nature of the German military and its utter disregard for the Rada's land program manifested itself in the following portion of the order: "In those locales where the peasants cannot cultivate all of the land and where there are still landowners, the latter are expected to seed fields but not in a manner which would interfere with the right to a legal division of land with the aid of the land committees. In such cases the peasants are not to hinder the landowners in the sowing."[43]

When the Rada protested, Eichhorn maintained that the

[43] The text of Eichhorn's order is to be found in Khristiuk, *op.cit*, II, pp. 201f., n. 23. Cf. Vinnichenko, *op.cit.*, II, pp. 320ff. Mumm claimed, in a note which he sent to Chancellor Hertling on May 15, that he had been informed that the order would be issued but did not participate in the issuance of it; he placed the responsibility for it squarely upon the military command. In this note he also expressed the opinion that the order should not have been issued. (See Mints and Eideman, *op.cit.*, p. 91.)

order had been prepared with the consent of the minister of agriculture, Kovalevsky. When Holubovich, Hrushevsky, and Liubinsky protested to Mumm on April 12, he reminded them that they could call themselves the government of Ukraine only because Germany stood behind them. The *Mala Rada*, after heated debate, adopted a resolution declaring that willful intervention by the armies of occupation in the social, political, and economic life of Ukraine was not permissible. Kovalevsky tendered his resignation, but the *Mala Rada* meeting on April 13 refused to accept it and instead instructed him to inform the Ukrainian population that Eichhorn's order was not to be executed. The foreign minister was directed to protest the order and all other acts of intervention. Eichhorn contended that he was not intervening but merely reinforcing the previous appeals of the ministry of agriculture regarding the spring planting.

This controversy placed an added strain upon German-Ukrainian relations and prompted Mumm to suggest to Berlin on April 18 that the substance if not the form of a general governorship be established and that the peasant (*khliborob*) demonstration against the Rada's agrarian policy, planned for April 28, could be capitalized upon to this end.[44] Mumm and General Groener did not differ appreciably at this point on whether or not a new government should be established but only on the time and method. Groener, who made all of Eichhorn's political decisions, desired immediate action but hesitated to overthrow the government without first obtaining the support of the foreign ministry. Yet Mumm vacillated and on April 16 sent a secret wire to Berlin in which he stated that "a change in governments would not in itself be unfortunate, but there are no suitable successors."[45] At the same time he expressed the opinion that in the event of risings it was

[44] Mints and Gorodetsky, *op.cit.*, pp. 71ff. On April 13, Mumm informed Berlin that "permanent collaboration with these men, who because of their socialist theories, cease to comprehend the real state of affairs, is impossible" (Mints and Eideman, p. 42).
[45] Mints and Eideman, *op.cit.*, p. 44.

124

possible that there would not be an adequate number of troops available to maintain order.

The issue was finally resolved on April 23, at a meeting held in Kiev and attended by General Groener, Baron Mumm, the Austrian ambassador Forgach, and two military plenipotentiaries. These men agreed that it was impossible to deal with the Rada "because of its tendencies" and Mumm, who had previously referred to the Rada as a "weak utopian communist government," reported to Berlin: "Insofar as it is possible a Ukrainian government should be preserved but one which must in its activities depend on the German and Austrian supreme commanders. The Ukrainian government must not hinder the military and economic undertakings of the German authorities."[46] The next decision which the occupation authorities had to make was the selection of a man to head the new government which would replace the Rada.

During the evening of April 24, Lieutenant General Paul Skoropadsky, a prominent landowner, met with General Groener for the purpose of discussing the conditions under which the occupation forces would support the new regime that he intended to establish. As nearly as can be determined, Skoropadsky was first contacted by a representative of the German command, a Major Hasse, on April 11 or 12, and subsequent preliminary meetings occurred on April 13 and 15. At the April 24 meeting the General was not promised German aid in the coup itself but was told that his government could expect support if he were to succeed in overthrowing the Rada and were to accept the conditions laid down by the military command. These conditions included acceptance of the peace treaty of Brest-Litovsk, the dissolution of the Rada and the banning of the Ukrainian constituent assembly until new elections could be held. The elections were to occur only if all unrest were terminated, and this would be determined in consultation with the German command. The Germans were willing to agree in principle to the organization of

[46] Mints and Gorodetsky, *op.cit.*, pp. 73f.

a Ukrainian army but qualified this by insisting that its strength and disposition be determined in agreement with the occupation authorities. All crimes committed against troops of the Central Powers and all violations of decisions of the military authorities were to be tried in military courts. All "untrustworthy" persons were to be removed from the civil service, and the land committees and other such local bodies were to be dissolved and replaced by responsible state organs of administration. The German and Austrian law regarding natural obligations in time of war (the right of the army to requisition) was to apply to Ukraine until appropriate legislation could be enacted. All limitations on the export of raw materials and manufactured goods were to be removed together with all railroad restrictions; a joint border control was to be established. The Germans also intervened in the agrarian sphere and demanded restoration of the right of ownership and payment for land received when holdings would be divided; large holdings were to remain, Ukraine was to agree to compensate Germany for the military aid rendered but the character and extent of the requital were to be determined later. A long-term economic agreement, with tariffs favorable to the Central Powers, was to be concluded in the future.[47] All cabinet appointees designated by Skoropadsky had to be personae gratae to the occupation authorities.

Skoropadsky accepted all of the important conditions laid down at this meeting and prepared to seize power. His conviction regarding the need for a new government was confirmed on April 24, when the wealthy Jewish financier and director of the Russian Bank for Foreign Trade, Abraham Iu. Dobri, disappeared. Dobri, who was a member of the financial commission which was negotiating a commercial agreement with the Germans, had favored the replacement of the Rada by a government which would reflect the distribution of economic wealth more accurately.

[47] *Ibid.*, pp. 74ff. Cf. Doroshenko, *Istoriia Ukraini*, II, pp. 30ff. and *Za Velich Natsii* (Lviv, 1938), pp. 27f.

He had also been accused of selling a sugar refinery to the Germans in violation of the laws of the Republic. It appears that he was kidnaped and taken to Kharkiv by agents of the Committee to Save Ukraine (*Komitet Poriatunku Ukraini*), a pro-Rada organization. At the time, the interior minister, Tkachenko, and other officials were accused of being accessories to the kidnaping. The wealthier citizens of Kiev appealed to the Germans, who regarded this as conclusive proof of the Rada's inability to maintain order. When Baron Mumm demanded Dobri's release by 6:00 p.m. on April 25, Premier Holubovich truthfully informed him that he knew nothing of the banker's whereabouts.

The obscure Dobri affair prompted Field Marshal von Eichhorn to issue his sweeping order of April 25, regarding the jurisdiction of military courts in Ukraine.[48] He posed the problem in these terms: "Irresponsible persons and organizations are attempting to terrorize the population. In violation of all law and right they are carrying out arrests for the purpose of intimidating those who, in the interests of the birthland and the newly-founded state, are prepared to work hand in hand with Germany." He ordered that all offenses against public order and all criminal acts be under the jurisdiction of the German military courts. All street meetings were forbidden, as well as all attempts to create disorder by means of verbal or journalistic agitation. Newspapers found guilty of this offense were to be closed. This order limited the jurisdiction of Ukrainian courts exclusively to civil cases.

Throughout April, Kiev was alive with rumors regarding the establishment of a new government. As the influence and prestige of the Rada declined, the Socialist Federalist party on April 27 withdrew its three ministers (justice, trade, and education) from the cabinet. The party was not involved in the conspiracy which resulted in the Rada's overthrow, but it cannot be denied that the resignation

[48] For the text of this order, see Doroshenko, *Istoriia Ukraini*, II, p. 32, n. 3 and Mints and Eideman, *op.cit.*, p. 52.

of its ministers further weakened the government. However, the party was justified in withdrawing from the cabinet because its ministers were responsible for the acts of the government but lacked authority commensurate with the responsibility which participation placed upon them.

Prior to this, on the night of April 26, the Germans disarmed the first Ukrainian division of *Sinezhupaniki* (bluecoats) composed of former Ukrainian prisoners of war in Germany. At the same time Mumm felt compelled to prevail upon General Groener not to proclaim a state of siege, since such a step would have created an unfavorable impression upon public opinion at home and in neutral countries.

. These new German acts of intervention in Ukrainian internal affairs caused the Rada to spend April 27 and 28 in stormy debate and bitter denunciation of the reactionary German military. The Ukrainian foreign minister, Nicholas Liubinsky, was unjustly criticized for not having obtained a German-Ukrainian agreement with the precise conditions of occupation clearly stated. There were threats of refusal to fulfill commercial agreements, especially that of April 23; the Germans were also promised peasant rebellions. Prussian Junkerdom and its imperialism were vehemently castigated. Premier Holubovich, in addressing the Rada, distinguished between the German military in Ukraine and the German government and incorrectly assumed that the former was pursuing its own policy in opposition to that of the latter.[49] Eichhorn was not removed as a result of the appeals and protests to Berlin.

[49] Hrushevsky also maintained this naiveté at least until April 21, on which day an article of his appeared in *Narodna Volia* (Popular Will) stating: "We have faith in the political sense of the German and Austrian governments. We do not believe that it will heed the voices of these sycophants [landowners] and the reports which under their influence local German and Austrian commanders refer to the high command." (Khristiuk, *op.cit.*, II, p. 161.) Others were guilty of the same unfounded optimism. Porsh, a Social Democrat, believed that the peasantry would deal with Eichhorn as it had with Kornilov and that three million German troops would be needed in order to hold Ukraine for the Central Powers. Vinnichenko, who had returned to Kiev for what was to be the last session of the Rada, believed that revolution would soon break out in Germany

Instead, the Rada chamber was invaded on the afternoon of April 28, by a detachment of armed German troops; the German officer in charge, speaking in Russian, ordered the members of the Rada to stand and raise their hands. In Vinnichenko's words, the Germans, who had been expected to conduct themselves as guests, were behaving in the manner of swine. Only Hrushevsky had the temerity to remain seated; a search of the members revealed that some had been carrying firearms. The purpose of the raid was to arrest the following ministers and officials: Michael Tkachenko, internal affairs; Nicholas Liubinsky, foreign affairs; A. Zhukovsky, military affairs; Nicholas Kovalevsky, agriculture; and Haevsky, a department head in the interior ministry. Only Liubinsky and Haevsky were present; Tkachenko avoided arrest by hiding, but his wife as well as Zhukovsky were apprehended later. These persons were arrested because of their alleged participation in the Dobri affair. The German troops did not disperse the Rada since it met again the next day in what was to be its final session. On the day of the Rada raid, the military command also issued an order directing labor organizations and the interior ministry to obtain permission from military headquarters before attempting to hold or sanction any May Day demonstrations.

Premier Holubovich protested to Mumm and asked if the German Government had approved of the act or had ordered the raid. The German envoy informed him that the officer in charge had acted independently. This explanation was subsequently adhered to by other German spokesmen and may have some validity since Eichhorn did send Holubovich a letter expressing regret over the arrests. In any case, it seems that the raid was not directly related to the coup being planned by Skoropadsky and his supporters.[50]

---

and Austria-Hungary. It is only fair to state that some of this confidence resulted from opposition to the occupation policy of the military which arose in the Reichstag and was led by such deputies as Erzberger, Scheidemann, and Noske.

[50] Skoropadsky, in the fragments of his memoirs published in *Khlibo-*

One of the prominent organizations behind the coup was the League of Landowners (*Soiuz Zemelnykh Sobstvennikov*) which was composed of Russified intermediate and large landholders who had little sympathy with the Ukrainian national movement. This body called a congress of agriculturalists in Kiev on April 29, which was attended by more than six thousand delegates from eight Ukrainian provinces. The objectives of this gathering were preservation of the principle of private ownership, the termination of socialist experimentation, and the dissolution of the Rada. Various speakers advocated the establishment of a dictatorial type of government. Apparently by prearrangement, General Skoropadsky appeared in a box in the auditorium and was given an ovation. The president of the Congress, Michael M. Voronovich, former tsarist governor of Bessarabia, then called upon the landowners to confer upon Skoropadsky the antiquated Ukrainian monarchical title of "Hetman." When the General reached the stage he was greeted with a tumultuous ovation after which he expressed his gratitude to the delegates "for having conferred [provisional] authority upon me."[51] He concluded his speech of acceptance with the following words: "You all know that anarchy is rampant everywhere and that only a firm authority can reestablish order. I shall rely for support upon you and upon the stable and prudent portions of the population, and I pray to God to grant me the strength and firmness to save Ukraine." The new Hetman, who had been "elected" by acclamation, was then carried about the auditorium on the shoulders of his admirers, who saw in him the salvation of their class.

The Ukrainian Democratic-Agrarian party, which was composed of prosperous peasants, did not participate in the

---

robska Ukraina (Vienna, 1924-1925), v, pp. 76f., maintained that there was absolutely no connection between the two events. Baron Mumm admitted on May 2, in a note which he sent to the foreign ministry in Berlin, that the violation of parliamentary privileges of Rada members had antagonized even the moderate Socialist Federalists as well as all of the leftist parties (Mints and Eideman, *op.cit.*, p. 60).

[51] Doroshenko, *Istoriia Ukraini*, II, p. 37.

"election" because it disagreed with the League of Landowners on two important issues. It favored agrarian reform whereas the landowners were not favorably disposed
towards the dissolution of their estates. The second issue
which divided the two groups was the question of the
existing government; the wealthier peasants were willing
to compromise with the Rada while the landowners wished
to replace it.[52] However, a more fundamental issue, the national question, divided the two organizations. The Democratic-Agrarian party was Ukrainian while the membership of the Landowners' League was lacking in national
consciousness and regarded Ukrainian independence as a
temporary phenomenon.

The Democratic-Agrarian party, which was much weaker
than the League financially, had called a congress of agriculturalists to meet in Kiev on April 28, and had held a
preliminary session on that day in a Kiev theater. The
general session, which was to meet on April 29, was forbidden by the German military on the basis of Eichhorn's
order of April 25, banning public gatherings and agitation.
It is significant that General Groener did not apply Eichhorn's order to the congress of the Landowners' League
which was meeting on the same day but under German
armed protection. Some of the wealthier peasants, finding
themselves locked out of their meeting hall, went to the
landowners' congress, where, if they were able to enter the
crowded auditorium, they participated in the shouting.
The Ukrainian Democratic-Agrarian party did not participate in the coup as a unit, although it cannot be denied
that the party, in criticizing the Rada, helped lay the
groundwork for a change in governments.

Although General Skoropadsky had been "elected" by
the landowners, something more ceremonious than mere
acclamation was necessary in order to establish the legiti-
macy of the new regime. Accordingly, the landowners were
instructed to be present on the afternoon of April 29 in
St. Sophia Square for the purpose of attending a pontifical

---

[52] *Ibid.*, p. 39. Cf. Shemet, *op cit.*, p. 70.

Te Deum (*moleben*). Prior to this, the new Hetman, attired in a black Cossack uniform, was anointed by Bishop Nicodemus in the old cathedral of Saint Sophia. The inhabitants of Kiev received the news of the establishment of the Hetmanate with nonchalance as well as with slight bewilderment since no one had held the title for 154 years.

While the new Hetman was being inaugurated, to the accompaniment of much bell-ringing, the Rada was holding its last session at which it belatedly adopted the constitution of the Ukrainian People's Republic, which originally was to have been ratified by the Ukrainian Constituent Assembly.[53] This dramatic but ineffectual final act typified the unreality and lack of political aptitude which prevailed in the Rada. This first modern Ukrainian parliament was not dispersed, although it recognized that it had been superseded by a new government. It did not prove to be a popular rallying point; instead, it collapsed quickly when slight pressure was brought to bear upon it. Several hundred of Skoropadsky's supporters, mostly Russian officers, under the command of General Dashkevich-Hor-

[53] This constitution was of the liberal democratic variety and provided for an All-National Assembly with one deputy representing 100,000 persons; the minimum age for deputies was to have been twenty. The Council of People's Ministers was to have been appointed by the head of the Assembly in consultation with other Assembly officials. A section of the document embodied the Rada's proposed system for dealing with national minorities. Russians, Poles, and Jews were accorded national-personal autonomy and other nationalities were enabled to qualify for it by presenting a petition with ten thousand signatures. Citizens of a given nationality were to form a national union which was to be entitled to receive state funds and to have its own constituent assembly, which was to determine the extent of competency of the union. Delegates to these constituent assemblies were to be elected by all citizens of the particular union who were twenty years of age; sex and religious faith were not to limit anyone's right to vote. Conflicts between the constituent assemblies of individual nationalities and the All-National Assembly were to be resolved by joint commissions in which both bodies were to have an equal number of votes. Decisions of such a commission were to be subject to confirmation by the All-National Assembly, and organs of the national unions were to be state organs. An administrative court was to decide jurisdictional conflicts between organs of a national union, organs of the state administration, and organs of other national unions. (For a full text of the constitution see Khristiuk, *op.cit.*, II, pp. 175ff.)

batsky, seized control of the various ministries during the night of April 29. The Rada's ministries were defended only by some Galician Ukrainians, members of the Sich Sharpshooters, who offered slight resistance. Three Hetmanites were killed in the coup, and by the early hours of the morning of April 30 Skoropadsky's forces were in control of all the government offices and the Sich Sharpshooters were disarmed.[54] The Ukrainian State (*Ukrainska Derzhava*) had replaced the Ukrainian People's Republic.

The immediate cause of the Rada's downfall undoubtedly was the debilitating influence of the Brest-Litovsk Treaty as well as an inability to please the German master. But the demise of this government can be correctly evaluated only in terms of the weakness of the Ukrainian national movement and the unfortunate circumstances which surrounded its emergence at the time of the Russian Revolution. The year 1917 was one in which many people failed to pay taxes; police power dwindled and soldiers deserted from the army in increasingly large numbers, often commandeering first-class rail accommodations and dispensing with the bourgeois formality of payment. The attempt to maintain the existing administrative apparatus in Ukraine would have proved to be difficult enough in itself without the insertion of the General Secretariat into the nexus of the administrative organization. In short, the year 1917 was hardly one in which to proclaim the rebirth of the Ukrainian nation.

The prevailing uncertainty of the period caused some of the Rada's spokesmen to advocate caution. Serhi Efremov, the first secretary of nationalities, was initially opposed to the establishment of the Secretariat because the problems which lay ahead of it were both manifold and

---

[54] Doroshenko, *Istoriia Ukraini*, II, p. 38. Vinnichenko described this change in governments in terms of the Ukrainian nationalist petit bourgeois democracy being succeeded by the non-Ukrainian upper middle class. The coup, in his opinion, was based on an alliance between the German command and a coalition of landowners, financiers, industrialists, and right-wing moderate elements inimical to the aims of the revolution and acting on the basis of immediate personal self-interest.

complex and, in the light of the Rada's meager resources, would only lead to the disillusionment of the masses, who awaited miracles. Boris Martos, the first secretary of agriculture, was willing to accept office solely on the condition that the Secretariat only "prepare the foundation" for autonomy and not actually attempt to exercise it; Vinnichenko agreed with Martos at the time in order to avoid a crisis.[55] Underlying the moderation of the men in the Secretariat was the belief that revolutionary Russia would not deny the Ukrainians the right to exist as a nation and would establish a new federative relationship based on mutual respect. There were also the urban Russian and Jewish minorities which served to check the extremists in the Rada. But the hesitancy which characterized many of the Rada's policies in 1917 was also undoubtedly related to the lack of widespread and sustained popular support.

This, in turn, reflected itself in the isolation of turbulent Kiev from the provinces. Although the Rada and its supporting congresses contained delegates from most of Ukraine, the actual authority of the Rada was confined to the banks of the Dnieper in the Kiev region and to the agrarian Right Bank. The Secretariat made no effort to establish contacts with the provincial commissars; while Petrograd bombarded them with telegrams, the Secretariat did not bother to answer correspondence. Nor did the secretaries general visit the provinces in their official capacity. Dmitro Doroshenko, the commissar for Chernihiv under the Provisional Government, accused his own Ukrainians of harming their cause: "if they had manifested as much energy in the development of their authority on the spot as they expended in struggling with the central government over the formal limits of autonomy it would have been easy to achieve the goals."[56]

The lack of contact between Kiev and the provinces was made inevitable by the absence of a well-organized adminis-

---

[55] For these two instances see Shulgin, *L'Ukraine contre Moscou*, pp. 120f. and Khristiuk, *op cit.*, I, p. 77, footnote.
[56] Doroshenko, *Moi Spomini pro Nedavne-Minule*, II, p. 25.

tration in the capital. This was due, in part, to the personal antagonism existing between the two Social Democrats, Vinnichenko and Petliura, which was accentuated by their disagreement over what the nature of the Ukrainian state was to be. There was also division between the three Ukrainian parties and the national minorities on the question of relations with the central government as well as on pressing social and economic issues. Agreement on basic policy is a prerequisite for the establishment of an administrative organization; men must concur on objectives before they can commence working together for their realization. Lack of such concurrence within the Rada prevented the development of a sound administrative organization.[57]

Another factor which contributed to the Rada's ineffectiveness was its lack of forceful and experienced leadership in the legislative, administrative, and military fields. In 1917 Vinnichenko was but thirty-seven years of age; Holubovich, his successor, was only thirty-two; while Doroshenko and Petliura were thirty-five and thirty-eight, respectively. Hrushevsky, the grand "old" man of the Ukrainian movement, was only fifty-one years old when he presided over the Rada. The Social Revolutionaries, the weakest Ukrainian party in terms of leadership, were led by two students, Paul Khristiuk and Nicholas Kovalevsky. Nicholas Shrah, a twenty-two-year-old student, was Hrushevsky's substitute as presiding officer.[58] Most of these men were

[57] An amusing personal experience recounted by Doroshenko in his memoirs illustrates the administrative confusion which prevailed in the Rada Government. After the Rada's return from Zhitomir in March, Doroshenko, much to his surprise, read in the Russian newspaper *Vechernia Novosti* (Evening News) that he had been appointed to the Ukrainian ambassadorship to Holland. Seven days later the same newspaper reported that he had declined the appointment. In the course of the interim Doroshenko had neither been consulted nor informed of the appointment and had consequently not declined the post. Finally he spoke with Hrushevsky and obtained a promise that he could have the position (*Ibid.*, II, pp. 8of).

[58] This is not to be construed as an indictment of youth, for the young man is often ready to attempt what his elders regard as impossible. This is a commendable characteristic, but it must be tempered by comprehension of the age-old dictum that politics is the art of the possible. Some men master this dictum at an earlier age than others, and it cannot be said

intellectuals experienced in theoretical disputation, literary endeavor, and scholarly research but hopelessly deficient in their knowledge of the art and science of politics—the endless struggle for power. Vinnichenko, although sincere, was hesitant to continue in office after August of 1917 when Doroshenko unsuccessfully attempted to form a Secretariat; yet he remained at the helm of the Ukrainian state during four of the most crucial months of its existence. When Kiev came under Bolshevik attack in January of 1918, the fatigued and harassed Vinnichenko resigned, shaved his mustache and whiskers, and disappeared. For this he was accused by some of cowardice, yet in all truthfulness his resignation and flight were but proof of the underdevelopment of the Ukrainian movement and not the cause of its failure.

Those who represented Ukrainian nationalism in Kiev during 1917 were not supreme. Their program was being challenged by inhabitants of Ukraine who did not share their views. The local Russian troops were loyal to the Provisional Government or became pro-Bolshevik, and Kiev, a predominantly Russian city, had a municipal government in which the Ukrainians held but twenty per cent of the seats. The municipal council, which was hostile to the Ukrainians, refused to allow the Secretariat to utilize the Savoy Hotel and later demanded rental fees which were beyond the Rada's ability to pay. During 1917 the Ukrainians were in a minority in all of the important municipal councils; in Katerinoslav they had eleven out of a total of 110 seats, while in Zhitomir they controlled only nine out of 98 seats; in Odessa's council, which had a membership of 120, the Ukrainians had but five votes.[59] Such anti-Ukrainian groups as the Gogol League of Little Russians (*Soiuz Malorosov imeni Gogolia*), the Russian National Union (*Russki Natsionalni Soiuz*), and the South

---

that older men have been gifted with a monopoly of it. The Rada's leadership was not unique in its youthfulness since the Russian Revolution was, in general, a period in which younger men predominated. Kerensky was but thirty-six years of age in 1917 and his colleague Tseretelli was a year younger; Trotsky and Stalin were both thirty-seven at the time.

[59] Fedenko, *op.cit.*, p. 75. Cf. Doroshenko, *Istoriia Ukraini*, 1, pp. 143f.

Russians (*Iugorossi*) opposed the Ukrainization of schools and other institutions. In August of 1917 the faculties of the University of Kiev and the Kiev Polytechnical Institute protested the "Ukrainization of Little Russia" on the grounds that the use of the Ukrainian language, because of its allegedly impoverished vocabulary, would retard the educational development of the people. The rector of the University, N. M. Tsytovich and the University Council were especially disturbed by the government's adherence to the Second Universal which they declared to be "dangerous to the interests of the whole Russian state and juridically incorrect."[60] Similarly, old judges and prosecuting attorneys continued at their posts and showed no desire to compromise with the Ukrainian movement.

Much of this opposition to the Rada had its source in the Russified Ukrainians who resided in the cities. The extent of Russification had been so great that all of the prominent persons in the Rada spoke Russian fluently. Whole families were divided internally on the question of acceptance of Ukrainian nationality or the retention of Russian. Vasili Vitalievich Shulgin, editor of the conservative Russian newspaper *Kievlianin* (The Kievan) and leader of the Russian National Union in 1917, was a sworn enemy of the Ukrainian movement and consistently charged the Rada with Ukrainizing the non-Ukrainian children. He preferred to be regarded as a Little or South Russian and during the civil war was with Denikin. Yet his nephew, Alexander Shulgin, was a prominent nationalist and became the first Ukrainian foreign minister. The Doroshenko family, descendent from a seventeenth century hetman, always spoke Russian and only rarely interjected a Ukrainian word into the conversation. However, young Dmitro Doroshenko discovered his Ukrainian nationality, served as foreign minister in 1918, and made himself worthy of being regarded as Hrushevsky's successor.[61] Many of the

[60] For excerpts from this protest see Eugene V. Spectorsky, *Stoletie Kievskago Universiteta Sv. Vladimira* (Belgrade, 1935), pp 61ff.

[61] A. Shulgin, *L'Ukraine contre Moscou*, pp. 17ff.; and Doroshenko, *Moi Spomini pro Nedavne-Minule*, II, p. 85. Vasili Shulgin maintained his anti-Ukrainian attitude even as an émigré; as late as 1939, in a brochure en-

delegates at the First Ukrainian Military Congress, which met in May, could not speak pure Ukrainian, but Vinnichenko observed that these were the most ardent "nationalists" since they were "fired with hate for those who had brought them to such a condition" of ignorance of their own language.[62] The cultural resources of the nation were so undeveloped that Ukrainian schools could not be established on a large scale until special courses were organized for the purpose of giving teachers a rudimentary knowledge of Ukrainian history, language, and literature. New Ukrainian textbooks had to be written or Russian texts rewritten. This widespread denationalization reduced the number of nationally conscious Ukrainians, especially among the intelligentsia, and probably more than any other factor was responsible for the failure of the Rada.

However, Vinnichenko did not explain the downfall of the Rada in terms of a lack of a fully-developed national consciousness. Instead, he concluded that the fundamental issue was socio-economic and that the basic error made by the Rada was its failure to be truly socialistic rather than bourgeois national republican-democratic. Bitterly attacking the Ukrainian socialists for having been unable "even to think of the ruination of the bourgeois state,"[63] he accused them of paying lip service to agrarian reform. He recalled that "in the [Third] Universal it is true we were radicals. But . . . in actuality we were not able to be such radicals."[64] This was because the men of the Rada were obsessed with legality and could not bring themselves to employ force as would have been necessary had they

---

titled *Ukrainstvuiushchie i My* (The Ukrainizers and We) published in Belgrade, he referred to the work of his nephew as "insurrectionary" and incorrectly charged that Ukraine was a product of Polish and German intrigue.

[62] Vinnichenko, *op.cit.*, I, p. 140.   [63] *Ibid.*, II, p. 107.

[64] *Ibid.*, II, p. 111. There is ample evidence to corroborate Vinnichenko's thesis. In the months immediately preceding the November Revolution, the expressions of disapproval of the Rada increased sharply. One of the more important of these was the Fourth Congress of the Ukrainian Social Democratic party which met in Kiev on October 13-17, and branded the Rada as "petit bourgeois nationalist."

sequestered bank funds. "In all frankness it can be said that we changed nothing of the substance of that state-form which prevailed during the time of the Provisional Government. We did not modify any of its foundations. We merely changed its national form—in place of the blue, white, and red tsarist tricolor we substituted our yellow and azure banner."[65]

As a Marxist, Vinnichenko desired to eliminate the role of the Church and unsuccessfully advocated that the civil marriage ceremony be the only legally required one. He assailed the Rada's use of "parades, crowds of priests, church bells, and *Te Deums* [at the proclamation of Universals] with all of the unpleasant comedy with which tsarism and the ruling classes hypnotized the blind strata of the population."[66] All of this he attributed to Petliura, whom he referred to as that "specialist in the matters of *Te Deums* and all other sorts of decorations and advertising."

Despite his dislike for Petliura, Vinnichenko did not regard him as personally responsible for the failure of the Rada although he did accuse the amateur military commander of foolishly believing that the adoption of red-colored caps by the Rada's troops would stiffen their resistance against the Bolsheviks. According to Vinnichenko, the soldiers who originally had supported the Rada with such ardor became apathetic when it failed "to liberate its toiling masses from the social oppression which was inimical to the nation and the toiling class."[67] The appointment of Nicholas Porsh as successor to Petliura failed to halt the Bolshevik advance. Vinnichenko believed that the fall of the Rada resulted not from mere military defeat but as

[65] *Ibid.*, II, p. 108. Vinnichenko is almost masochistic in his self-criticism, but his analysis cannot be disregarded in view of the important role which he played during 1917.

[66] *Ibid.*, II, p. 115.

[67] *Ibid.*, II, p. 158. This assertion is undoubtedly true, but there is also the fact that the Rada's military forces had never been numerous or well-trained. In the words of a prominent secretary in the Rada: "There were individual military units with Ukrainian national insignia, but there was no army. In the process of 'Ukrainization' it melted like snow in the sun." (Khristiuk, *op.cit.*, II, p. 120.)

a result of forces which were greater than any single individual, and he stated that neither Alexander of Macedon nor Napoleon could have saved it. "The sole remedy was not to contradict the inclinations of the masses, to agree to their desire to change the government and its social policies, and in this way to preserve this government in national-Ukrainian hands and not develop in the masses conflict between the national and social idea."[68]

In the manner of a modern Haroun Al-Raschid, but belatedly, Vinnichenko, following his resignation, spent eight days traveling incognito south from Kiev. During this journey he discovered the extent of the bankruptcy and sterile parliamentarism of the Rada which was so remote from actuality. At this time the Rada, rather than the Bolsheviks, represented the Ukrainian national movement and it was only natural that the population came to regard with hostility everything Ukrainian as exemplified by the Rada. This antipathy provided the final proof which Vinnichenko needed to support his contention that the end of the Rada began, not when it invited the Germans in, but when it broke with its own masses by failing to cope with the landowners, industrialists, and bankers. The period of the Russian Revolution was one in which social and economic issues ultimately took precedence over the purely national struggle, and Ukraine was no exception.

The Rada, in the early months of its existence, enjoyed considerable peasant support because it was generally expected to come to grips with the crucial agrarian problem.

[68] *Ibid.*, II, p. 219. Even Khristiuk, a Social Revolutionary and no admirer of Vinnichenko, admitted that "the Central Rada . . . did not demonstrate in this social and economic field of revolutionary creativeness that boldness, decisiveness, foresight, and perseverance which it manifested in the national-political struggle" (Kristiuk, I, p 106). However, in explaining the fall of the Rada, Khristiuk adopted a partisan view by placing much of the responsibility on the Social Democrats especially because of their tardiness in relinquishing control of the cabinet to the Social Revolutionaries. He also stressed the greater wealth and resources and the more numerous experienced military personnel which the Council of People's Commissars had at its disposal. The absence of defensible geographic frontiers between Ukraine and Russia was also regarded by Khristiuk as a factor which facilitated the victory of the Bolsheviks (II, pp. 132ff.).

The average peasant was concerned with obtaining additional land far more than he was with such intangibles as autonomy and federalism.[69] To him, socialism meant obtaining land from the landowner without payment. The First Ukrainian Peasants' Congress, dominated by the Social Revolutionaries, unanimously adopted a resolution advocating the abolition of private ownership of land (to be applied in practice only to the large estates), transfer of all land to the land fund without compensation to owners, and distribution of it to those who could till it with their own hands on the basis of a norm to be established in the future.[70] The Social Democrats finally took a stand on the agrarian question by favoring nationalization of the land, but the Social Revolutionaries opposed them on the grounds that it would place too much economic power in the hands of the government. The two parties also disagreed on the size of the agrarian norm which was to be established; the Social Democrats were willing, even after the issuance of the Third Universal, to allow 135-acre holdings to be exempted from the reform, while the Social Revolutionaries wished to lower the limit substantially.[71] These differences resulted in procrastination and inaction which by November destroyed much of the confidence of the peasants in the Rada; only a swift and decisive agrarian reform could have convinced them that this was their government.[72]

In terms of the criterion of *immediate* success, the Ukrainians were attempting the impossible: achievement

[69] Arnold Margolin, *Ukraina i Politika Antanty* (Berlin, 1923), p. 43 Cf Hrushevsky, *La lutte sociale et politique en Ukraine*, pp 5f.

[70] Khristiuk, *op.cit*, I, pp 100f

[71] *Ibid.*, II, p 59 Doroshenko, *Istoriia Ukraini*, I, pp 191f. contains excerpts from the announcement made by the Minister of Agriculture exempting from reform holdings less than fifty *desiatinas* (135 acres) in size

[72] However, it must be borne in mind that the Ukrainian idea had not been discredited in the eyes of the peasants In the elections for the All-Russian Constituent Assembly held in the Poltava province during the autumn of 1917 the Ukrainian Social Revolutionaries received an overwhelming majority based on complete returns—727,247 out of a total number of 1,149,256 votes See Oliver H Radkey, *The Election to the Russian Constituent Assembly of 1917* (Cambridge, Mass, 1950), pp. 29ff.

within a single year of the transformation of a national group into a nation state. This is a development which normally unfolds itself only gradually, but the adverse political circumstances brought on by the November Revolution and the termination of the war with Germany compelled the Ukrainians to proceed to nominal independence with exceptional rapidity. Nations are not created by proclamations but result from a slow process of growth. The initial fervor which greeted the Rada in the spring of 1917 and manifested itself in crowds, oratory, resolutions, congresses, parades, banners, and religious processions was deceptive in that it was not exclusively or, for the most part, even predominantly national. In 1917 the rebirth of the Ukrainian nation was not an accomplished fact. Relatively few of the inhabitants of Ukraine were fully conscious of their nationality. Two and a half centuries of union with the Russians had left their mark, and many peasants, although retaining their language, still described themselves as *Ruskie.* It was this which, in part, prompted Vinnichenko to reveal that "truly, we were like the gods at this time attempting to create from nothing a whole new world."[73] No words illustrate better than these why the year 1917 proved to be an inauspicious time in which to launch the movement for national liberation.

[73] Vinnichenko, *op.cit.*, 1, p. 258.

CHAPTER IV
The Interlude of the Hetmanate

I am neither a Germanophile, nor a Francophile, nor an Anglophile but love only my Fatherland, desiring its welfare, and regarding myself as obligated to utilize every possible means of saving it and to collaborate with all who are sincerely willing to aid it.

Hetman Paul Skoropadsky (1919)

THE political transformation which accompanied the coup of April 29 profoundly shocked the young nationalistically-inclined socialists who during the preceding year had been endeavoring to govern Ukraine. These advocates of the republican form of government could only regard the Hetmanate of General Paul Petrovich Skoropadsky as an anachronistic political monstrosity, reactionary in the national as well as in the social and economic spheres.

This attitude was prompted in large measure by the General's social background and by his association with the Imperial Russian regime. The ancestral estate of the Skoropadsky family, "Trostianets" in the province of Poltava, was but one of many landholdings owned by the fabulously wealthy Hetman. Born on May 3, 1873, the son of a colonel in the tsar's cavalry guards, he attended the fashionable Pages' School from which he ultimately emerged as an officer. In 1897 he married a wealthy niece of P. N. Durnovo, a prominent Russian arch-conservative and minister of the interior. In 1906, after having participated in the Russo-Japanese War, he was promoted to the rank of colonel and placed in command of the twentieth Finnish regiment of dragoons. Entering World War I as a major general, he emerged as a lieutenant general in command of the 34th army corps and had also had the privilege of serving as an aide-de-camp to Nicholas II. This was hardly the career of a Ukrainian nationalist.

Some of the more moderate supporters of Skoropadsky regarded as proof of his national loyalty the fact of his being a collateral descendant of Hetman Ivan Skoropadsky, who was the elected chief of the Zaporozhian Cossacks from 1709 to 1722.[1] His enemies also seized upon this ancestry in an attempt to discredit him by pointing out that Ivan had led the dissidents who in November of 1708 refused

[1] Hetman Ivan Skoropadsky had two daughters and no male descendants. General Paul and Hetman Ivan had a common ancestor in Fedir Skoropadsky, who died in 1648 in the battle of Zhovti Vodi (Yellow Waters) fighting the Poles. For a genealogy of the family see *Za Velich Natsii, op.cit.*, pp. 5off.

to follow Hetman Ivan Mazepa in his dangerous policy of alliance with Charles XII of Sweden, a policy which ended in disaster at the battle of Poltava. Closer collaboration between Ukraine and Muscovy resulted from the battle, and Peter the Great even succeeded in persuading the weak and gentle Hetman Ivan Skoropadsky to give one of his daughters in marriage to a Russian grandee, Peter Tolstoy, so as to strengthen the existing ties between the two peoples. In April of 1722, several months before the death of Ivan Skoropadsky, Peter the Great established the Little Russian Board and, in effect, deprived the Hetman of the last vestiges of authority.

Another argument which the opponents of General Skoropadsky's regime employed was based on the attitude which he had adopted towards the Rada in 1917. As a soldier he felt duty-bound to promote the war effort, and as a landowner he naturally did not favor the abolition of private ownership which was being advocated in the Rada. The General Secretariat reciprocated by suspecting him of desiring to become military dictator. Skoropadsky's 34th army corps had become the first Ukrainian army corps when it was Ukrainized, despite the General's hesitation which was prompted by what he regarded as the unpleasant association of socialism and nationalism in the Rada. He was further distrusted by the secretary for military affairs because of his election in October of 1917 at Chihirin to the post of "honorary Hetman" of the *Vilne Kozatstvo* (Free Cossacks). This was a spontaneous semi-military movement which had arisen during the summer for the purpose of preventing banditry in the villages as a result of the breakdown of the police. The Rada did not attempt to utilize this source of support, and by autumn it had come under the influence of Skoropadsky.[2]

[2] Any study of the Hetman regime encounters difficulties because of the existence of two main types of literature dealing with it: the deprecatory and the panegyrical A case in point is the obscurity which surrounds the activities of the General during the latter part of 1917. He and his supporters have contended that he attempted to organize resistance to the Bolshevik advance and even resigned the command of the first Ukrainian

Dissatisfied with the Rada, Skoropadsky was unable to organize any extra-governmental forces to oppose the Bolshevik invasion of Ukraine in January 1918. During the brief Bolshevik occupation the bald General disguised himself in worker's clothes, sewed his wedding ring and St. George's Cross in his sleeves, and grew a beard. Later he went into hiding in Kiev. The arrival of the German occupation forces enabled the General to emerge from hiding and discard his assumed name. He immediately began to advocate the establishment of a firm dictatorial authority (*tverda vlada*) to cope with anarchy and came into contact with the Ukrainian Democratic Agrarian party and the League of Landowners.[3] Underlying his effortless coup was the conviction that a new government must not be based on those segments of the population who have nothing to lose but rather on those endowed with property and having a stake in the maintenance of order.

Upon assuming office on April 29, Skoropadsky issued an edict (*hramota*) in which he proclaimed himself "Hetman of all Ukraine." He recalled that the blood of the sons of Ukraine had recently been flowing in prodigious quantities and that the Ukrainian State had been on the brink of disaster but was saved by the Central Powers. It had been hoped that political and economic order would be restored under the returning Rada: "But these hopes were not realized. The former Ukrainian government did not achieve the political reconstruction of Ukraine because it was completely incapable of doing so. Disorder and anarchy continue in Ukraine; economic ruin and unemployment are increasing and becoming more widespread with

---

army corps because he believed that this action would enable the Rada to supply that unit of 60,000 men and prevent its dissolution. It is doubtful, however, whether any measure could have prevented the decomposition of the corps. Critics of the Hetman have claimed that he refused to allow the *Vilne Kozatstvo* to defend the Rada in Kiev against the Bolsheviks. He was also accused of resurrecting old Cossack customs and attire for the purpose of drawing the attention of the men away from more significant matters. Cf. the excerpts from the Hetman's memoirs published in *Khliborobska Ukraina, op.cit.*, v, pp. 31ff.

[3] Supra, pp. 130f.

each passing day, and now before the once prosperous Ukraine there looms the specter of famine."

Proclaiming himself to be a "true son of Ukraine," Skoropadsky "resolved to answer the call and to assume temporarily complete authority."[4] He declared the Central Rada, the Mala Rada, and all land committees to be dissolved and removed all ministers and their immediate aides from their positions. All other civil servants were told to remain at their posts in the various ministries. The Hetman promised to issue an electoral law for the election of members of a Ukrainian parliament (*soim*), and, in accordance with the wishes of the occupation authorities, he declared that "the right of private ownership, as the foundation of culture and civilization, is reinstituted *in toto* and all ordinances of the former Ukrainian Government and of the Provisional Russian Government, so far as they affect property rights, are abrogated." Not wishing to alienate the intermediate and wealthier peasants, the Hetman promised to transfer land from the large owners to the landless agriculturalists at actual value. He also pledged himself to protect the rights of the working class and especially to improve the working conditions of railroad employees.

The form of the new government was that of a dictatorship; this was evident in the decree which the Hetman issued for the organization of the Provisional Government of Ukraine which was to operate until the convocation of the parliament. According to this law, governing authority was to reside exclusively in the Hetman; he was empowered to make all cabinet appointments and had an absolute veto over all legislation. Legislative authority was placed

[4] For the text of the edict see Doroshenko, *Istoriia Ukraini*, II, pp. 49f. For an English translation, see James Bunyan, *Intervention, Civil War, and Communism in Russia, April-December, 1918* (Baltimore, 1936), pp. 16f. Traditionally, the Cossack Hetmans issued universals, but Skoropadsky desiring a complete break with the Rada which had issued four such documents, issued a *hramota* instead. Many nationalists regarded this change in terminology as indicative of the extent of Muscovite influence in the new government. Vinnichenko stated that it was issued in Russian and not in Ukrainian.

148

provisionally in the cabinet and remained there throughout the thirty-three-week period during which the regime
was in existence. Freedom of speech and of assembly
"within the limits of the law" were proclaimed; freedom
of worship was also recognized, although the leading (state)
church was declared to be the Orthodox Christian. While
the Hetman was commander-in-chief of the army and navy
and, in theory, a veritable dictator, his lack of decisiveness
and his willingness to be influenced by ministers and aides
appreciably reduced his authority.

Immediately following the coup, Nicholas Ustimovich,
a lover of horses little known in nationalist circles, was
appointed provisional premier; he held the office for only
a day because of his failure to entice the Socialist Federalists
into the cabinet despite an offer of seven portfolios which
he made to them. On April 30 he was succeeded by Nicholas Prokopovich Vasilenko, a Constitutional Democrat and
member of the law faculty of the University of Kiev, who
also attempted in vain to obtain the support of the Socialist Federalists. These efforts to secure the participation
of Ukrainian moderates in the cabinet were made at the
Hetman's insistence. On May 2 the Social Democrats, Social
Revolutionaries, and Socialist Federalists responded by
sending a delegation to General Groener, apparently after
having discovered who the real masters of Ukraine were.
The delegates informed the General that socialists could
participate in the cabinet only if there were a complete
change in the government and in agrarian policy accompanied by the voluntary dissolution of the Rada, establishment of a new provisional legislative body to be known
as the State Council (*Derzhavna Rada*) representing all
segments of the population, and convocation of the Ukrainian Constituent Assembly as soon as peace and order were
restored.[5]

[5] Doroshenko, *Istorua Ukrami*, II, pp 54f The Rada had finally set the
convocation of the constituent assembly for May 12, 1918. In January, 172
of the 301 delegates had been elected and the Rada had intended to hold
elections for the remainder in the spring Voting was based on general,
direct, equal, and secret suffrage without reference to sex, religion or na-

149

Groener informed the socialists that the Germans had not participated in the coup and that a return to the Rada was out of the question since the new government had already been accorded recognition by Berlin. He contended that Ukraine was still independent and that socialist participation in the cabinet was desirable. When questioned about the recent arrests in the Rada, Groener claimed that the German Command possessed information regarding the organization of a conspiracy; he denied that the arrests were made with the knowledge of the Command. The Ukrainians left this meeting dissatisfied; apparently they had not yet fully comprehended the extent of the anti-socialist reaction which had accompanied the entry of German troops into Ukraine.

After this meeting Alexander Shulgin and Serhi Efremov, prominent Socialist Federalists, sent Groener a note in which they stated that the Russophile monarchist coup had occurred "with the understanding and support of the German command." They were willing to accept Skoropadsky only as a provisional president of a Ukrainian republic under the Rada's constitution of April 29; later the constituent assembly would elect a new Hetman who would be a titular executive. Socialist Federalist participation, they declared, could be had only if the Ukrainian parties were given a majority of the portfolios including the premiership, foreign affairs, agriculture, and education. Their candidate for premier was Serhi Shelukhin, the jurist; for the post of foreign minister they proposed Viacheslav Lipinsky, who later became Ukrainian ambassador to Austria-Hungary.[6] However, the formation of Vasilenko's cabinet was almost completed and Groener responded to the Ukrainian demands with a laconic "zu spät," convinced that the Socialist Federalists would eventually enter the government on any terms. All that they could expect was three or four portfolios. The socialist parties then decided

tionality and with proportional representation. The April coup, of course, prevented the assembly from meeting.

[6] *Ibid.*, ii, pp. 55ff.

that if any of their members wished to enter the cabinet they could do so upon resigning from the party.

The May 3 cabinet originally contained no men who were prominent in the Ukrainian national movement. Vasilenko held the foreign affairs and education portfolios as well as the premiership. Other ministers included Anton Rzhepetsky, a banker, who held the finance portfolio; Julius Wagner, minister of labor and formerly a professor of zoology at Kiev Polytechnical Institute; Boris Butenko, a railroad official who was given the transportation portfolio; and George Afanasev, state controller and former director of the Kiev branch of the state bank. Significantly, there was no ministry for national minorities in the cabinet similar to that of the Rada. Vasilenko was soon succeeded by Fedir Andrievich Lizohub, a dignified, bearded landowner from Chernihiv and Poltava who was a Zemstvo official in the latter province. The new premier was an Octobrist in his political attitudes and was not a Ukrainophile although he was too intelligent to be a Ukrainophobe.

The May cabinet acquired one nationalist with an unimpeachable reputation when Dmitro Doroshenko accepted the post of acting minister of foreign affairs at the price of relinquishing his membership in the Socialist Federalist party, which regarded the regime as "absolutist and anti-democratic." However, most of the nationalists regarded his action as opportunistic and refused to follow suit. Instead, they organized the Ukrainian National Political Union (*Ukrainski Natsionalno-Derzhavni Soiuz*) the purpose of which was "to save threatened Ukrainian statehood and to consolidate all forces for the purpose of creating an independent · Ukrainian state." The Union was composed of various organizations, including the Socialist Federalists, the Democratic Agrarians, the Independentists-Socialists (a small group of nominal socialists who advocated absolute independence), and the postal, telegraphic, and railroad workers. The Social Democrats and Social Revolutionaries participated but only in a consultative capacity. The Union commenced its policy of criticism by presenting a memorial to the Hetman on May 24, in which it charged that the cabinet was non-Ukrainian in its composition and political orientation. The presence of numerous Russian Kadets and Octobrists, it was claimed, made it impossible for the cabinet to enjoy the confidence of the broad masses. The memorial also criticized the recent bans on workers' and peasants' as well as on Zemstvo congresses which made the government appear to be ignorant of the occurrence of the revolution. It accused the minister of education, Vasilenko, of being a Russian Kadet and blamed the minister of justice for failing to Ukrainize the courts. The growth of anarchy and disorder in the villages and the spread of Bolshevism were attributed to the Hetman regime, and the solution supposedly lay in the establishment of a Ukrainian national government which would not favor capitalists and landowners.[7]

The Union next issued an appeal to the German people on May 30, in which it claimed that the Russian and Jewish bourgeoisie and the Polish landed gentry had always been enemies of Ukrainian independent statehood because it would spell an end to their privileged status. It alleged that these groups could see their salvation only in the provocation of a conflict between the Ukrainians and Germans. The Union accused the German Command of participating in the coup and termed the Lizohub cabinet "Little Russian," composed of persons who were "Ukrainian by blood but Muscovite in spirit." Calling upon the Germans to abide by the Treaty of Brest-Litovsk by not allowing the army to intervene in internal affairs, the Union asked that the army be compelled to cease supporting the "Muscovite minority" and that a Ukrainian national cabinet be established in the interests of peace and order.[8]

The government encountered further embarrassment on May 30, when a strike of civil service employees occurred in the ministry of agriculture. Under the Rada many socialists who believed in the abolition of private ownership

[7] Ibid., II, pp. 103ff.   [8] Ibid., II, pp. 107ff.

of land found their way onto the payrolls of the ministry. The strike was precipitated when Kolokoltsov, the Hetman's minister of agriculture, ordered a reorganization which resulted in numerous dismissals affecting these partisan employees. The strikers demanded the use of the Ukrainian language in the ministry, the reinstatement of dismissed workers, the dismissal of all "Russificators" recently hired by Kolokoltsov, and the removal of all troops from the ministry. Employees from some of the other ministries joined the strike, but the government refused to accept these demands and by June 1 the workers returned to their jobs.

Meanwhile, Petliura had been devoting his time to obtaining control of the All-Ukrainian Union of Zemstvos for the purpose of utilizing this organization in his campaign against the Hetman regime. The All-Ukrainian Congress of Zemstvos, which met in mid-June, developed into a center of opposition to the government. On June 16 it sent a protest to Skoropadsky, declaring that the peasantry was convinced that the old order was being restored. It criticized punitive expeditions, the widespread arrests and the denial of civil liberties, requisitioning, the burning of villages, oppression of Zemstvo and *Prosvita* (Enlightenment) societies, and opposition by reactionary clergymen to the Ukrainian effort to obtain an autocephalous Orthodox Church. The Congress demanded the removal from office and trial of all officials guilty of violating laws, the re-establishment and full guarantee of civil liberties, the renewal of organs of local self-government, the immediate convocation of a provisional legislative council, and the holding of elections for the Ukrainian Constituent Assembly. It concluded its protest in a threatening manner by refusing to accept responsibility for the possible results of a breach between the central government and the people.

When this protest failed to elicit a change in policy on the part of the regime, Petliura, as head of the Kiev provincial zemstvo and the All-Ukrainian Union of Zemstvos, appealed directly to Baron Mumm by letter, informing him that numerous Ukrainian leaders had been arrested. He stated that the Germans were responsible for some of these arrests and that such actions were not promoting Ukrainian-German friendship. In appealing to the German people and to their ambassador in Kiev, Petliura and the Ukrainian National Political Union were undermining that very independence in the name of which they claimed to be acting. Apparently they were not opposed in principle to German intervention if it were exercised on their behalf.

However, the German Command had no intention of unseating the current government which was rapidly establishing an administrative organization of a somewhat higher caliber than that of the Rada.[9] The Hetman took up residence in the former home of the provincial governor at 40 Institutska Street. The cabinet, which was a legislative as well as an executive body, held its daily sessions under the Hetman's portrait in this closely guarded building. These meetings, usually presided over by Skoropadsky, began at eight in the evening and often lasted till the early hours of the morning or, on occasion, till dawn. The work load which this arrangement imposed upon the ministers was unusually heavy. The Hetman himself was isolated from the administration; this condition was due in part to his loquacity as well as to the fact that he had a weakness for the ceremonial aspects of government and often spent the whole of the day receiving visitors and delegations rather than coming to grips with affairs of state.[10]

Yet these shortcomings were not in themselves disastrous since the regime was completely under the control of the

[9] Some opposition to the coup did develop in the German Reichstag from the socialist deputies Vice Chancellor Friedrich von Payer, in addressing the Main Committee on May 4, defended the coup on the grounds that a Ukrainian Committee of Safety (apparently the Committee to Save Ukraine) was considering the massacre of a number of German officers. He also stated that the arrests made in the Rada were a blunder and that the subordinates responsible for them had been removed. (Cf. *New York Times*, May 6, 1918)

[10] A. Maliarevsky, "Na pere-ekzamenovke P. P. Skoropadsky i evo vremia," *Arkhiv Grazhdanskoi Voiny*, II, pp. 105-142, contains a critical account of the administration of the Hetman regime.

occupation authorities. Skoropadsky stated in a note to Mumm on May 10: "I regard it as necessary for the good of my fatherland-Ukraine to go honestly and openly hand-in-hand with Germany."[11] The Hetman, like his ancestor, ruled in name rather than in fact although he had some consolation in adopting the title of "Serene Highness" (*Ioho Svitlist* or *Iasnovelmozhnist*), which was as archaic as the German "Durchlaucht." He also wore a dagger, concluded some of his edicts with an "Amen," and often employed the first person plural in them rather than the singular in referring to himself.

Such practices only reaffirmed the conviction of the leftist socialists that this was a reactionary regime, an instrument of the landowners and capitalists, utilized and valued by them as an apparatus of their class rule for the purpose of exploiting and enslaving the toiling masses.[12] Hrushevsky later attacked the Hetman regime as "bourgeois" in the same way in which the Bolsheviks had previously assailed his government. The socialists linked the Hetman with the Union of Industry, Commerce, Finance, and Agriculture (*Soiuz Promyshlennosti, Torgovli, Finansov i Sel'skogo Khoziaistva*), usually referred to as *Protofis*. This organization had presented its demands to the Rada during the week preceding the coup and appreciated the change in governments which followed.[18] The Hetman Government did not restrict the activities of the *Protofis* in any way; instead, it appeared to express sympathy with the organization. Premier Lizohub, the minister of trade

---

11 Doroshenko, *Istoriia Ukraini*, ii, p. 211.

12 Khristiuk, *op cit.*, iii, p 123.

18 The demands presented to the Rada included the establishment of closer economic ties between Ukraine and Russia, basing the activities of the ministry of trade and industry on close consultation with the representatives of trade and industry, a balanced state budget, and the reaffirmation of the principle of private ownership and the termination of socialist experimentation and workers' control of industry. It also took the stand that the immediate introduction of Ukrainian as the official language would retard economic reconstruction and alienate many intellectuals and capable workers whose services the government needed For the text of the *Protofis* program see Iu. Kreizel, *Professionalnoe Dvizhenie i Avstro-Germanskaia Okkupatsiia* (Kiev, 1924), pp. 14ff.

and industry, Sergei Gutnik, and the ministers of transport and finance attended the *Protofis* congress which was held in May.

In contrast to this was the policy which the government employed in dealing with those segments of the population which had supported the Rada. When the Second Ukrainian Peasants' Congress met on May 8-10, German troops invaded the first session and arrested the members of the presidium and credentials commission, including Fedir Shvets, a geologist who later became a member of the Directory Government. The Congress was compelled to adjourn to the Holosiivski forest on the outskirts of Kiev, where it demanded the convocation of the constituent assembly, declared Ukraine to be still a people's republic, and protested the return of land to the landowners. Several days later, on May 13, the Second Ukrainian Workers' Congress met secretly to demand a Ukrainian People's Republic, the convocation of the constituent assembly, transfer of all land into the hands of the toiling people without compensation, re-establishment of the eight-hour day, worker control over industry, and freedom of speech and press. The Ukrainian Social Democratic party held its fifth congress secretly in mid-May at the same time that the Social Revolutionaries met illegally for their fourth congress. The latter declared the Hetman Government to be "the result of the forcible usurpation of authority by elements which do not enjoy support in the territory" and resolved to oppose it and demand the convocation of the Ukrainian Constituent Assembly. The Katerinoslav city council, which overtly opposed the government, had to be dispersed, and a congress of municipalities which was to meet on May 9 was banned by the premier. Municipal government in Ukraine then reverted to the pre-revolutionary pattern.[14]

Spokesmen for the government continually denied that it was reactionary, autocratic, and an instrumentality of the

[14] For these instances of repression see Khristiuk, *op.cit.*, III, pp. 15ff. and Doroshenko, *Istoria Ukraini*, II, p. 265.

landowners and capitalists, as the socialists claimed. As early as May 10, the cabinet issued a statement in which it pledged itself to promote the development of Ukrainian culture and to ensure the rights of the Ukrainian language in schools and public institutions. On the same occasion it asked for support rather than criticism of its efforts to restore order, and threatened to take strong measures against its opponents. As the summer progressed, and pleas for "work instead of politics" became more frequent, the cleavage between the government and the socialists widened.

A vain attempt to effect a reconciliation was made by the foreign minister, Dmitro Doroshenko, who accepted the portfolio only because he wished to further Ukrainian national interests. It was not difficult for him to assume office under the Hetman since he was not fully cognizant of the economic and social consequences of the revolution. However, he realized that he was, in his own words, "a hostage from Ukrainian democracy in the camp of the enemy"; this led him to make the artificial and useless distinction between internal and external politics. He conveniently decided that he would not participate in cabinet discussions or voting which pertained to domestic affairs. For more than a month he remained "a mute witness," not signing cabinet minutes and expressing himself only on questions of foreign policy. This dichotomy broke down when he began to receive numerous letters from the provinces requesting that he obtain the release of arrested persons who were prominent in the Ukrainian movement. In this way he was compelled to participate in internal affairs and interpellate his colleagues regarding these excesses.[15]

15 Doroshenko, *Moi Spomini pro Nedavne-Minule*, III, pp. 54ff. All human groupings, including governments, are composed of conflicting and sometimes totally contradictory elements. This prevents many intellectuals from joining political parties or affiliating themselves with political movements because they believe that in doing so they will compromise their intellectual honesty and find it necessary to serve as apologist for every act of the group, whether they approve of it or not. The case of Doroshenko illustrates well the proposition that the very process of association causes participants in

The policy of repression which the Hetman Government pursued was prompted by the opposition which arose from the Ukrainian national socialists. Their attitude was based in large part on their inability to accept General Skoropadsky as a sincere Ukrainian. Vinnichenko, for instance, described the Hetman as "a Russian general of Little Russian origin, . . . a sentimental degenerate, will-less but with romantic dreams and large landholdings all over Ukraine."[16] These youthful opponents of the regime saw the Hetman's restoration of private property not as the foundation of culture per se, but of bourgeois capitalist culture and civilization. The rigid government censorship of the press and the closing of such newspapers as *Borotba* and *Narodna Volia* only served to reinforce the convictions of the socialists who met in the coffee houses and eating establishments on Fundukleivska Street to express their resentment.

Kiev at this time was teeming with well-dressed Russians who had fled from the Bolshevik-dominated North, as had the Hetman's wife and children, and who no longer hesitated to wear elegant attire in public for fear of being labeled "bourgeois." It was again possible to purchase expensive articles if one possessed money. The "Mother of Russian Cities" abounded with prostitutes and speculators, and its theaters and cafes were filled to overflowing.[17]

Many of the Russians who came South obtained employment in the various ministries of the Hetman Government. Some Ukrainian nationalists believed that sixty per cent of the officers in the gendarmerie had served in the same

it to compromise themselves since they cannot possibly approve of every act committed by their colleagues.

[16] Vinnichenko, *op cit*, III, p. 16. Nor were the nationalists convinced of the sincerity of the Hetman's ministers. Nicholas Halahan states that Premier Nicholas Vasilenko was referred to by some persons as "Nik-Myk" because he habitually commenced to sign his Christian name in Russian (Nikolai) rather than in Ukrainian (Mykola), correcting himself only after he had allegedly revealed the novelty of his Ukrainian nationality. (*Z Moikh Spominiv, op.cit.*, IV, pp. 49f)

[17] Roman Goul, "Kievskaia Epopeia," *Arkhiv Russkoi Revoliutsii* (Berlin, 1921), II, p. 60.

capacity prior to the revolution. These persons desired employment not because they were nationalists but because they could further their careers in a regime which at the time appeared to be a stabilizing force. Most of the large landowners were willing to tolerate the existence of the Ukrainian State only so long as the circumstances of international politics made it necessary; their real objective was the utilization of Ukraine as a base for the struggle against the Soviet Government and the revolution. Many regarded the regime, with its paying of lip service to Ukrainian traditions, as nothing more than a "farce" or "operetta" while the more outspoken of them dismissed it as *chepukha* (nonsense).

The counter-revolutionary character of the government especially manifested itself in the sphere of provincial and district administration when the position of commissar, which had existed under the Russian Provisional Government and the Rada, was supplanted by that of *starosta* (elder). This seemingly insignificant titulary change in itself revealed the nature of the regime. The complete disorganization of all local administration at the time of the Rada's return early in March prompted and enabled landowners to assume authority and to organize mercenaries and adventurers into punitive expeditions for the purpose of repossessing their property which had been seized by the peasants. The Hetman endeavored to bring an end to all violence and re-establish responsible organs of local government by appointing propertied non-Ukrainian persons as elders for the provinces and districts (*poviti*). Probably the worst appointment was that of Ivan Chartorizhsky for the province of Kiev; he had acquired a reputation as a Ukrainophobe during the war when he was governor of Russian-occupied Ternopil and referred to the Ukrainians as *Mazepintsi* (followers of Mazepa). Dmitro Doroshenko, the leading apologist for the Hetmanate of 1918, has admitted that the appointments of elders were made hastily and "were not always fortunate" ones; he also contended that successful efforts were made to remove some of the more obnoxious officials.[18] Skoropadsky was aware of the problem and on July 8 sent a letter to Premier Lizohub, who concurrently held the interior portfolio, informing him that local officials were acting contrary to the policies of the government in Kiev; he also complained that his agrarian program was being widely misinterpreted and was providing material for anti-governmental agitation, as was the ministry's inability to cope with speculators. This action prompted Lizohub to resign from the ministership of the interior and concentrate his energies exclusively on the premiership.

The charges which the nationalists hurled against the Hetman, his ministers, and the civil service were not unfounded. Yet the condition of accepting them at face value is the denial of the proposition that human affairs are characterized by complexity and that the motives underlying human behavior cannot always be easily isolated. It is impossible to state categorically that all participants in any aggregation of human beings, whether it be a political party, a religious group, or a coalition cabinet, are acting on the basis of the same motive. There is always the real possibility that men with conflicting views may collaborate. if only for the purpose of attempting to proselytize their colleagues or utilize them for their own ends. This condition compels the honest observer to conclude that the sweeping accusations of the nationalists were not without bias.

However, their position was understandable when viewed in the light of the activities of Igor Kistiakovsky, who succeeded Lizohub as minister of the interior. This Moscow lawyer bore the responsibility for the numerous arrests of Ukrainian leaders on the grounds that they were "bolsheviks." When visitors began to call on Vinnichenko at Kaniv, where he was residing during the summer, the

18 Doroshenko, *Istoriia Ukraini*, II, p. 260. Both Vinnichenko (III, p. 67, n. 1) and Khristiuk (III, p. 39, n. 1) give long lists of provincial and district elders, mostly with Russian surnames, as proof of the Russian character of the Hetman Government.

minister incorrectly concluded that the former premier under the Rada was conspiring to overthrow the Hetmanate; this led to his arrest on July 12, which was the religious feast day of Saints Peter and Paul. After having been brought to Kiev, he was released on the following day. The arrest, although of short duration, further discredited the government in nationalist circles.

Skoropadsky himself recognized the need for a limited Ukrainization of the regime, and in July instructed Dmitro Doroshenko to negotiate secretly with three prominent conservative elderly Ukrainians and attempt to persuade one of them to accept the premiership. The first person consulted was Professor Dmitro I. Bahaly, a former rector of Kharkiv University and a member of the State Council of Imperial Russia since 1906; he declined because he preferred to spend his last years writing a six-volume history of Ukraine. Doroshenko then went to Chernihiv and offered the premiership to seventy-one-year-old Elias Liudvikovich Shrah; when he complained about the behavior of local officials, Doroshenko informed him that he could rectify matters by accepting the offer. When Shrah refused, the foreign minister called on his sixty-year-old uncle, Dr. Peter Iakovlevich Doroshenko, who also declined the post because of his age.[19]

The attempts to Ukrainize the government were hindered by the arrest of Petliura on July 27. Dmitro Doroshenko immediately attempted to obtain his release, and the Hetman originally was willing to give Petliura a diplomatic sinecure abroad in order to remove him from Ukraine while the government was consolidating its control over the country. This plan had to be discarded in the last days of July when tension between the government and its enemies reached new heights as a result of the assassination of Field Marshal von Eichhorn. Petliura's release was finally arranged by justice minister Andrew H. Viazlov on the meaningless condition that he refrain from participating in any conspiratorial activity.

[19] Doroshenko, *Moi Spomini pro Nedavne-Minule*, III, pp. 74ff.

During July the anti-Hetman forces became consolidated when the National Political Union was transformed into the Ukrainian National Union (*Ukrainski Natsionalni Soiuz*) when the Social Democrats and the moderate Social Revolutionaries entered the new organization. Early in August its statute was approved; it contained the following objectives: establishment of a strong and independent Ukrainian state; a legal government responsible to parliament; democratic suffrage on a direct, general, equal, secret, and proportional basis; and the defense of the rights of the Ukrainian people and their state in the international sphere. The Union was composed not only of political parties but also of peasant, professional, labor, and cultural organizations as well as student groups. Organizational policy was determined by the general assembly which met when summoned; component parts of the Union were to abide by assembly decisions unless they declared their inability to do so. The first president of the Union was Andrew V. Nikovsky, a thiry-three-year-old Socialist Federalist who edited the newspaper *Nova Rada*, but on September 18 he was succeeded by Vinnichenko.[20]

One of the demands which the National Union continually made was that Ukrainian be the sole official language; this, of course, meant the exclusion of Russian. The nationalists were willing to compromise temporarily by allowing all public employees until January 1919 to acquire a knowledge of the language or face the alternative of dismissal. Skoropadsky himself did not know literary Ukrainian although he did speak the village vernacular, and during 1918 he made rapid progress in acquiring a knowledge of the former. Yet in 1918 the Hetman was more at ease while speaking Russian, and during the period of the Hetmanate Doroshenko conversed with him exclusively in that language.

Other prominent figures in the regime besides the Hetman had difficulty with the Ukrainian language. The senile

[20] Doroshenko, *Istoriia Ukraini*, II, pp. 386f. Cf. Khristiuk, *op cit*, III, pp. 87f.

and deaf state controller, George Afanasev, issued an order to the employees in his department instructing them to write all reports exclusively in Russian. Iovenko, the director of the state printing plant, refused to speak Ukrainian. Doroshenko rationalized such activities on the grounds that a newly established state must hire experienced and capable administrators rather than philologists. He contended that under the Rada the criterion employed in hiring civil servants and Zemstvo employees was a candidate's reputation as a Ukrainian revolutionary socialist. Thus it was inevitable that the men of the Rada, who were now no longer in power, should criticize the government. They had not proved themselves to be capable administrators and sincerely believed that this qualification was of secondary or tertiary importance.

Many persons in opposition circles were further displeased by the failure of the Hetman to prevent the trial in a German military court of several Social Revolutionary ministers who had been implicated in the inane kidnaping of Dobri.[21] The failure of ex-premier Holubovich to stand up under the browbeating tactics of the German prosecutor brought him a two-year sentence. He unnecessarily feigned guilt, probably in order to protect the other defendants. Haevsky, a department head in the interior ministry, and P. Bohatsky, head of the Kiev militia, received prison sentences of one year each, as did two militia officials, Kraskovsky and Osipov. The Rada's minister for military affairs was sentenced to two years and six months. These men were all freed when the Hetmanate was overthrown in December.

Yet, despite these unfortunate occurrences, considerable progress was made during the Hetmanate in the Ukrainization of education. This took place even though most educated persons of Ukrainian descent spoke Russian at the time. In the elementary schools there was very little difficulty since the village teachers already knew the vernacular;

---

[21] Supra, pp. 126f. Also see Khristiuk, *op.cit.*, III, p. 41, n. 1.

all that was required was the introduction of new texts in Ukrainian. On the secondary and higher levels the problem was more highly complicated by the absence of the necessary literature in Ukrainian for each academic discipline as well as by the shortage of experienced professors capable of delivering their lectures in Ukrainian. Ukrainization of the latter stages of the educational process could not be accomplished by decree. The minister of education, Nicholas Vasilenko, understood this and pursued a policy of moderation.[22]

The government appropriated more than three million *karbovantsi* for summer courses which would enable teachers to acquire a knowledge of Ukrainian culture. When district elders opposed the courses on the grounds that many teachers were opposed to the Hetmanate, Premier Lizohub ordered them not to interfere with the program. By the autumn of 1918 there were in operation approximately 150 Ukrainian gymnasiums, most of which were newly established; of this number only three were in Kiev. The government also established 350 scholarships for Ukrainian students. On August 1, the ministry of education issued an order compelling Russian secondary schools to provide compulsory learning of Ukrainian language, history, and geography for several hours per week.

These measures failed to satisfy the opponents of the regime who, when in power, had themselves failed to accomplish as much. They desired that all Russian gymnasiums in Ukraine be Ukrainized immediately. Vasilenko was unwilling to precipitate a clash between the two cultures and add to the animosity which already existed. When it was decided that the new Ukrainian State University was to be housed in the buildings of the artillery school on the outskirts of the city, some of the national socialists objected and demanded that the Russian University of Saint Vladimir in the center of Kiev be transformed into the state university.

22 Doroshenko, *Istoriia Ukraini*, II, p. 339.

This new institution had an enrollment of three thousand students distributed among the following four faculties: historical-philological, physical-mathematical, law (including political economy, civil and canon law, and statistics), and medicine. The dedicatory exercises, held on October 6, were attended by the Hetman, who appeared in the costume of his office, which included a white satin coat and a sable cap decorated with ostrich feathers. The Very Reverend Vasil Lipkivsky, who was later to become Metropolitan of the Ukrainian Autocephalous Orthodox Church, celebrated a *Te Deum* and delivered a lengthy address which some of the audience, and especially the envoys of the Central Powers, found tedious and boring. The Russian Metropolitan of Kiev, Anthony Khrapovitsky, addressed the audience of two thousand in Russian; he aroused considerable dissatisfaction by employing the term *Malorusski* (Little Russian), resented by all nationally conscious Ukrainians, and upon completing his speech was greeted with general silence. At these ceremonies the Hetman read the edict of establishment and was thanked by the rector, Professor Feoktist Sushitsky.

A second Ukrainian university was opened at Kamianets-Podilsk on October 22, 1918; its rector was Ivan Ohienko, professor of theology, who became a metropolitan in the Ukrainian Orthodox Church in Kholm during World War II under the monastic name of Ilarion. This institution was temporarily housed in the building of the Kamianets Technical School. In accordance with Vasilenko's policy, the three Russian universities in Kiev, Kharkiv, and Odessa were to remain undisturbed on the condition that they establish special chairs in Ukrainian language, literature, and history. The regime further demonstrated its good faith by appropriating two million *karbovantsi* for textbooks, and the Hetman himself decreed that scholarly dissertations submitted in all institutions of higher learning could be written in Ukrainian as well as in Russian.

Steps were also taken to organize a Ukrainian Academy of Sciences. Hrushevsky refused to accept the presidency of this body since it would have been conferred upon him by the Hetman who had dissolved the Rada over which the historian once presided. The position was finally accepted by the mineralogist, Vladimir Vernadsky, father of Professor George Vernadsky, the noted American historian of Russia. The first members of the Academy were not named until November, when the downfall of the regime was but a matter of days. If the government had existed longer, the Academy would have been organized into three sections: the historical-philological with twenty-two members, that of the physical and mathematical sciences with thirty members, and that of the social sciences with twenty members.[23]

In the cultural sphere Natalie M. Doroshenko, the wife of the foreign minister, was instrumental in founding the Ukrainian State Theater in Kiev, where Ukrainian dramas, including the works of Vinnichenko, were presented. Plans were also made to Ukrainize the Kiev opera by translating many of the libretti in the repertoire into Ukrainian. This program also involved obtaining the services of singers of Ukrainian descent who had been performing in Moscow and Petrograd. The collapse of the Hetmanate brought these worthwhile efforts to an end.

Further evidence regarding the Ukrainian nature of the regime is to be found in the law on Ukrainian citizenship which was enacted on July 3 by the Hetman and his cabinet. Prior to this a special commission had drafted the proposed law; its membership included Professor Eugene V. Spectorsky, rector of the Russian Saint Vladimir's University in Kiev, as well as Vasilenko, Lizohub, Dmitro Doroshenko, and the sociologist, Bohdan Kistiakovsky. The law automatically conferred citizenship upon all Russian subjects residing in Ukraine unless they made known to local officials within one month their desire to retain Russian citizenship. Persons born in Ukraine but not residing there at the time could become citizens by signifying

23 *Ibid.*, p. 363. Cf. Doroshenko's *Moi Spomini pro Nedavne-Minule,* III, p. 86.

their intention at the nearest consulate. The act also recognized birth, marriage of a woman to a Ukrainian citizen, and naturalization after a residence of eight years as means of acquiring citizenship.[24] The oath of citizenship took the following form and, significantly, did not contain a pledge of allegiance to the person of the Hetman:

"I promise and swear always to be true to the Ukrainian State as my Fatherland, to protect the interests of the State, and with all of my strength to further its glory and development even to the extent of giving up my life. I promise and swear not to recognize any Fatherland other than the Ukrainian State, to fulfill sincerely all duties of citizenship, to submit to its government and to all authorities established by it, always bearing in mind that the welfare and development of my Fatherland must take precedence over my personal interests."

On the basis of this law many persons born in Ukraine who had no national consciousness adopted Ukrainian citizenship for the sole purpose of fleeing from the Bolshevik-controlled North. At the same time some individuals, such as Vasili Shulgin, found the very idea of a Ukrainian citizenship to be repugnant; they fled to the Don and Kuban regions, where the Russian anti-Bolshevik movement was gaining momentum.

Thus there were those who regarded the Hetmanate as Ukrainian while the nationalists believed it to be the very antithesis. The position of the latter resulted from the fact that prior to the revolution the number of nationally conscious Ukrainians was very small. These men spoke literary Ukrainian fluently, subscribed to the available Ukrainian periodicals, and belonged to *Prosvita* societies or to one of the small Ukrainian political parties. They formed a compact and exclusive "in" group, a narrow sect of a few thousand who regarded themselves as the only true Ukrainians. An ordinary resident of the territory could qualify only if he adopted their political views and acquired

[24] For the text of the law on citizenship see Doroshenko, *Istoriia Ukraini*, II, pp. 158ff.

167

knowledge of the literary tongue. Dmitro Doroshenko discarded this conception of "nationality" in 1918 contending that "if there was some reason for this division between the 'pure' and the 'impure,' the 'conscious' and the 'unconscious' in the pre-revolutionary period, all cause for it disappeared after the revolution when the national rebirth became not a literary but a living fact, when it became necessary to build not a party but a state."[25] What was needed in 1918 was a new and broader conception of Ukrainian nationality which would have included persons who could hardly speak the language.

The inability of the nationalists to adopt this attitude and concede that civil service appointments should be based on merit rather than on national and social consciousness caused them to refuse to participate in the cabinet on any terms other than their own. These included the purging of all non-nationalist and anti-socialist elements. The young nationalists of the Rada also found displeasure in the advanced age of many of the Hetman's ministers; Premier Lizohub was sixty-seven, while Vasilenko and Afanasev were fifty-one and seventy, respectively.

Although the Hetman was but forty-five, the socialists ascribed to him the same conservatism which is generally associated with advanced age. Skoropadsky had informed a group of visiting teachers on June 29 that he had not assumed the heavy burden of the Hetmanate for personal gain but only so that Ukraine could be free and independent. Here it cannot be denied that the Hetman was thinking of independence in terms of separation from Bolshevik-dominated Russia, which had no respect for the principle of private property. Had he been satisfied with mere independence, the Rada would have met his requirements. Undoubtedly economic interest rather than nationalism was the primary motive so far as the Hetman and most of his supporters were concerned. Doroshenko admits this in stating that: "The Hetman and his government were supported only by those elements in Ukrainian society

[25] Doroshenko, *Moi Spomini pro Nedavne-Minule*, III, p. 53.

who valued statehood, order, and peace in themselves and not necessarily in a Ukrainian national form, and for whom the independence of Ukraine appeared to be the sole means of salvation rather than a constant national ideal. They understood the Ukrainian state in a broad territorial sense rather than in a restricted national sense."[26] They were patriots in the sense that they were attached to their birthland and at the same time wished to have it remain in the form which would provide them with maximum material and psychic satisfaction. However, they were not nationalists and did not share that sense of exclusiveness which characterizes those to whom the nation is the supreme ideal.

In the final analysis, the attempt to determine objectively whether economic interests or nationalist sentiment characterized the regime can only lead to the conclusion that the former appear to have taken precedence over the latter. Yet the nationalist factor was present, and honest efforts were made throughout the summer and autumn to Ukrainize the cabinet. Doroshenko has contended that Skoropadsky was compelled to appoint Russophile ministers when the Ukrainian parties refused to support him.[27] As foreign minister, Doroshenko attempted to retain Ukrainians in the service of his ministry. Ukrainians were in a majority in the transport ministry and in the ministry of health, headed by V. G. Liubinsky. Even nationalists who were opposed to the Hetmanate and its policies found employment in the government.[28]

All of the attempts to make the regime more palatable to the leaders of the National Union failed to unseat Premier Lizohub. Doroshenko's inability to persuade a conservative nationalist to accept the premiership caused him to en-

---

[26] Doroshenko, *Istoriia Ukraini*, II, p. 86.

[27] This thesis is corroborated by another capable participant, Arnold Margolin, who in his *Ukraina i Politika Antanty*, p. 66, also expresses the opinion that the nationalist boycott of the Hetman cabinet was an error

[28] A case in point is that of Nicholas Halahan, who became a department head in the ministry of public health and rationalized his acceptance of the post on the grounds that it was "non-political" (Halahan, *op.cit.*, IV, pp. 55f.)

deavor to obtain portfolios for moderates like Alexander Lototsky and Peter Stebnitsky. They refused to assume the posts without the consent of the Socialist Federalist party. Doroshenko then arranged for the Hetman to meet secretly with the leaders of the National Union on October 5. Subsequent negotiations led to a reorganization of the cabinet which gave the nationalists six portfolios but only from mid-October to November 15. The impossibility of a genuine compromise was evident in the statement of Interior Minister Igor Kistiakovsky, who in addressing a meeting of provincial elders on September 19 said: "I regret to state that among Ukrainians there exist groups who place primary importance on revolutionary seizures of power and on the principle of socialist internationalism. It is necessary to regard them as pseudo-nationalists. With them nationalism is but a protective coloring which must not deceive the ministry of internal affairs."[29]

The Hetman and Doroshenko were not alone in desiring Ukrainization of the cabinet. On June 29, Baron Mumm informed Lizohub of the desirability of introducing some *couleur locale* into the regime. The motive of the Germans in this case was prevention of the reunion of Ukraine with Russia, a reunion which could not be accomplished unless a nationalist separatism was assiduously fostered.[30] Another factor which undoubtedly prompted the Germans to concern themselves with cabinet reform was the growth of terrorism and general uncertainty during June.

On the morning of June 6, large powder and munitions stores exploded in series in Kiev, killing two hundred persons and injuring a thousand more. Women fainted, horses ran away, and persons with heart disease dropped dead. Eight days later a fire of undetermined origin swept through a large portion of the waterfront in the lower part of the city. Only an abating of the wind made it possible for the fire to be brought under control; ten thousand persons were left homeless. On July 31 munitions stores on

[29] Doroshenko, *Istoriia Ukraini*, II, p. 263.
[30] Mints and Eideman, *op.cit.*, p. 75.

Dalnitska Street in Odessa exploded, killing several hundred persons.

The culminating act of terrorism was the assassination of Field Marshal von Eichhorn on July 30 by the twenty-four-year-old Russian Social Revolutionary sailor, Boris M. Donskoi, who was acting on orders from the party's central committee in Moscow. This drastic step resulted from the conviction that the imperialistic German military was threatening the revolution by assuming the role of gendarme of bourgeois society in Ukraine. The party had also been responsible for the murder of Count Wilhelm von Mirbach-Harff, German ambassador to Moscow, on July 6. The murder of Eichhorn was accomplished by means of a bomb which also killed the marshal's adjutant, Captain von Dressler. The assassin and his two accomplices, Irene Kakhovskaia and Gregory Smoliansky, entered Ukraine from Russia late in May in elaborate disguise, with the explosives concealed in their clothing. Donskoi, who made no attempt to flee from the scene of his crime, was hanged on August 10; his body was then displayed for several hours as a warning. Following the Marshal's death, the Hetman personally expressed sympathy to Baron Mumm and sent a message of condolence to Kaiser Wilhelm.[31]

Several Ukrainian Social Revolutionaries planned to assassinate the Hetman at Eichhorn's funeral, but pressure from the police and the military compelled them to flee. This attempt was not unique; the Hetman's residence always had the appearance of an armed camp because of the innumerable threats which were made on his life. Kiev was rife with rumors of conspiracies, and plots were continually being uncovered. When Skoropadsky visited Ger-

[31] For a description of the preparations and the initial failure, see Kakhovskaia's *Souvenirs d'une révolutionnaire* (Paris, 1926), pp. 63ff. For a brief account in Russian, see her "Terroristicheski Akt protiv generala Eikhgorna," *Letopis Revoliutsii* (Berlin, 1923), I, pp. 215ff. Cf. Doroshenko, *Istoriia Ukraini*, II, pp. 119ff. Kakhovskaia was also arrested and sentenced to death, but was saved by the collapse of the German Empire. This collapse made it impossible for the Kaiser to sign the death warrant—a legal prerequisite for the execution of a woman.

many in September 1918, Baron Mumm found it necessary to send a confidential message to Berlin, warning the foreign ministry to maintain secrecy until the time of departure from Kiev in order to avoid an attempt on the Hetman's life by means of railway sabotage.[32] Similar circumstances early in June had caused Eichhorn to abandon his planned trip to Odessa.

The railroad workers' organizations were an imporant source of opposition to the regime. In mid-July they launched a nation-wide strike which was not purely economic in its origin since the government was prepared to meet their wage demands; it was not ready, however, to grant wider powers to the central union of railroad workers. The occupation forces, who had feared such a strike as early as May, kept their supply trains operating, and within ten days the strike front commenced to break. In the ensuing disorganization, large numbers of rail workers and strike committee members were arrested.

The Germans, quite naturally, desired to decrease unrest and agitation since they were detrimental to the economy which meant so much to the war effort of the Central Powers. Some of the local commanders employed severe measures of suppression. The commandant in Kharkiv, acting quite ironically on May 1, forbade all gatherings on streets and in public places and set the minimum sentence for violators at three years, although under extenuating circumstances this sentence could be reduced to six months; persons instigating strikes of workers, advocating the use of force against the government, or hindering rail transport were to be sentenced to death.[33] Other local German commanders throughout Ukraine issued similar although less harsh orders, and in Katerinoslav the threat was made to deport all strikers and replace them with unem-

[32] Mints and Eideman, op.cit., pp. 134f.
[33] Mints and Gorodetsky, op cit., p. 80. For a detailed study of the trade union movement during the Hetmanate, see Iuri Kreizel, op.cit., which contains ample evidence to support the conclusion that labor was dissatisfied with Skoropadsky's regime. However, it is of little use to the student of the national movement.

ployed Austrians. Many industrialists took unfair advantage of the occupation and abrogated prior wage agreements by extending the length of the working day and by reducing wages.

While many of the local officials of the Hetman Government were not sympathetic with labor, the central administration in Kiev did take steps to gain the confidence of the industrial worker. It permitted two congresses of railroad workers to be held; one was composed exclusively of Ukrainians, while the other was territorial and included representatives from the national minorities. It also allowed the First All-Ukrainian Conference of Workers' Organizations to meet in Kiev during the week of May 21-27. The lack of national consciousness among the urban proletariat in Ukraine was reflected in the fact that the Ukrainian socialist parties controlled only seven per cent of the delegates at the Conference. Only 45 of the 539 delegates were Bolsheviks, but the conference, which was conducted almost exclusively in Russian, demanded the eight-hour day, collective agreements, and factory committees.[34]

The difficulties which the regime had with urban workers were of secondary importance when compared with the dissidence manifested by the peasantry. The Hetman inherited this problem from the Rada, which had been unable to cope with the punitive expeditions of the landowners engaged in seizing the tools, implements, and livestock which the peasants had expropriated in 1917. During the preceding winter, the Hetman's own ancestral home had been destroyed by peasants. His edict of April 30 caused local officials to order the restoration of property to former owners and forbid land committees from interfering with the disposition of land. These orders caused numerous uncoordinated local peasant revolts to break out during May and the first half of June; landowners' property was set on fire and many paid with their lives as well. The most

[34] See *Pervaia Vseukrainskaia Konferentsiia Profsoiuzov*, compiled by Iuri Kreizel (n p., 1924). M. Iavorsky, *op cit.*, p. 55 is probably in error in stating that the Bolsheviks had more than seventy supporters at this Conference.

serious of these uprisings occurred in the Zvenihorodka, Tarashchansk, and Uman districts in the Kiev province and were under the leadership of George Tiutiunnik and the Social Revolutionary Nicholas Shinkar. Revolts of lesser intensity took place in the Chernihiv, Poltava, Katerinoslav, Kreminchuk, Mirhorod, Chihirin, and Mohiliv regions. Landowners who managed to survive appealed to the occupation authorities, and new punitive actions were undertaken; in some instances whole peasant villages were burned as a result of shelling by German artillery. Some Ukrainian reports have placed the German losses sustained in these suppressions at 19,000 officers and men.[85]

A number of responsible Germans, including Dr. Paul Rohrbach and the consul general in Odessa, did not hesitate to admit that dissatisfaction with the government could be reduced appreciably only if the peasants received land quickly. German insistence together with the *Jacqueries* prompted the cabinet to adopt Agriculture Minister V. Kolokoltsov's provisional agrarian law on June 14. This act enabled any person to sell land which he owned; it also empowered the State Land Bank to purchase and resell land. The statute fixed the maximum size of landholdings of "one physical or juridical person" at 67.5 acres (25 *desiatinas*). Organizations of individuals cultivating the soil on a cooperative basis could acquire the maximum amount for each member. However, this act was a failure because it did not deal with the crucial problem of dividing the large estates. It contained no provision regarding the price at which land was to be sold and did not make it possible for the poorer peasants to make purchases.

When a delegation of Democratic Agrarian party members called on the Hetman on June 21, asking for order and conditions conducive to peaceful labor, he stated that agrarian reform would be forthcoming. He cautioned them

---

[85] For an account of the agrarian disorders, see N. M. Mogiliansky, "Tragediia Ukrainy," *Arkhiv Russkoi Revoliutsii* (Berlin, 1923), XI, pp. 97ff. Cf. Khristiuk, *op.cit.*, III, pp. 51ff. The *New York Times* printed a brief dispatch from Stockholm on July 3, which reported exaggeratedly that "Kiev peasants have killed all landlords"

in pointing out that the historical and juridical aspects of the problem had to be taken into consideration. He also observed that there was insufficient land to satisfy the needs of all of the peasantry and concluded that Ukrainian industry would have to be developed in order to create gainful employment for this human surplus. Available landed estates were to be purchased by the State Land Bank. A subsequent statute, enacted on August 23, formally established the Bank and provided it with a reserve fund of fifty million *karbovantsi* for making purchases as well as mortgage loans to individual peasants.

These moderate measures were inadequate for a period of such immoderation. The resulting general peasant unrest prompted the cabinet on July 8 to enact a law for combatting disruption of the rural economy. The law empowered provincial agrarian commissions to issue, with the supervision and consent of the ministry of agriculture, mandatory decisions regarding the utilization of agricultural equipment and livestock if, in their opinion, they were not being employed efficiently. The discretion granted to the commissions was of sufficient breadth to include the disposition of human labor engaged in operating the implements and the establishment of wage rates. In short, the peasant was placed at the service of the landowner; violators of commission decisions were to be punished with a jail sentence of up to three months or a fine of up to 500 *karbovantsi*.[36]

The Hetman was caught between the need to supply the Central Powers and the demands of his rural subjects for land. No amount of lip service paid to the ideal of a "healthy peasantry endowed with land" could mitigate the harmful effects of the law of July 8. The policy of General Skoropadsky was designed to create a large number of small and relatively prosperous landholding peasants over an extended period of time in the manner of Stolypin; this was commendable and would have provided a substantial social basis for the political order, but under the circum-

[36] For the text of this law see Khristiuk, *op.cit.*, III, pp. 58f.

stances it proved to be too dilatory and evolutionary. Too many of the officials of the regime were unable to comprehend the profundity of the social impact of the revolution of the preceding year; they ignored the fact that the peasants had seized the land during 1917 and would now naturally resent having to pay for it even though many of them had considerable savings as a result of the inflation and the lack of manufactured goods. The bankruptcy of the Hetman's agrarian policy became apparent early in November, when the cabinet adopted the program of Volodimir Leontovich, the landowner turned minister of agriculture. It provided for the compulsory sale of large estates to the State Land Bank but exempted all landholdings of economic significance up to 540 acres (200 *desiatinas*) in size as well as all estates producing beet sugar. This measure confirmed the arguments of the anti-government agitators and was a source of the peasant support which was enjoyed by Vinnichenko's and Petliura's rising against the Hetmanate.

In part, the Hetman's agrarian policy, as it developed in practice, was related to the demands which the Central Powers made upon the Ukrainian economy. The Hetman had inherited a series of economic agreements which the Central Powers had concluded with the Rada. The first of these had been made on April 9 and provided for the delivery of more than a million tons (60 million puds[37]) of grain as well as fruits and fats by July 31. A second agreement, concluded on April 11, obligated the Rada to provide 400 million eggs by July 31; a third, arranged two days later, committed the Ukrainians to supply 50 thousand tons of horned livestock with the stipulation that the average weight of the animals be 541.5 pounds. The Ukrainians also agreed to furnish more than 27,000 tons of potatoes. These three separate agreements were incorporated into a general treaty which was signed in Kiev on April 23 by Mumm, Forgach, and Nicholas Porsh.[38] On the

[37] One pud = 36.1 pounds (U.S.)

[38] Doroshenko, *Istoriia Ukraini*, II, pp. 292ff. Cf. Mints and Gorodetsky, *op cit.*, pp. 65ff.

176

following day, General Groener met with Skoropadsky to discuss the establishment of the Hetmanate.

The new regime failed to meet the monthly delivery schedules which were incorporated into the April 23 agreement, and the Germans, who had promised to send agricultural machinery and coal to Ukraine, were also unable to meet their obligations. This agreement expired unfulfilled on July 31, and it was not until September 10 that a new treaty was signed. The new accord, which was to continue until July 1919, stipulated that thirty-five per cent (two million tons) of Ukrainian grain production be exported together with two million fowl, as well as butter, cheese, fats, eggs, and more than 45,000 tons of sugar. A supplementary financial agreement provided that Germany print 11,500,000 *hriven*[39] by January 1, 1919, for circulation in Ukraine. Of this amount the sum of 1,600,000 *hriven* was to be retained by the Central Powers for the use of their armies and officials in Ukraine; the Ukrainian Government was to be compensated for this in part in marks and kronen which were to be deposited in the German and Austrian state banks but could be spent only during the year following the conclusion of a general peace. In this way the Hetmanate was to be compelled to pay the costs of the occupation.

The burden of the occupation was felt throughout the economy which was already disrupted by revolution and civil war. In 1918 the prices of manufactured goods rose to twenty-four times their 1912 cost in accordance with the corresponding inflation of the currency. Coal production in the Donets Basin declined during the first six months of 1918 to 5,176,000 tons, in comparison with an output of more than fifteen million tons for the first half of 1917

[39] The value of the *hrivnia* was equal to half that of the *karbovanets* or old ruble; the former was supposedly valued at 8.712 parts of pure gold and the latter at twice that amount. Actually this currency was based not on bullion but on a 400 million *karbovanets* loan which the Central Powers made to Ukraine on May 15. Half of the loan was in kronen and half in marks with the *karbovanets* valued at two kronen or 1 1/3 marks. Cf. *Texts of the Ukraine "Peace"* (Washington, 1918), pp. 153f.

despite the collapse of the tsarist government. The lowest monthly production occurred in May 1918 when less than half a million tons were mined.[40] The general economic retardation which resulted was especially evident in the industrial segments of the economy. During the first half of May the number of unemployed rose to a quarter of a million, most of which were in the Katerinoslav, Kharkiv, and Kherson regions. By June 1 this number had declined to 180,600, but continued large-scale unemployment prompted the cabinet on August 5 to appropriate two and a half million *karbovantsi* for public works. Extensive plans were also drawn up for the construction of new rail lines and public buildings in Kiev, as well as for dredging portions of the Dnieper rapids.

Yet public works programs, while providing employment and preventing the urban worker from starving, could not provide the manufactured goods which the peasant wanted in return for his deliveries of agricultural products to the Germans. Instead, he received worthless currency which only served to accentuate his dissatisfaction with the regime and to decrease the economic aid which Ukraine could render to the Central Powers.

The country had been divided into two zones of occupation at Baden on March 29, 1918, with the Germans receiving the better portion, including the northern part of Ukraine as well as Taurida, the Crimea, Tahanrih, and Novorossiisk. In May they occupied the Donets Basin in order to ensure a coal supply for Ukraine. The Austrians, who were somewhat slower, occupied southwestern Volynia, Podolia, Kherson, and part of Katerinoslav. They did not have troops in Kiev and could influence the German Command and the Hetman Government only through their envoy, Count Forgach. Mutual suspicion on the part of the two powers undoubtedly limited the effectiveness of the occupation. Field Marshal Alfred Krauss, the Austrian commander, was convinced that Berlin intended to subjugate Ukraine permanently and utilize it as a route to

40 Mints and Gorodetsky, *op.cit.,* p. 133.

Mesopotamia and Arabia via Baku and Persia; he also feared that Austria would have to give up Odessa and Katerinoslav to its stronger ally.[41] The Germans at the same time suspected the Hapsburgs of promoting the candidacy of Archduke Wilhelm for the Ukrainian throne and of desiring to unite the whole Ukrainian nation, including Eastern Galicia and Northern Bukovina, into a crown province. The Archduke was a prominent Ukrainophile and had learned to speak the language fluently; he acquired the name of Vasil Vishivani (Basil the Embroidered) as a result of the elaborate blouses which he wore.[42] Skoropadsky's fear that he would be succeeded by the Archduke drove him into closer collaboration with the Germans whose military power he understandably appreciated.

The efficacy of the occupation in economic terms was reduced by the inability of the Central Powers to furnish Ukraine with the manufactured products which it needed and expected. At Brest-Litovsk they, together with the Ukrainian delegation, had overestimated the supplies which would be available and had not taken into account the widespread Bolshevik requisitions which occurred during February. This situation led to a very one-sided commercial relationship which the Austrians intensified by being able to export little else but mineral water. A fuel shortage constantly hampered Ukrainian industry and transport despite the German shipment of 21,428 carloads of coal into the country between April and September. The uncertainty of property rights caused agricultural productivity to decline, and the produce available for export was often delayed because of the lack of rolling stock.

[41] Mints and Eideman, *op.cit.*, pp. 71ff.

[42] Rumors concerning the Archduke's acceptance of the Ukrainian throne prompted the Emperor Karl to warn him in May of 1918 that such action could antagonize Germany at a time when Austria-Hungary was badly in need of food supplies. The Emperor advised him not to take any "decisive steps" because "under present conditions it is difficult to determine what is the actual will of the majority of the Ukrainian people" (Mints and Eideman, p. 154). The Archduke survived World War II, but in the autumn of 1947 he was reported to have been arrested in Vienna by Soviet occupation authorities.

The occupation was regarded as unprofitable by some observers since its fruits were obtained at the cost of immobilizing half a million German and Austrian troops stationed in Ukraine. This caused both Vienna and Berlin to consider withdrawing their forces in mid-August.[43] However, this step was not taken. Later Count Ottokar Czernin, one of the prime architects of the *Brotfrieden*, defended the occupation and regarded the total food imports from Ukraine as "not inconsiderable." These included thirty thousand carloads of foodstuffs shipped officially as well as fifteen thousand carloads more "smuggled unofficially." While these imports did not meet the expectations of the occupation authorities, they did prevent a serious famine in much of Central Europe.[44]

The economic and political dependence of the Hetmanate upon Germany did not preclude its having some of the trappings if not the substance of a sovereign state. One of these political embellishments was the ministry of foreign affairs. Foreign minister Doroshenko, struggling against overwhelming odds, endeavored to implement a foreign policy which would serve the interests of the Ukrainian State. His cardinal objective was to terminate the German guardianship in the shortest possible period of time and to use it in the interim for the reunion of what he regarded as Ukrainian irredentas in Kholm, Bessarabia, the Kuban, and the Crimea. The second foreign policy objective was the obtaining of recognition from neutral countries and, if possible, from the Entente Powers. The third aim was the conclusion of peace and the delimitation of the frontier with Soviet Russia.

The achievement of these goals would have been difficult even if the occupation authorities had cooperated with the regime in every way. Instead, they chose not to pursue a clearly defined positive policy in Ukraine; this error can

[43] Mints and Gorodetsky, *op.cit.*, pp. 176f.
[44] Count Ottokar Czernin, *In the World War* (London, 1919), pp. 255f. Cf. Gustav Gratz and Richard Schüller, *The Economic Policy of Austria-Hungary during the War in its External Relations* (New Haven, 1928), p. 136.

probably be attributed to the preponderance of the politically unschooled military. They opposed the organization of a separate Ukrainian army until the end of the summer and did not support the Ukrainian irredentist claims. Doroshenko, who was no Germanophobe even after the fall of the regime, later complained that "the German Government, as if intentionally, sent to Kiev persons who had no understanding of Ukraine, took no interest in her and who looked down upon the whole matter of Ukrainian statehood."[45]

These men commenced to accuse the Ukrainians in May and June of violating the terms of the Brest-Litovsk Treaty in respect to grain deliveries. The charge, which was not without basis, was repeated by the Vienna press in June. The motive of the Austrians in raising the issue was to escape having to fulfill two obligations which they had assumed in February only because of the dire food shortage. The more humiliating commitment which Czernin made was incorporated into a secret protocol appended to the treaty. In this document the Rada's delegation and the Austrians affirmed their respect for national minorities and the former committed its government to enact legislation protecting the rights of Germans, Poles, and Jews in Ukraine. The Austrians promised to introduce a bill in their parliament by July 20, providing for the unification of Eastern Galicia and Northern Bukovina into a separate Ukrainian province.[46]

The protocol was an integral part of the whole Brest-Litovsk Treaty and its validity was contingent upon the fulfillment of all conditions in the peace settlement, including the grain deliveries. Only two copies of the text of the protocol existed and these were deposited in the Ukrainian foreign ministry and at the Ballplatz. However, Alexander Sevriuk, the Rada's youthful diplomat, violated the condition of secrecy in March when he indiscreetly in-

[45] Doroshenko, *Moi Spomini pro Nedavne-Minule*, III, p. 7.
[46] For the text of the agreement see Doroshenko, *Istoriia Ukraini*, II, pp. 215f. or Mints and Eideman, *op.cit.*, pp. 77f.

formed some of the Galician politicians in Vienna of the provisions of the document. When Polish deputies in the Austrian parliament learned of the protocol, they immediately protested. They were opposed to the division of Galicia into Polish western and Ukrainian eastern portions especially because the capital of the latter would have been in the then Polish city of Lviv. The Ballplatz then demanded and otained the Ukrainian copy of the protocol by insisting that it be deposited in the German foreign ministry. At the time, Berlin agreed to surrender it to Vienna if the partition of Galicia were carried out; in the event that partition did not take place, the text was to be returned to the Ukrainians.

The Austrian plan to renounce the protocol took shape on July 4, when Count Forgach, who had been Vienna's minister to Belgrade prior to the war, informed Skoropadsky that his government was going to annul the agreement because it concerned an Austrian internal matter. The Hetman protested, but two days later Forgach threatened that he would bring about the removal of Doroshenko if any notes of protest were issued by the Ukrainian foreign office. Acting quickly, the Austrians persuaded the Germans to burn the Ukrainian copy of the protocol on July 16 in Berlin. Viacheslav Lipinsky, the Hetman's ambassador to Vienna, sent futile notes of protest to the Austrian foreign minister, Count Burian, on July 24 and 28. The Hetman, who did not learn of the burning of the document until early in September, had no alternative but to acquiesce; his failure to obtain German support compelled him to inform Forgach on August 7 that he would bow before superior force but only under protest.

Relations between Kiev and Vienna were subjected to additional strain when the Austrians refused to abide by that portion of the peace treaty in which they recognized the Ukrainian claim to Kholm. This ethnically mixed region had a slight Ukrainian and Bielo-russian majority and lay west of the Bug River. In March the Rada had appointed Alexander Skoropis-Ioltukhovsky as its commissar for Kholm and Pidliashe, but the Austrian troops, which occupied the five southern districts, refused to grant him and his staff entry. This policy was based on Vienna's fear of losing Polish support, but it did not meet with the approval of the Germans, who allowed Skoropis-Ioltukhovsky to enter the northern portion of the disputed region. German support enabled Kiev to refuse to accept the Bug River frontier which the Austrians and Poles desired, but the inability to agree on the frontier enabled the Austrians to refuse to ratify the peace treaty.[47] The insistence of the Ukrainians was of no practical value. When the Dual Empire crumbled, the Austrian officers in Kholm allowed the representatives of resurrected Poland to assume authority and intern Skoropis-Ioltukhovsky and his aides.

This incident and the concurrent collapse of the Skoropadsky Government symbolized the futility of a puppet regime's attempting to conduct foreign relations. Yet, despite this failure, the Hetmanate must be commended for having established a diplomatic corps whose general ability and size was an improvement over that of the Rada. Ukraine's first foreign minister, Alexander Shulgin, had not been able to send diplomatic representatives to the Entente Powers late in 1917, but his successor after Brest-Litovsk, Nicholas Liubinsky, did appoint ambassadors to the Central Powers. Their brief tenure was cut short by the coup of April 29. The Rada's ambassador in Berlin, Alexander Sevriuk, resigned and went to Switzerland. Andrew Iakovliv was recalled from Vienna, and Nicholas Levitsky, who represented the Rada in Constantinople, tendered his resignation when the Social Democratic party

---

[47] Instruments of ratification were exchanged in Vienna but only with the other three Central Powers. Bulgaria assumed the initiative on July 15, and was followed by Germany on July 24, and by Turkey on August 22, 1918. The refusal of the Austrians to ratify the treaty was indicative of their suspicion of the Hetmanate and their fear that a strong Ukraine would be in a position to annex Eastern Galicia and Northern Bukovina as well as Carpatho-Ukraine. They were undoubtedly conscious of the possibility that Skoropadsky, in assuming the title of "Hetman of all Ukraine" could have, in effect, been claiming every irredenta.

forbade its members to hold positions in the new government.

The Hetman's foreign ministry made two ambassadorial appointments which did not meet with the approval of the nationalists. The first of these was the designation of Baron Fedor Rudolfovich Shteingel as ambassador to Germany. The bearded Volynian baron, who had been a member of the First Duma and who had served a three-month jail sentence for having signed the Viborg Manifesto, was firmly convinced of the necessity for having federal ties with Russia, but he agreed to repress his sympathies and work for Ukrainian independence. This did not prevent him from conducting the business of the embassy in Russian. The other unsatisfactory appointment was that of Michael A. Sukovkin as ambassador to Turkey; he did not leave Kiev until October and adopted an anti-Ukrainian position with the fall of the Hetmanate.

These appointments were counterbalanced by the decision to send a sincere non-socialist nationalist, Viacheslav Lipinsky, to represent the Hetmanate in Vienna. He had been a Polonized Ukrainian but had retained his Latin-rite Catholic faith even after rediscovering his nationality. His first-hand knowledge of both the Dual Empire and the Polish nation prompted the Directory Government, which succeeded Skoropadsky, to retain him at this post despite his membership in the Democratic Agrarian party. An equally good choice was made in sending Alexander Shulgin to represent the Ukrainian State in Bulgaria.

Tsar Ferdinand reciprocated by sending Professor Ivan Shishmanov as his ambassador to Kiev. This Slavist and historian had taught at the University of Sofia and had served as minister of education in Bulgaria for four years, commencing in 1903. He was an ardent Ukrainophile and a member of the Shevchenko Scientific Society in Lviv; his wife, Liudmila, was the daughter of Michael Drahomaniv, the prominent Ukrainian émigré publicist. To Shishmanov belonged the distinction of being the first envoy of the Central Powers to employ the archaic title of "Serene Highness" in addressing the Hetman; prior to this the German and Austrian ambassadors had addressed him as "Seine Exzellenz" rather than as "Durchlaucht." Titles mattered relatively little to these men since they were actually the masters of the situation. The occupation authorities continually intervened in Ukrainian internal affairs and protests from Ukrainian citizens were always being referred by Doroshenko to the German embassy, with the request that soldiers guilty of excesses be punished and that restitution be made. When this approach failed to achieve results, Doroshenko attempted to shift the scene of German-Ukrainian relations from Kiev to Berlin for the purpose of obtaining access to the foreign ministry and the Kaiser. Premier Lizohub and the Hetman visited Germany for the same purpose and Baron Shteingel's post assumed added importance. Doroshenko later concluded that by the end of the summer the most important issues were being resolved in Berlin.[48]

The importance of relations with Germany did not cause the Ukrainian foreign office to neglect events in the remainder of Russia. The Don region, which contained a considerable Ukrainian population, was of especial interest to the Hetmanate. Early in May, Major General Peter N. Krasnov was "elected" *ataman* (military commander) and

[48] Doroshenko, *Istoriia Ukraini*, II, p 136. The Hetman arrived in Berlin on September 4, for the purpose of obtaining German permission for the organization of a Ukrainian army and control of the Black Sea fleet. He was met at the station by State Secretary Richard von Kühlmann and proceeded to the Hotel Adlon. On the following day he and Baron Shteingel called on Chancellor Hertling. Skoropadsky then went to Kassel to meet the Kaiser and be decorated with the Order of the Red Eagle. These two doomed rulers, in the final fleeting days of their reigns, exchanged good wishes and drank toasts; the Hetman expressed the hope that the political and economic ties between the two countries would be strengthened and toasted the Kaiser's health and "the glorious future of the valiant and faithful German people." Other events on his itinerary were the horse races at Grunewald and visits to the Cologne cathedral and the Krupp Works at Essen On September 9, he paid homage to von Hindenburg and von Ludendorff and four days later visited the Kiel naval base, where he spent a half hour in a submerged submarine. On the afternoon of September 17, he returned to Kiev, bearing the indelible stamp of a German puppet (Doroshenko, *Istoriia Ukraini*, II, pp. 381 ff.).

became, for all practical purposes, dictator of the Don. A non-national independent state was proclaimed, but its existence was to be terminated when all Russia would be free of Bolshevik rule. General A. Cheriachukin was sent to Kiev to represent the Don. General Skoropadsky became interested in this movement because it provided support for his policy of containing and, if possible, overthrowing Bolshevism. Yet the agreement on this one objective was beclouded by Krasnov's claim to Tahanrih, Starobilsk in Kharkiv province, and to Lugansk with its munitions industry. The *ataman* also stated that he was willing to recognize Ukrainian independence only until "the re-establishment, in some form or other, of a united Russia." When Lizohub and Doroshenko protested and insisted that Ukraine was to remain independent, Krasnov claimed that relations between the two states would not be harmed by the reunification of Russia, but hastily added that such a step would be unthinkable without the participation of both the Don and Ukraine.

Despite the existence of these real differences, the Hetman was compelled to come to terms with Krasnov if he wished to secure an ally and reduce the length of the Soviet Russian-Ukrainian frontier. If the independence of the Don had not been recognized by Ukraine, the Council of People's Commissars would have claimed the right to represent it in the Russian-Ukrainian peace negotiations which had commenced in May. The modus vivendi which the two states arrived at was incorporated into the Ukrainian-Don treaty of August 8, in which both signatories recognized each other's independence and sovereignty. The former provincial frontiers for Katerinoslav, Kharkiv, and Voronezh were re-established as the Ukrainian-Don frontier, with several slight modifications, one of which gave Mariiupil to Ukraine; Tahanrih, Rostov on the Don, and much of the Donets Basin were placed in the Don State. Each high contracting party agreed to accord to the irredenta of the other linguistic, educational, and cultural rights. Both states also obligated themselves not to conclude any treaty with another state or with a military organization which would be detrimental to their mutual interests. A mixed commission was to be established in order to preserve the economic unity of the Donets Basin.[49] This agreement provided a basis for the shipment of considerable quantities of Ukrainian military supplies to the Don.

A similar anti-Bolshevik movement began to develop in the Kuban region which lay south of the Don. The Ukrainian minority in the Kuban caused the Hetman Government to take an interest in the Volunteer Army which Generals Michael V. Alexeiev and Anton Denikin, who were not sympathetic with the idea of Ukrainian independence, were organizing there. A delegation of Ukrainians from the Kuban visited Kiev early in June and discussed the union of the region with Ukraine even though the Don, which lay between, was opposed to this. Plans were made to prevent Denikin from obtaining control of the Kuban. This was to be done by transporting 15,000 Ukrainian troops, under the command of General Natiev, in a shore-to-shore operation from the Azov coast to the Kuban in order to seize Ekaterinodar (now Krasnodar) ahead of Alexeiev. A local rising of Ukrainians was to take place simultaneously. The plan failed when a ranking Russian official in the Ukrainian war ministry, whose identity cannot definitely be established, obstructed the movement of General Natiev's troops long enough to enable Alexeiev to take Ekaterinodar in August several weeks prior to his death. Once the city fell, the German military forbade the Ukrainian expedition and the Kuban remained under the control of Denikin's Volunteer Army.

Ukrainian interest in the Don and Kuban regions was overshadowed somewhat by the concern which the Hetman manifested over the Crimea in June when the German occupation authorities sponsored a Russian Crimean terri-

[49] *Ibid.*, pp. 192f. The Ukrainian National Union objected to the treaty at its meeting on August 30, claiming that it surrendered a million and a half Ukrainians to the Don and was a betrayal of the principle of national unification. For the text of the protest see Khristiuk, *op.cit.*, III, p. 109.

torial government headed by Lieut. General Suleiman
Sulkevich. As in the Don, this government's independence
was to be terminated with the reunification of Russia.
The Ukrainian opposition to Crimean independence was
prompted by economic and strategic interests as well as by
the fact that Sulkevich's hostile attitude towards Ukraine
could develop into a threat to its independence. During the
summer an embargo was placed on all goods entering
Crimea except those consigned to the German occupation
forces. This measure prevented the peninsula's fruit pro-
ducers from obtaining the sugar needed for the preservation of their crop. Faced with tremendous losses, the Crimean Government promised to unite with Ukraine on
the condition that the embargo be lifted. The delegation
which it sent to Kiev in September obtained autonomy for
the peninsula which included a territorial legislature and
military force as well as the appointment of a state secretary
for Crimean affairs in the Ukrainian cabinet.[50]

The Hetmanate met with much less success in attempting to assert its control over Bessarabia. Rumania had an-
nexed the region in March 1918, but this had not prevented
the Rada from sending Nicholas Halahan as its envoy to
Jassy, the provisional capital at the time. He was unable
to obtain *de jure* recognition from the Rumanians, and,
upon returning to Kiev and finding the Hetman in power,
he resigned even though asked by Doroshenko to remain
at the Jassy post.[51] The Hetman Government severed diplomatic relations with Rumania and on May 11 imposed an
economic embargo at the Dniester which was lifted only
when Jassy protested to the Germans. Late in the summer
Doroshenko consented to open negotiations for a com-

[50] Doroshenko, *Istoriia Ukraini*, II, p. 214. Cf. "Krymskoe kraevoe
pravitel'stvo v 1918-19 godakh," *Krasnyi Arkhiv*, XXII, pp. 92ff. The Hetman's foreign ministry subsidized Ukrainian publications in the Kuban
and in the Don in order to stimulate national consciousness. In the
Crimea it financed three newspapers.

[51] Halahan, *op.cit.*, IV, pp. 11ff. The Rada's envoy, like other Ukrainian
diplomats of the time, found it necessary to travel to the Dniester River
frontier under guard. He described vividly his crossing the frontier in a
Rumanian freight car sent from Bendery especially for his use.

mercial agreement largely because this could provide a means of contacting diplomats of the Entente who were still at the Rumanian court. A stillborn agreement was signed with Rumania late in October, but the Hetman's inability to raise a large army precluded the possibility of regaining Bessarabia.

The Ukrainians were compensated for this diplomatic defeat by the peace negotiations which Soviet Russia was compelled to carry on with them in Kiev during the late spring and summer. The Germans had insisted upon the inclusion of the following (sixth) article in the March 3 Treaty of Brest-Litovsk: "Russia agrees to conclude peace immediately with the Ukrainian People's Republic and to recognize the treaty of peace concluded between that state and the four Central Powers. Ukrainian territory shall be evacuated without delay by the Russian Army and the Russian Red Guard. Russia shall cease all agitation or propaganda against the government or public institutions of the Ukrainian People's Republic."[52]

The Red Army was withdrawn, but Ukrainian Bolshevik forces continued to wage war against the Rada Government. When the latter protested to the Council of People's Commissars on April 1, it received a reply which stated that the conflict was actually between different segments of the Ukrainian people and was not Russo-Ukrainian in nature. An armistice with the Russian Bolsheviks was finally signed when their Ukrainian comrades were driven out of the country and found it necessary to seek refuge in the north.

The Soviet delegation to Kiev was headed by Dmitri Z. Manuilsky, a native of Volynia who was fluent in Ukrainian, and Christian Rakovsky. The Bolsheviks were housed, much to their dismay, in the inferior Hotel Marcel, which was a haven for girls and their suitors; this arrangement resulted from malice as well as from the acute housing shortage. The Ukrainian delegation was headed by the noted jurist, Serhi Shelukhin, who, despite the fact that

[52] Khristiuk, *op.cit.*, II, p. 116.

he was as fluent in Russian as he was in his native tongue, insisted that all Russian statements made in the course of the negotiations be translated into Ukrainian. He was assisted by Igor Kistiakovsky and later by Peter Stebnitsky.

The negotiations commenced on May 23 in the Pedagogical Museum. Shelukhin immediately rejected the Soviet credentials because they did not state the nature of the treaty which was to be concluded and did not define the component political units of the Russian Soviet Federated Republic. On the following day Rakovsky declared that the nature of the treaty was evident from all of the preliminary diplomatic correspondence, and a long discussion followed regarding the juridical character of Soviet Russia. The dispute over credentials was renewed on May 31, even though new and more explicit documents arrived. Rakovsky refused to recognize that the negotiations were being conducted by two sovereign states; he was willing to concede only that the Brest-Litovsk Treaty obliged Russia to conclude a peace with Ukraine. He based his position on the contention that the lack of extensive recognition of Ukrainian independence on the international plane left the matter undetermined. The dispute was terminated on June 2, when it was agreed that both Russia and Ukraine were independent.

A preliminary agreement was signed on June 12, providing for the suspension of all hostilities and the lifting of all restrictions on the exit of Ukrainian citizens from Soviet Russia and Russian citizens from Ukraine. Consulates of the Hetmanate were established in approximately thirty Russian and Siberian cities to facilitate the southward flow of population; a Soviet consulate was opened in Kiev. Postal, telegraphic, and rail communication was resumed between the two countries, and the Russians agreed to return all locomotives and rolling stock seized during the Bolshevik retreat. This initial accord was nullified somewhat by the clash which occurred when the negotiators commenced to discuss the question of the Soviet-Ukrainian frontier.

The disputed areas included the northern districts in Chernihiv province and the western and southwestern districts of Kursk and Voronezh provinces. Rakovsky appeared to be willing to allow the local population to decide the issue. Shelukhin claimed that the people were not adequately informed in order to vote correctly, and accused the Bolsheviks of having coerced the inhabitants of the disputed areas to express a desire for annexation by Russia. His ideal was an ethnographic frontier in principle but with economic and strategic needs also taken into consideration. The summer dragged on, and the mutual bitterness was intensified. With each passing day the possibility of an agreement on the frontier diminished. Shelukhin correctly charged the Bolsheviks with employing delaying tactics and engaging in propaganda against the Ukrainian Government. He also complained of violations of the armistice and of the failure to return rolling stock.

The Ukrainians reduced the area under consideration when Shelukhin informed the Bolsheviks on August 15 that a treaty had been concluded with the Don, delimiting the southeastern Ukrainian frontier. On October 3, they made a final proposal and granted some territorial concessions to the Bolsheviks in the hope of resolving the issue within four days or breaking off negotiations temporarily. On October 7, Rakovsky stated that the new proposal necessitated his returning to Moscow for consultation. While Manuilsky remained in Kiev, several Soviet diplomatic officials were arrested for having carried on agitation against the Hetmanate. This incident prevented the resumption of negotiations, and on November 3 Moscow ordered Manuilsky to withdraw all Soviet diplomatic personnel from Ukraine. The Hetman's officials held the future Soviet Ukrainian foreign minister and representative in the United Nations at the frontier until the Ukrainian consuls had returned safely from Russia.

The failure of these artificial peace talks can be attributed to the Bolshevik appraisal of this period as one of transition. This conclusion was undoubtedly corroborated by the deterioration of the German position on the Western front and the knowledge that Skoropadsky, being without any real army, could not continue in power after the military collapse of the Reich. In order to facilitate the fall of the Hetmanate, Manuilsky encouraged the leaders of the Ukrainian National Union when they came to him in order to obtain support for their projected insurrection against Skoropadsky. He informed Vinnichenko and his colleagues verbally that Moscow could aid only indirectly by increasing the military activity on the Russo-Ukrainian front and diverting the attention of the regime's few troops. He also promised to recognize the new Ukrainian Government and to refrain from intervening in the internal affairs of the Independent Ukrainian People's Republic. In return, Vinnichenko agreed to legalize the Ukrainian Communist party.[53]

The attitude of the Ukrainian socialists which made such an agreement possible was related to the growth of pro-Bolshevik sentiment in the left wings of both the Social Democratic and Social Revolutionary parties. Yet this did not prevent Vinnichenko from simultaneously negotiating with Skoropadsky for the reorganization of the cabinet along democratic national lines in accordance with Woodrow Wilson's recommendations regarding Germany. On October 5, Vinnichenko, together with Andrew Nikovsky and Fedir Shvets, went secretly to the Hetman's residence at Doroshenko's behest in order to present him with a list of ministerial candidates. After some discussion it was decided that Lizohub would continue as premier, but agreement could be obtained neither on the number of portfolios to be assigned to the Ukrainians nor on the

[53] Vinnichenko, *op.cit.*, III, pp. 158f. The meeting occurred in the quarters of Vasil Mazurenko, a Social Democrat who was employed in the Hetman's finance ministry. He confirmed Vinnichenko's account in an article which he wrote for *Chernaia Kniga* (edited by A. G. Shlikhter. Ekaterinoslav, 1925), p. 277. Both Doroshenko and Shelukhin were later convinced that the peace talks failed because of the treachery of the Ukrainian National Union. Doroshenko attempted unsuccessfully to transfer the sessions to the quiet provincial town of Nizhin in order to divorce them from the turbulence of the capital.

candidates. At this time Vinnichenko enjoyed great popularity, as was demonstrated on the following day at the
opening of the Ukrainian State University when the applause accorded him was not equalled by that given any
other speaker. This support enhanced his bargaining power
and enabled him to delay the formation of the new cabinet
for more than two weeks. His position was further strengthened when Baron Mumm was ordered on October 10 to
direct Skoropadsky to Ukrainize the cabinet.[54] The motive
of the Germans was their desire to promote Ukrainian
separatism and the resultant weakening of Russia now that
they were losing the war.

The sense of strength which the leaders of the National
Union undoubtedly experienced at this time was evident
in the following passage from a declaration which they
issued in mid-October:

"We do not regard the present cabinet in Ukraine as
having full authority or as being the legal representative of
the Ukrainian State. The present cabinet of ministers, made
up largely of former officials of the autocratic Russian
regime and alien to the people nationally and inimical to
it politically and socially, has support only in the numerically small circles of large landowners and captains of industry. It does not and cannot comprehend the new basis
of life which is embracing the whole world."[55]

The nationalists had been saying this all summer, but
their words asumed real meaning when the cabinet learned
of the secret negotiations which the Hetman was conducting with the National Union. Tension manifested itself
among the ministers and a cabinet crisis was finally precipitated in mid-October when ten of them petitioned Premier
Lizohub regarding the role which Ukraine would play in
the forthcoming peace conference.

The group of petitioners included education minister
Vasilenko; Sergei N. Gerbel, the minister of supply; Wagner, minister of labor; Kolokoltsov, minister of agriculture;

---

[54] Mints and Eideman, *op.cit.*, p. 136.
[55] Khristiuk, *op cit.*, III, p. 112.

Zinkivsky, the minister of cults, as well as state controller Afanasev and finance minister Rzhepetsky. These men wished to aid Russia at the peace conference, help her to defeat Bolshevism, and then establish a federative relationship. In short, they desired to wage war against the Bolsheviks in the name of a reunited Russia. The other six ministers—Lizohub, Kistiakovsky, Doroshenko, Butenko, George Liubinsky, and General Rogoza—rejected the notion of a large reunited Russia and were of the opinion that Ukraine should speak only on her own behalf at the conference. It is possible that the crisis could have been averted, at least temporarily, if Gutnik, the minister of trade and industry, had not published the petition in the Russian newspaper *Kievskaia Mysl* before it was discussed at a meeting of the cabinet. This arbitrary step was the final event leading to the cabinet's dissolution on October 18.

Within a week a coalition cabinet was formed with Lizohub as premier. It included such anti-Ukrainians as Gerbel and Rzhepetsky, but Gutnik, the villain of the crisis, was succeeded by Sergei F. Mering, a landowner and sugar refiner. Vinnichenko's National Union had originally demanded eight portfolios but in the end accepted the following five: education, Peter Stebnitsky; cults, Alexander Lototsky; agriculture, Volodimir Leontovich; justice, Andrew Viazlov; and labor, Slavinsky. Doroshenko, although remaining as foreign minister, was not a candidate of the National Union.

The new cabinet immediately encountered serious difficulties. One of the first official acts of Vladimir E. Reinbot, Kistiakovsky's successor as interior minister, was to prohibit a meeting of the Democratic Agrarian party. It was only due to the personal intercession of the Hetman that the gathering met on October 26. Soon Vinnichenko stated that the National Union could not accept responsibility for the actions of the cabinet and had no alternative but to oppose it. He demanded the convocation of a parliamentary body (*soim*) representing the workers and peasants, the release of all political prisoners, the organization of a Ukrainian army and the termination of press censorship and restrictions on the right of free speech.

But Vinnichenko's voice was drowned out by the scurrying for shelter brought on by the impending defeat of the Central Powers. Bulgaria had withdrawn from the war late in September, and as the Dual Empire commenced to disintegrate. Prince Max of Baden became chancellor of Germany under the guise of democratization. The collapse of the Soviet-Ukrainian peace negotiations meant war with the Bolsheviks in the event of the withdrawal of the forces of occupation. Disorganization had already set in, especially among the men in the Austrian army who wished to return home in order to participate in the creation of the new political order. All this disturbed the Hetman. Early in October he had inquired regarding the possibility of a withdrawal of the troops of the Central Powers from Ukraine since this would have serious consequences for him unless there was time to obtain support from the victorious Entente Powers. Initially, the Germans opposed such a step, but by mid-October they were persuaded of its usefulness, especially if the Entente Powers would allow Ukraine to remain independent and if the German occupation forces were directed to perform police functions.

As a result of this change in policy, Doroshenko was sent to Berlin on October 22 to obtain the retention of German troops in Ukraine until a Ukrainian army could be formed. He also sought more positive German support for the annexation of Kholm and intended to discuss the appointment of Serhi Shelukhin as successor to Shteingel. Doroshenko, one of the last official guests to be wined and dined by the Imperial German Government, was informed by State Secretary Wilhelm Solf that Germany could do little for Ukraine and that it would be wise to go to London and Paris. After having conversed with Prince Max of Baden about the differences between the Russian and Ukrainian languages and having obtained assurance that German troops would remain, the Ukrainian foreign minister went to Switzerland to establish contacts with representatives of the Entente.[56]

Prior to this the Hetman had sent Dr. E. K. Lukasevich to Bern for the same purpose, giving him the rank of chargé d'affaires. Ukrainian consulates were established at Zurich and Geneva; the latter was headed by Eugene Sokovich, who had been minister of transport in the last Rada cabinet. Actually Switzerland had not recognized Ukraine although there was some Swiss interest in developing commercial relations between the two countries on the basis of *de facto* recognition. Doroshenko's colleagues were able to do little in Switzerland and the foreign minister himself was unable to do anything. Upon arriving in Bern he learned from a French journalist that he was no longer foreign minister; a new cabinet had been established, headed by Sergei Nikolaeveich Gerbel, former Ukrainian plenipotentiary representative at the Austrian Command in Odessa.

Another equally unsuccessful attempt to obtain the support of the Entente was the mission to Jassy made by Ivan Korostovets, former tsarist ambassador to Peking. On November 7, he saw Saint-Aulaire, the French envoy, and Sir George Barclay, who represented Great Britain; they were willing to speak with him only as a private individual since their governments did not recognize Ukraine. Korostovets maintained that Ukraine desired to remain neutral, but the Entente diplomats pointed out that Doroshenko was in Berlin at the time and that the Hetmanate was allied with the Central Powers. His request for Entente occupation forces to replace the Germans resulted in no definite commitment. Instead, he was directed to inform his government that all Germanophiles had to be replaced by persons in whom England and France could have confidence.[57]

[56] Doroshenko, *Moi Spomini pro Nedavne-Minule*, III, pp. 82ff.

[57] Doroshenko, *Istoriia Ukraini*, II, pp. 409f. Korostovets was also directed to undertake a mission to England and the United States while Nicholas M. Mogiliansky was sent to Paris only to arrive there after the collapse of the regime.

The establishment of the Gerbel cabinet was a vain effort on the part of the Hetman to gain favor with the Entente Powers. Gerbel, a landowner who had served as governor of Kharkiv province during the Imperial regime, had been minister of supply in the Lizohub cabinet and now held the agriculture portfolio as well as the premiership. The only person in the new cabinet who could pass as a nationalist was education minister Volodimir P. Naumenko, a historian and publicist who had edited *Kievskaia Starina* (Kievan Antiquity) prior to 1907. The appointment of Gerbel as premier marked the abandonment of all efforts to arrive at a settlement with the nationalists.

The *raison d'être* of the new cabinet was the fulfillment of the new policy of federation with the future non-Bolshevik Russia. The Hetman hoped his policy would convince London, Paris, and Washington of his good faith and loyalty. The new orientation was promulgated on November 14 in an edict in which the Hetman observed that the end of the war necessitated creating the basis for a new life. This shift was rationalized in the following terms:

"When compared with the other remaining parts of long-suffering Russia, Ukraine has had the most fortunate fate. Ukraine was the first to establish a basis for law and order. With the friendly support of the Central Powers she has maintained [internal] peace until the present. Being sympathetic with Great Russia and all its sufferings, Ukraine has attempted with all of its strength to aid its brethren, tendering them a broad hospitality and supporting them in the struggle to restore firm political order in Russia.

"Before us now stands a new political task. The Allies have long been the friends of the former great and united Russian State. Now . . . the conditions of its future existence have definitely changed. The former vigor and strength of the All-Russian State must be restored on the basis of the federative principle. In this federation Ukraine deserves to play one of the leading roles because from Ukraine law and order spread throughout the country and within her borders for the first time the citizens of former Russia, humiliated and oppressed by Bolshevik despotism, were freely encouraged. . . . Ukraine must take the lead in the matter of the establishment of an All-Russian federation the final goal of which will be the restoration of Great Russia. . . .

"Deeply convinced that any other policy would mean the destruction of Ukraine, I appeal to all who cherish her future to unite about me and stand in defense of Ukraine and Russia. I believe that in this sacred, patriotic cause you, citizens and Cossacks of Ukraine, and the remainder of the population will render sincere and strong support.

"I hereby commission the newly-formed cabinet to undertake the execution of this great historic task in the very near future."[58]

The edict had one immediate result in that it enabled Vinnichenko's National Union to launch its insurrection at a moment which was psychologically opportune because it demonstrated the allegedly Russian character of the Hetmanate.

Actually the edict only precipitated but did not cause the insurrection which the National Union had been planning since the late summer. The Hetman had become panicky and, knowing that the nationalists were planning to overthrow him, forbade a National Congress which the Union had called for November 17. The edict did not elicit the support of the anti-Bolshevik Russians who were certain at the time that the Allies would restore Russia in any case.

[58] Khristiuk, *op cit.*, III, pp 120f. The new orientation was foreshadowed by Lizohub in an interview which appeared in the *Berliner-Tageblatt* of August 19, while the premier was visiting Germany. At the time he was reported to have stated that ruling circles in Ukraine were not opposed to federation with Russia if based on the Pereiaslav Treaty of 1654. When the National Union protested, Lizohub accused the German journalists of having misinterpreted his remarks, but this explanation satisfied neither the Ukrainian nationalists nor the Russians in Ukraine. Another strong indication of a change was the November 3 meeting of Skoropadsky with General Krasnov at Skorokhodovo between Kharkiv and Poltava. At the time Krasnov stated that the Hetman had the task of gathering together the portions of the former Russian Empire since "now again, as a millennium ago, the eyes of all of the better people of Russia are upon Kiev."

It only served to antagonize the nationalists and hasten the fall of the Hetmanate.[59]

The center of the insurrection was at Bila Tserkva, where the Sich Sharpshooters had been reassembling in the course of the autumn with the consent of the Hetman Government even though it had disarmed these Galician troops at the end of April. They entered the Hetman's army with the consent of the National Union which wanted Ukrainian elements in it because the war ministry was overstaffed with Russians. In all probability the Sharpshooters and their commander, Colonel Eugene Konovalets, claiming to be non-partisan and having as their sole goal the establishment of an independent Ukraine, were prompted to join the rising as a result of the edict* of November 14, which they regarded as a betrayal of Ukrainian statehood.[60]

These Galician Ukrainians provided the initial armed force for the insurrection, but the political leadership emerged from the National Union on the night of November 13, when a secret meeting was held in room number six of the Hetman's ministry of transport at 34 Bibikovsky (later renamed Shevchenko) Boulevard. Vinnichenko presided and informed the small group of conspirators that Skoropadsky was preparing to issue an edict proclaiming federation with Russia. It was decided that a Directory of five members be established to head the insurrectionary government. Vinnichenko, who represented the Social Democrats, was elected to the presidency of this body while Simon Petliura, who was at Bila Tserkva, was elected in

[59] The Ukrainian Democratic Agrarian party, finding it impossible to accept the policy of federation, attempted in vain to convince the Entente Powers that all nationalist opposition to Skoropadsky was not socialist. See Victor Andrievsky, *Z Minuloho* (Berlin, 1923), II, part one, pp. 194f.

[60] Col. Eugene Konovalets, *Prichinki do istorii Ukrainskoi Revoliutsii* (2d ed.; n.p., 1948), pp. 9ff. According to this apologia, the Sharpshooters finally pledged allegiance to the Hetmanate because they regarded it as an independent Ukrainian government. However, at the time of the April 29 coup the twenty-six-year-old commander had refused to support the Hetman because the latter was surrounded by Russian officers. When Konovalets went to the German Command that same night he was informed that failure to aid Skoropadsky would result in the disarming of the Sharpshooters.

absentia to represent the Sich Sharpshooters although he was not a member of that military unit. Fedir Shvets, the third permanent member, was a nominal Social Revolutionary. Opanas Andrievsky and Andrew Makarenko, the latter of whom was designated by the railway workers' union, assumed office on a provisional basis.

One of the first acts of the Directory was the issuance of a proclamation, printed copies of which appeared on the streets of Kiev during the next night. It called the Ukrainian people to arms and to order and charged the Hetmanate with desiring to restore landowner-bureaucratic reaction. The Hetman was branded as "a coercionist and usurper of popular authority. His whole government is declared to be inactive because it is anti-popular and anti-national."[61] He and his ministers were publicly advised to resign immediately in order to preserve peace and prevent bloodshed. All Russian officers in Ukraine were told to surrender their arms and leave the country or be forcibly deported. The hope was expressed that the soldiers of the democratic German Republic would not intervene in this internal struggle, and the Hetmanites were threatened with "vengeance which no one will be able to stop" in the event of an attack upon Ukrainian democracy.

"Who stands for the oppression and exploitation of the peasantry and of labor, who wishes the rule of gendarmes and secret police; who can witness with equanimity the executions of peaceful students by bestial Russian officers— let him stand with the Hetman and his administration for a single, indivisible Russia against the will of the Ukrainian People's Republic.

"All others, honest citizens, Ukrainians as well as non-Ukrainians, must stand with us as a friendly armed force against criminals and enemies of the people, and then all the social and political achievements of revolutionary democracy will be restored. And the Ukrainian Constituent Assembly shall firmly strengthen them in the free Ukrainian land."

[61] For the text of the proclamation see Khristiuk, *op.cit.*, III, pp. 131f.

Within a day all of the members of the Directory were in Bila Tserkva with the exception of Makarenko, who was hiding in Kiev. Meanwhile, Petliura, in an arbitrary manner which was characteristic of him, issued his own Universal referring to himself as supreme commander and calling upon "all Ukrainian soldiers and Cossacks to fight for the independence of Ukraine against the traitor, the former tsarist servant, General Skoropadsky."[62] He informed every citizen that it was his duty to arrest the General and deliver him to Republican authorities; he also threatened to punish persons aiding the Hetman in any attempt to flee from the country. After having defined his own role in the rising, Petliura turned to the operational problem of moving the Sharpshooters and the increasing number of peasant volunteers towards the capital.

In attempting to do this he encountered a serious obstacle in the German troops who were still in Ukraine. After several armed clashes an agreement was concluded with the troops in the Bila Tserkva area by which the Directory promised not to attack the Germans or impede their evacuation if they did not intervene in the internal Ukrainian struggle. The forces of the Directory moved to Fastiv and then to Vinnitsa but found it necessary to halt their advance when the German Command decided to hold Kiev. This step was prompted by the Hetman's claim that Petliura was a bandit, as well as by the insistence of the nominal French vice consul in Kiev, Emile Henno, in Odessa at the time, who ordered the Germans to prevent the Directory from taking the capital. A line of demarcation was established between the Ukrainian forces, who were located southwest of Kiev, and the Germans in the city.

The resulting stalemate caused the Social Democrats in Kiev to organize a revolutionary committee headed by V. M. Chekhovsky, who became the first premier under the Directory. Headquarters were established in a school building on Stepanivska Street, but the committee's plans

62 *Ibid.*, p. 133.

were upset when it learned that some of the Hetman's troops had scheduled a rising for the night of November 22. A delegation was sent to Colonel George Kapkan, who commanded the rebel troops; he claimed that it was impossible to postpone the revolt but promised the committee a thousand rifles and ammunition. Kapkan informed the committee that he was going to seize the Austrian consulate and utilize it as his headquarters. Once action commenced with the firing of a rocket in the botanical gardens, the committee was to send some of its men to the consulate; admission was to be obtained by means of the password, "Uncle Tom."

Thus the scene was set for two comic episodes which demonstrated the ineptitude of the local leadership. The first occurred when the janitor of the school locked the revolutionary committee in the building and caused its membership to lose much valuable time in obtaining egress. This was followed by the rebuff which was administered to its representatives upon their arrival at the Austrian consulate. When they asked for "Uncle Tom" they were informed that no such person resided there, and when they became insistent the soldiers on guard drove them off. The rising collapsed almost before it commenced when the colonel failed to deliver the arms he had promised to the committee.[63]

The failure of the coup allowed Skoropadsky to continue as the nominal ruler of Kiev so long as the remaining German forces were willing to prevent Petliura from taking the capital. The policy of federation with Russia had caused the Hetman to increase the control which pro-Denikin Russian officers were exercising over his dwindling military establishment. As this became more evident the nationalist elements deserted the Hetmanate in increasing numbers until only a force of Russian officers remained to defend the regime. Thus the balance was held by the

[63] Halahan, *op cit.*, IV, pp. 73ff. Halahan was a member of the revolutionary committee and at the same time remained as an employee in the Hetman's ministry of health.

German forces, and their action finally resolved the situation and knocked the few remaining props out from under the Skoropadsky Government. Realizing the futility of remaining in Ukraine, the German Command in Kiev sent representatives to Kazatin to meet with General Michael Grekov, who had deserted Skoropadsky, and Dr. Osip Nazaruk, both of whom negotiated for the Directory. On December 12, an agreement was signed providing for German neutrality and withdrawal from Kiev.

The revolutionary committee of the Social Democrats then staged a second rising inside the city which proved to be successful since the agreement reduced the Hetman's armed forces to a few small Russian units. In desperation Skoropadsky called up all civil servants capable of bearing arms. Yet the anti-government forces did not assume authority with any degree of rapidity because their units inside the capital were not coordinated with each other or with the Directory's army which was advancing on the city. The Directory's forces, led by Colonel Konovalets, entered Kiev on December 14 and established a military government after brief sporadic fighting with the Russian officers. The lack of contact between the insurgents within the city and Konovalets was evident in the way in which the latter's officers searched and disarmed many of the former.[64]

This division and misunderstanding between the victors could have provided General Skoropadsky with but little satisfaction. The sands had run out. He had played his brief and bitter role. Having cast his lot with that of his protectors, he was now compelled to share their fate. On December 14, he signed the following instrument of abdication: "I, Hetman of all Ukraine, have employed all of my energies during the past seven and one-half months in an effort to extricate Ukraine from the difficult situation in which she finds herself. God has not given me the strength to deal with this problem and now, in the light of conditions which have arisen and acting solely for the

[64] *Ibid.*, pp. 87f.

good of Ukraine, I abdicate all authority."[65] Three days later the Directory termed his acts treasonable and criminal, confiscated all of his movable and immovable property in Ukraine, and declared him to be beyond the protection of the law. Disguising himself in a German uniform, the Hetman remained in Kiev a few days and then left for Germany together with his wife, who was dressed as a nurse.

This escape was symbolic of the whole regime and its utter dependence upon the army of occupation from the first moment of its existence. In this respect it was no different from the Rada in its last days, although Hrushevsky, writing in 1920, seemed to neglect this similarity when he declared that the Hetmanate "would not have lasted a single day without German troops."[66] The Hetmanate was not instituted, as was the Rada, during a period of free interchange of ideas, and General Skoropadsky did not assume office by will of the people. Alien and archaic to the bulk of the population, especially because of its opposition to rapid social reform, the Hetman's Government was doomed from the beginning. Paradoxically, the Hetmanate, which in the seventeenth century had opposed vested interests, was now being utilized by many as a reactionary dike to halt the swift incoming tide of social and economic revolution. It was the resulting failure to agree with the large Ukrainian parties on social and economic objectives, far more than their doubts regarding the Hetman's nationalism, which prevented the government from obtaining their badly needed support.

The émigré supporters of General Skoropadsky, in the years following the fall of the regime, claimed that the

[65] Sviatoslav Dolenga, *Skoropadshchina* (Warsaw, 1934), p 140. Also Mints and Gorodetsky, *op.cit.*, pp. 216f. For a dramatic but not fully objective treatment of some of the factors present in the last days of the Hetman's regime and in the initial period of Directory rule see the play, "Days of the Turbins," by Michael Bulgakov; an English translation of this drama can be found in *Six Soviet Plays* (Boston, 1934) edited by Eugene Lyons.

[66] Hrushevsky, *La lutte sociale et politique en Ukraine*, p. 25.

Hetmanate was more positive than any other Ukrainian government of the period because it embraced all society and endeavored to serve the interests of all classes. They glorified the brief tenure of their idol and contended that the Directory could not have carried on its struggle against the Bolsheviks without the material resources which were amassed during 1918.

These assertions may be challenged to the same extent that the nationalists questioned the General's national consciousness while he was in power. Yet, even the Hetman's enemies could not deny the fact that he became a figure of greater stature in the national movement as an émigré than he had been during 1918. He became very fluent in the Ukrainian language and, despite his official abdication, renewed his claim to govern Ukraine. His enemies argued that he lacked the right to do this since he was only a private individual after December 14, 1918. Vienna became the center for his organization, the Ukrainian Union of Agrarian Statesmen (*Ukrainski Soiuz Khliborobiv Derzhavnikiv*). Here Viacheslav Lipinsky wrote his *Letters to Brethren Agriculturalists* (*Listi do Brativ-Khliborobiv*) in which he championed the Hetman's cause on the grounds that only his form of government could save Ukraine.

Skoropadsky took up residence at Wannsee outside of Berlin shortly after having reunited his family in Lausanne late in 1919. When the regime fell, his children had been in the Crimea, where they commenced an eleven-month period of wandering through Rumania, Turkey, Greece, and Italy until they learned of their parents' survival. At Wannsee the Hetman lived comfortably and directed the activities of his followers. Here, surrounded by icons and portraits of Ukrainian hetmans, he reared his younger children in a spirit of Ukrainian patriotism and especially concerned himself with his heir and younger son, Hetmanich Daniel Skoropadsky. The Hetman left no doubt in the minds of his supporters regarding the succession to his claim to rule when on May 16, 1933, he issued the following testament (*zapovit*):

"History compels Me to make certain that the Ukrainian State established by Me in 1918 shall continue on to the full and happy realization of our national-political task. In our particular circumstances it is necessary to ensure the extended and persistent effort of a line of generations. Although I still possess strength and energy and the impulse to combat, I must nevertheless make certain that after Me there will be secured uninterrupted Leadership of our Cause.

"And for this purpose on this day of the sixtieth year of My birth I solemnly pronounce My Will:

"After Me the Leadership of our Cause and all rights and obligations of the elder in our Family pass to My Son Daniel.

"I instruct My Son Daniel to stand steadfastly to the end of His life at the head of the Cause of the Hetmanite State, and I instruct all Hetmanites to aid Him faithfully in this."[67]

The issuance of this document did not signify the Hetman's retirement. He had witnessed one horrendous human upheaval and was destined to die in the midst of another. In mid-April of 1945, during the last days of Hitler's Third Reich, the Hetman was fleeing by rail to Obersdorf in Bavaria and while en route was killed when the train was bombed by Allied planes. Thus a colorful but spent career was brought to an end.

The Hetman had not been without error and during the brief period of his tenure was very much the victim of circumstances. Yet his contribution to the Ukrainian national movement in 1918 and in the years that followed has passed beyond dispute. His regime was Ukrainian in name and in many respects also in fact, and his activities undoubtedly caused many persons in Western Europe to

[67] John Esaiw (ed.), *Za Ukrainu, podorozh V. P. Hetmanicha Danila Skoropadskoho do zluchenikh derzhav Ameriki i Kanadi* (Edmonton, 1938), p. 23.

become aware of the existence of the Ukrainian people. Although maligned and neglected by many, General Skoropadsky cannot be denied the niche which is rightfully his in any consideration of Ukrainian efforts to achieve independent statehood.

CHAPTER V

The Republican Revival

Seek not misfortune for it will inevitably search you out.—*an old Ukrainian proverb*

If the will of each man were free, that is, if each could act as he chose, the whole of history would be a series of disconnected accidents.—COUNT LEO TOLSTOY, *War and Peace* (Epilogue)

THE termination of the war in Western Europe provided the Eastern Ukrainians with an opportunity to overthrow the Hetman and restore the Republic. In Galicia the Western Ukrainians had been no less aware of the opportunities for change which would occur with the dissolution of the Dual Empire. Prior to the war, the Ukrainian deputies in the Austrian parliament had waged an unending campaign to obtain greater privileges for their constituents. By 1907 the Galician Ukrainians had twenty-eight seats in the parliament and those of Bukovina had five, but this did not give them representation which would be regarded as comparable to that enjoyed by the Poles.

This weakness and the cooperation between the Poles and Austrians made it impossible for the Ukrainians to achieve their primary objective—the division of Galicia into separate Polish and Ukrainian provinces centered at Cracow and Lviv, respectively. So long as Galicia remained as a single province, the Ukrainians would be in a minority in its diet and in the civil service. Some of them had realized this as early as May of 1848 when they convened a supreme council (*Holovna Rus'ka Rada*) in Lviv and vainly petitioned the Crown for a separate province. While they were recalling how ancient Halich had enjoyed independent status in the thirteenth century following the collapse of Kievan Rus, the Poles in the Dual Empire were busy claiming that the language of Eastern Galicia was nothing more than a Polish dialect. This argument, backed by Polish voting strength and Vienna's desire not to antagonize Russia, doomed the Ukrainian proposal and, in the end, ensured the unity of Galicia until the fall of the Hapsburgs in 1918.

While the Western Ukrainians failed to attain their political goals within the framework of the Dual Empire, they occasionally were able to obtain educational rights which included the establishment of several Ukrainian chairs in the University of Lviv (Lemberg). However, the increasingly numerous demands of the Ukrainians for the

211

use of their language in the university placed an additional strain upon their relations with the Poles. In March of 1906 a small riot occurred between the Polish and Ukrainian students when the latter forced entry into one of the institution's halls and held an unauthorized rally protesting the compulsory use of the Polish language. A similar meeting, held in January of the following year, prompted some of the Ukrainians to administer a severe beating to the secretary of the university, who was a Pole. The riot which ensued led to the arrest of more than one hundred Ukrainian students and caused the Poles to stage a window-breaking demonstration before various of the Ukrainian buildings in Lviv. When the senate of the university petitioned the government in 1910, asking it to make Polish the sole medium of instruction the Ukrainians in the student body called a mass meeting and demanded that the institution remain at least nominally bilingual until they could obtain a separate university. The Poles constructed a barricade in order to prevent the several hundred participants from leaving the university building. The Ukrainians threw themselves on this barricade, and in the mêlée which followed one of their number was killed while 128 were arrested and given sentences ranging from two weeks to three months.[1] Although the Ukrainian deputies in Vienna later pressed the demand for a separate university, such an institution was never established under Austrian rule.

The advent of World War I was regarded by some Galician Ukrainians as an opportunity to further the national cause; such men as Nicholas Vasilko, who headed the deputies from Bukovina, favored the annexation of all Ukraine by Austria while others believed that the victory of the Central Powers would lead to independence. However, it

[1] For these and similar instances see Vasil Mudri, *Borot'ba Za ohnishche Ukrainskoi kul'turi v Zakhidnıkh zemliakh Ukraini* (Lvıv, 1923). During the trial which followed the 1910 riot the defendants left the courtroom while the charges were being read in Polish and returned only when the Ukrainian translation was being delivered.

cannot be said that they enjoyed any real alternative to supporting the Austrian war effort since passivity on their part would have been capitalized upon by the Poles, who would quickly accuse them of treason. Pro-Allied sympathies were rare although in April 1918 Vasil Paneyko, editor of the Lviv newspaper *Dilo*, vacationed in Switzerland and, upon returning, proposed to Dr. Constantine Levitsky, a leading parliamentarian, that there be formed a Galician-Ukrainian legion composed of prisoners who had been fighting on the Italian front and who were in Allied prison camps at the time. This proposal was rejected because it was feared that such a step would provoke the Central Powers into employing repressive measures, especially since they had occupied all of Russian or Eastern Ukraine.[2]

The military situation was a matter of great interest to the Galicians, and they did not hesitate to defend the Rada Government. The Social Democratic deputy, Semen Vitik, warned the Central Powers on March 7, 1918, not to requisition but to allow the Rada to deliver foodstuffs. The fall of the Rada caused the Galician National Democratic party's committee to adopt unanimously a resolution censuring the German Government for having intervened in the internal affairs of the Ukrainian Republic in violation of obligations which it had assumed at Brest-Litovsk. The resolution also called for the cession of Kholm to Ukraine and the unification of Eastern Galicia and Northern Bukovina.[3] On July 19, Dr. Levitsky, in an address delivered before the parliament in Vienna, criticized the government's failure to ratify the Brest-Litovsk Treaty and its refusal to allow the Hetman's officials into that portion of the Kholm region which was occupied by Austrian troops.

These protests were as ineffective as the Austrian Government's futile attempts at self-preservation, and by August the committee of the National Democratic party realized this and commenced to hold secret meetings in order

[2] Dr. Constantine Levitsky, *Veliki Zriv* (Lviv, 1931), pp. 52f.
[3] *Ibid.*, pp. 49ff. contains the text of the resolution.

to lay plans for the assumption of authority in Eastern Galicia. Soon a cleavage developed between the parliamentary representatives, who believed that Vienna would allow the Ukrainians to govern the province, and the committee members, who believed that it would be necessary to employ force. Several days prior to the issuance of Emperor Karl's manifesto of October 16, which provided for the transformation of the Empire into a federal union of free peoples, the Ukrainian deputies called a congress of prominent legislators and party leaders to meet in Lviv on October 19, for the purpose of organizing a Ukrainian People's Council (*Ukrainska Narodna Rada*). The preliminary congress proceeded to take measures which were necessitated by the inability of the Council to convene prior to November 3. It enacted a statute of five articles for the Council and proclaimed that assembly to be "the constituent body for all of the ethnographic territory of that portion of the Ukrainian people which lives within the Austro-Hungarian monarchy." This meant that an attempt would be made to include Carpatho-Ukraine within its jurisdiction at the expense of Hungary.

The Poles in Cracow were intent upon preventing the Ukrainians from asserting control over Eastern Galicia. The desire of the Lviv Ukrainians to present the Poles with a fait accompli, together with their lack of confidence in the ability of their parliamentarians in Vienna to obtain a peaceful transfer of authority, caused them to decide to seize power. A final effort was made on October 31 to avoid the use of force; on the afternoon of that day Dr. Levitsky headed a delegation which called on the governor of Galicia and requested him to relinquish authority. His refusal to comply caused the Ukrainians in Lviv to amass their forces commanded by Colonel Dmitro Vitovsky.

That night a thousand Ukrainian soldiers, most of whom were theoretically still in the Austrian army, seized the principal buildings in Lviv and ran up the Ukrainian flag on the city hall. The Galician leaders met as the Ukrainian People's Council and issued a proclamation to the Western

214

Ukrainian people, informing them that they were now masters in their own land but also appealing to them:

"The fate of the Ukrainian State is in your hands. You shall stand as an impregnable wall and you shall repulse all inimical attempts upon the Ukrainian State.

"Until the establishment of organs of state authority according to legal procedure Ukrainian organizations in towns, districts, and villages should assume all state, territorial and local offices and govern in the name of the Ukrainian People's Council."[4]

The Council assumed command over all soldiers of Ukrainian nationality and called on them to maintain order and protect the railroads and postal and telegraphic facilities. The Council also assured all citizens, irrespective of their nationality or religious affiliation, of equality of civil, national, and religious rights. All laws not in fundamental opposition to the Ukrainian State were declared to be valid and binding, and a constitutional assembly based on universal suffrage was promised "as soon as the existence of the Ukrainian State shall be secured and strengthened."

Proclamations are more easily written than endowed with substance, and that of the People's Council was no exception. The predominantly Polish citizenry of Lviv soon rallied and commenced to attack the Ukrainian forces, compelling Vitovsky to resign his command on the morning of November 3. The continuous street fighting with the Poles caused the Galicians to turn to Hetman Skoropadsky for aid, and on the morning of November 5 Dr. Osip Nazaruk and an engineer, Shukhevich, left Lviv for Kiev. There they obtained an audience with the Hetman, who expressed his willingness to aid the Western Ukrainian Government but did not wish to become involved in a dispute with Warsaw. Skoropadsky proposed to aid the Galicians and at the same time avoid entanglement with the Poles by allowing the Sich Sharpshooters to cross the

4 *Ibid*, pp. 140ff.

Zbruch River independently and then declaring them to be excluded from the army of the Hetmanate. Nazaruk consulted with Vinnichenko and learned that an insurrection was being planned and that the withdrawal of the Sharpshooters to Galicia would undoubtedly cause it to fail. This information prompted them to send Shukhevich to the Hetman with a request that he send only half of the Sharpshooters across the Zbruch. In Bila Tserkva, which was the seat of the revolt, the predominantly Galician Sharpshooters decided not to send any of their men to the defense of Lviv since the possession of Kiev was of far greater import.[5]

The entry of the Directory's forces into Kiev on December 14 and Petliura's triumphal arrival several days later overshadowed the struggle which the Western Ukrainians were waging against the Poles over the possession of Eastern Galicia. The Directory had the larger territory as well as greater manpower at its disposal, and this meant that more was expected of it. A declaration issued by it on December 26 proclaimed Ukraine to be free from punitive expeditions, gendarmes, and the other repressive institutions of the ruling classes which had characterized the Hetmanite regime.[6] The Directory recognized collective labor agreements, the right to strike, and the eight-hour day, and it declared itself to be the provisional government of the revolutionary period. The landed and industrial bourgeoisie were accused of bringing disorganization and ruin to the country and as non-toiling exploiters were deprived of a right to a voice in the organization of the new order. It was proposed that a Congress of Toilers be convened for the purpose of determining the exact form which the

[5] Dr. Osip Nazaruk, *Rik na Veliki Ukraini, spomini z Ukrainskoi revoliutsii* (Vienna, 1920), pp. 6ff. Konovalets, *op.cit.*, pp. 13f. corroborated the account given by Nazaruk and defended the decision of the Sharpshooters' Council on the grounds that the fate of Ukraine would be determined in the center and not on the peripheries; he reasoned that the loss of Eastern Ukraine would also mean the loss of Lviv even if the Poles were driven out of the city.

[6] For the text of the declaration see Khristiuk, *op.cit.*, IV, pp. 15ff.

new government would assume. The peasantry was promised that it would regain what the Hetmanite regime had requisitioned, and a commitment was made to combat speculation and establish state and worker control over industry to ensure "healthy and useful economic development for the people."

The content of this declaration can be attributed to Vinnichenko, who was the president of the Directory. The international revolutionary tenor of the document was evident in the following passage:

"Standing firmly and unswervingly on the road to social reform, the Directory believes it necessary to state explicitly that it will take the necessary steps to avoid all anarchic, disorganized, and unsystematic forms of this reconstruction. The Directory will regard itself as obliged to view these great tasks within the context of the socio-historical and international conditions prevailing in Ukraine at the present time and also with respect to the best forms of social reform attained by world and especially by Western European toiling democracy."

Indeed, many of the nominal Social Democrats regarded the Directory's program as "almost Bolshevik," and Petliura, who commanded the armed forces of the new government, was not in complete accord with the objectives as stated in the declaration. He and Vinnichenko had clashed in the Rada Government during the previous year, and when the latter proposed in November that political commissars be attached to the army he was accused of intervening in military affairs and introducing Bolshevism into the armed forces. Vinnichenko later believed that Petliura, in issuing his own universal at Bila Tserkva, had given the rising a personal rather than a truly revolutionary, programmatic character.

This clash of two dominant personalities explains, in part, the use of the collegial titular executive. Both Petliura and Vinnichenko had considerable support, but at the time neither man was able to command enough confidence to don the mantle of dictatorship. Nor was any effort made to reconvene the Rada and invite its former president, Hrushevsky, to serve as a titular executive. This decision to commence with a totally new form of government, predominantly Social Democratic, can be attributed to the belief that Hrushevsky and his Social Revolutionaries were discredited by the collaboration with the Germans prior to the Skoropadsky coup. Hrushevsky, who was uneasy because of the predominance of the military in the new government, later charged that the Rada was not restored because of its Social Revolutionary majority.

Whatever élan the Directory possessed was undoubtedly provided by Vinnichenko and Petliura since the other three members were mere accessories. A non-Bolshevik coalition cabinet was formed on December 26, under the leadership of Volodimir Chekhovsky, a Social Democrat, who also held the foreign affairs portfolio. This cabinet was the real executive in name rather than in fact because much of whatever authority there was resided in the office of the commander of the occupation forces, Colonel Eugene Konovalets. His men were quick to act and did not hesitate to requisition the automobile of almost any civilian official. Konovalets later maintained that he had advocated nonintervention by the military in politics, but the Sharpshooters apparently were caught in the treacherous crosscurrents of the Directory's internal politics and for a considerable period were incapable of deciding whether to follow Vinnichenko or Petliura. Some of them proposed to Vinnichenko that he become dictator and rely on their support, but his refusal to accept this suggestion finally caused them to throw their strength behind his rival. Vinnichenko was suspicious of the Sharpshooters' motives and even feared that they would arrest him if he were to attempt to carry out his program which included the establishment of a soviet, although a non-Bolshevik, regime for Ukraine.[7]

[7] Konovalets, *op cit.*, pp. 24ff.

This mistrust was not altogether imaginary. The Galician Sharpshooters lacked a sense of social consciousness —a fact readily admitted by Konovalets. Their primary desideratum was independent national statehood for Ukraine, and this caused some of the leftists to brand them as "chauvinists." At that time, as in the years that followed, there was much confusion regarding Bolshevism and its adherents; often anyone who advocated rapid change was conveniently marked with this label. The general uncertainty and lack of precise criteria easily led to the employment of drastic preventive measures if there were any doubts regarding one's loyalty. It was under such circumstances that the Sharpshooters, on the night of December 20, raided the offices of the Central Bureau of Trade Unions at 19 Triokhsviatitelska Street. It was alleged that Bolshevik agents were meeting there; the search produced some labor literature which so incensed the men that they burned the organization's library and files, blackening the street with ashes.[8]

The Sharpshooter command also issued an order directing that all signs in the Russian language be changed to Ukrainian within three days. Serhi Efremov, a Socialist-Federalist, attempted to criticize this policy in a newspaper article, but publication of it was forbidden by the censor, Dr. Osip Nazaruk. The Russian newspapers in Kiev were closed for having opposed Ukrainian independence; when permission was asked to re-establish them, the publishers were informed that one-third of the content would have to be in Ukrainian. Such a condition was manifestly unfair at the time since there was a dearth of experienced journalists capable of employing the new official language.

However, such matters soon lapsed into insignificance as the result of the Directory's instability. This was due to the fact that it had a rival in the Bolshevik Provisional Workers' and Peasants' Government of Ukraine which arose under the leadership of George Piatakov. During the period

[8] *Ibid* , pp. 31f. Cf. Khristiuk, *op.cit.*, IV, p 25, n. 1.

Vilna

Mogilev

Minsk

Warsaw

Brest-
Litovsk

Pinsk

Chernihiv

Lublin

Kholm

Sarnı

Korosten Bazar

Nizhin K

Lutsko

Rıvne

Zhıtomır

Fastıv

KIEV

L

Tarnow

Peremyshl

Lviv

GALICIA

Radıvılıv
Brodı
Kremıanets

VOLYNIA

PODOLIA

Lıubar
Starokons-
tıantınıv

Berdıchıv
Kazatın

Bıla
Tserkva

Kanı

Cherkassı

Drohobıch

Ternopil

Proskurıv

Vinnitsa

F

CARPATHO-

Strıy (Stryj)

Zbruch

Prešov

Uzhorod

Stanıslavıv
Kolomeıa

Chortkıv
Husıatın
Kamianets-
Radılsk
Khotın

Zhmerınka

Mohılıv

Uman
Zıatkıvtsı

Olhopıl

UKRAINE

Khust

BUKOVINA

Cuernivtsı

Dniester

Balta

Debreczen

Jassyo

Kıshınev

Tıraspıl
Roz-
Bendery dılna
Odessa

Prut

UKRAINE

...... *ethnographic frontier*
claimed by Ukrainian governments

Briansk
Orel
Tambov
Saratov
Kursk
Voronezh
ach
Kharkiv
Starobilsk
Tsaritsyn
(Stalingrad)
Poltava
Lugansk
(Voroshilovgrad)
Kreminchuk
Dnipro
Katerinoslav
(Dniepropetrovsk)
Don
ad
ohrad)
Rostov
Riho
Oleksandrivsk
(Zaporizhia)
Tahanrih
Nikopil
Gulyai Pole
Mariupil
iv
Melitopil
Volga
Kherson
AURIDA
Ekaterinodar (Krasnodar)
Simferopol
Feodosiia
Novorossiisk
Sevastopol
Yalta
LACK   SEA

GLOSSARY OF IMPORTANT PLACE NAMES*

Ukrainian	*Russian*
Kiiv	Kiev
Kamianets-Podilsk	Kamenets-Podolsk
Chernihiv	Chernigov
Bila Tserkva	Belaia Tserkov
Kharkiv	Kharkov
Lviv	Lvov
Rivne	Rovno
Fastiv (also Khvastiv)	Fastov
Proskuriv	Proskurov
Ternopil	Tarnopol
Melitopil	Melitopol
Stanislaviv	Stanislavov
Katerinoslav	Ekaterinoslav (Dnepropetrovsk)
Lisavethrad	Elisavetgrad
Sevastopil	Sevastopol
Tahanrih	Taganrog
Kreminchuk	Kremenchug
Krivi Rih	Krivoi Rog
Olexandrivsk (Zaporizhia)	Alexandrovsk (Zaporozhe)
Pavlohrad	Pavlograd
Konstiantinohrad	Constantinograd (Krasnograd)
Mariiupil	Mariupol
Mikolaiv	Nikolaev
Nikopil	Nikopol
Tiraspil	Tiraspol
Rozdilna	Razdelnaia
Nizhin	Nezhin

* In most instances throughout this work the Ukrainian transliterated place names have been employed However, often the Russian form has been used for cities in which large numbers of non-Ukrainians reside.

of the Hetmanate the Ukrainian Bolsheviks had found it necessary to seek exile in Moscow. There on July 5, 1918 they held their first party Congress and organized themselves as a segment of the Russian Bolshevik party. This step was taken under Russian influence but was preceded by a bitter struggle which occurred in April at a conference held in Tahanrih during the retreat. The Ukrainian Bolsheviks were divided into two groups—those who favored the establishment of a separate Communist party of Ukraine coordinated with that of the Russians and those who desired the party to be integrated with and led by Moscow. The advocates of an independent party came from Kiev and were headed by George Piatakov, Volodimir Zatonsky, and Nicholas Skrypnik. The proponents of Russian leadership were led by E. Kviring and were centered in the Katerinoslav unit of the party. This cleavage resulted in part from the fact that the two groups had been dealing with different enemies; that in Kiev had had to cope with the nationalism of the Rada, while Kviring's group was faced with the anti-Bolshevism of the Don Cossacks in the East. At Tahanrih the Kiev group won out by defeating the proposal to adopt the title of "Russian Communist party of Bolsheviks in Ukraine" and enacting, instead, a resolution by which it entitled itself the "Communist party of Bolsheviks of Ukraine."[9]

At Moscow the substance of this decision was modified because exiles, like all guests, must be polite and not contradict their hosts. It is also probable that more of the Ukrainian Bolsheviks realized by that time that they could never hope to regain control of the country without the aid of their Russian comrades. The seventy-two delegates at the July Congress heard an address delivered by Bela Kun in which the future head of the Communist regime in Hungary called for an international civil war. Lengthy analyses of the situation in Ukraine under the Hetmanate were presented and the necessity of insurrection was stressed

9 Iavorsky, *op cit.*, p 50.

together with the danger of giving the movement a national rather than a class character. Kviring spoke on Russo-
Ukrainian relations and pointed out that Russia obtained
seventy per cent of its coal, three-quarters of its pig iron,
and nine-tenths of its sugar from Ukraine, while the latter
did not possess its own texile industry or petroleum resources. He concluded that Ukrainian independence had
no economic basis and could be brought about only with
the aid of an external imperialism; a resolution supporting this position was adopted on July 10. Significantly, the
Congress two days later unanimously resolved that the
party would not have relations with Russian Social Revolutionaries, Mensheviks, Jewish Bundists, Ukrainian Social
Democrats or Ukrainian Social Revolutionaries.[10]

This uncompromising position was reaffirmed in mid-
October at the party's second Congress which also met in
Moscow and was attended by more than one hundred
delegates who represented five thousand party members.
At that time Stalin was elected to the Central Committee
of the Communist party of Ukraine. This step, together
with the other results of the exile, indicated the extent to
which the Ukrainian Bolsheviks were dependent upon
the Moscow Council of People's Commissars. They were
able to establish themselves as the government of Ukraine
only with the aid of Red Army units. When the Bolshevik
invasion of Ukraine commenced late in December, Chekhovsky sent a note of protest to Chicherin, the Soviet foreign commissar. The latter denied that regular Soviet forces
were invading Ukraine. He caused some of the officials
of the Directory to believe that their government was being attacked by the Ukrainian Communists, led by George
Piatakov and George Kotsiubinsky, who, ostensibly, were
acting independently. Chicherin, in his reply of January
6, 1919, made it clear that his government did not approve
of the Directory or its policies:

[10] For the texts of the various resolutions see *Pervyi S'ezd Kommunisticheskoi Partii (bolshevikov) Ukrainy*, ed. M. Ravich-Cherkassky (Kharkiv,
1923).

"The expression in your radio-telegrams of your desire to find a peaceful settlement in the matter can apply only to the conflict between the Directory and the toiling masses of Ukraine who strongly desire the introduction of a soviet order. This is the same struggle of the toiling people which is being waged for its complete liberation in Latvia, Esthonia, Poland, and Bielo-russia against the government of exploiters and oppressors, both native and foreign, and against their agents and servants."[11]

Chicherin censured the Directory for suppressing soviets and prohibiting strikes and denied that the Council of People's Commissars opposed Ukrainian independence; as proof of Moscow's friendship he cited the warm greetings which it had sent the Soviet Government of Ukraine in February of the preceding year when it had driven the Rada out of Kiev.

On January 9, 1919, Chekhovsky and the members of the Directory sent a reply to Chicherin in which they main-

---

[11] For the text of the note see Khristiuk, op.cit., IV, pp. 35f. Christian Rakovsky, who was also in exile in Russia at this time with the Bolshevik government of Ukraine, published an article in the January 3, 1919, issue of Izvestiia under the title, "A Hopeless Matter" (Beznadezhnoe Delo). In it he contended that the ethnographic differences between Russians and Ukrainians were "in themselves insignificant" and that Ukrainians preferred to have their official documents published in Russian although he promised that the Soviet Authority would actually create the conditions under which Ukrainian national consciousness would flourish. However, Rakovsky made the slip of employing the term "Little Russian" in referring to the 94 per cent of the population of Ukraine which was engaged in agriculture at that time. He referred to the Directory as the Rada and declared it to have been "paralyzed from the day of its birth" as retribution for the sins of the Rada in connection with the German occupation. Rakovsky went on to predict that the Allies would overthrow the Directory as the Germans had the Rada and cited the Anglo-French agreement of December 1917 which he claimed gave Ukraine to France and the Caucasus to England as protectorates. Yet despite these attacks on the Directory, Rakovsky felt it necessary to assure the Ukrainians that the "danger of russification under the existing Ukrainian Soviet Authority is entirely without foundation" and that the Ukrainian workers and peasants would obtain their own schools, to the extent that they require them, from the Soviet Authority and not from the "newly-baked officials" of the Ukrainian intelligentsia who allegedly wished to create conditions for their own "bureaucratic rule."

tained that his denial of the invasion was a result of "either a willful distortion of the truth or of a complete lack of information." The Ukrainians denied that the invaders were Ukrainian or even completely Russian since they had obtained evidence that Mongols and Magyars were also in the invading Soviet army. The Directory accused Moscow of intervening in Ukrainian affairs and of desiring to return the country to the status of a Russian colony; it rejected the Russian demand that authority be placed in the hands of an infinitesimal urban minority—the Bolsheviks. Moscow was given forty-eight hours in which to answer whether or not it could cease all operations against the Ukrainian Republic and its toiling people. If the answer was in the affirmative, Moscow was to state whether or not it would agree to withdraw all of its troops from Ukrainian territory. The Directory expressed its willingness to engage in peace talks and commercial relations if these conditions were accepted. Failure by Moscow to respond within the forty-eight-hour period was to be regarded as a declaration of war.[12]

Chicherin answered with a reiteration of his previous denial and declared the Directory's demands to be "object-less" and its allegations to be calumniatory. He termed the conflict a civil war—"the natural result of the internal struggle which is being carried on in Ukraine between the workers and poor peasantry, on the one hand, and by the Ukrainian bourgeoisie, on the other." The Soviet foreign commissar protested the Directory's attempt to represent the urban and industrial proletariat as foreigners and as harbingers of Russian imperialism; he contended that the proletariat was merely struggling for its own political and economic liberation. Noting that some officials of the Directory Government had expressed a desire to come to terms with the Ukrainian Communists, Chicherin concluded that "such attempts on your part are proof that you regard the Ukrainian Communist party as the real

[12] Khristiuk, op.cit., IV, pp. 37f.

representative of the Ukrainian workers and peasants."[13] He reaffirmed his original demand that the Directory change its policies, and also proposed Moscow as a meeting place for peace talks with extra-territoriality and a direct wire to Kiev provided for the Ukrainian negotiators.

The proposal attracted the support of a number of leading officials in the Directory Government, including Chekhovsky and Vinnichenko. They sent a small delegation, headed by Semen Mazurenko, and instructed it to seek a settlement even at the price of accepting the soviet form of government in Ukraine in place of what might be termed parliamentarianism. The delegation was also empowered to conclude an economic agreement as well as a military union with the Bolsheviks, who, in return, were to cease their invasion, recognize Ukrainian independence, and accept the government which would be established by the Congress of Toilers. The willingness of some of the men in the Directory to obtain a modus vivendi with Moscow can be understood only in the light of the growth of an anti-bourgeois revolutionary radicalism in both of the leading Ukrainian parties.

The Social Revolutionaries had divided as early as June of 1918 when the left wing decided that the Rada had been bourgeois and that it had failed to stress the international solidarity of the working masses. The left wing obtained control of the party's central committee and accused the ousted right wing of placing Ukrainian statehood above all else and of advocating a parliamentary and evolutionary socialism rather than the revolutionary type based on a violent class struggle. The rightists accused their antagonists of not devoting enough attention to the idea of a Ukrainian state and of desiring an understanding with the Russian revolutionary parties. This intra-party conflict resulted in the refusal of the left-wing central committee to participate in the National Union which overthrew the Hetmanate and established the Directory.[14] Pethura did

[13] *Ibid.*, IV, pp. 38f.   [14] *Ibid.*, III, pp. 23ff.

receive the support of the right Social Revolutionaries, but the leftists were in disagreement with him and could not stomach the dominance of the exclusively nationalist military elements in Kiev after the Directory entered the city.

A similar cleavage appeared in the Ukrainian Social Democratic party at its sixth congress which met in Kiev on January 10-12, 1919. The defeated left wing, led by Michael Tkachenko, Vasil Mazurenko, and A. Pisotsky, advocated a workers' and peasants' government of soviets and a socialist republic. The left also desired an agreement with Moscow and believed that the Russian proletariat, although temporarily blinded by chauvinism, would ultimately collaborate with the Ukrainian urban and village proletariat and poorer peasantry. The right wing, led by Vinnichenko and Nicholas Porsh, held that the time was not ripe for a socialist revolution because Ukraine was primarily an agrarian country. It was thought that Western Europe, because of its high level of industrial development, would have to assume the leadership of a truly socialist revolution. The absence of a native Ukrainian proletariat, it was argued, meant that the recognition of the soviet form of government would deliver Ukraine into the hands of the Bolsheviks. As an alternative the right wing proposed that a "toiling democracy" be maintained and that the future government be established by the Congress of Toilers. This caused the left wing to secede and establish an independent faction with its own organ, *Chervoni Prapor* (The Red Banner), published under the slogan, "Proletariat of all countries, unite."

The left Social Democrats were in the position of criticizing both the Directory and the Bolsheviks. They could not condone the Soviet invasion, and at the same time they desired an independent Ukraine with a government to the left of that of the Directory. They were willing to accept the dictatorship of the proletariat as an ultimate goal but believed that in the beginning it would have to include the revolutionary peasantry. The Bolsheviks of Ukraine and Russia were regarded as enemies of the national movement and were also feared because of their lack of scruples. Yet, paradoxically, the leftists were in favor of negotiating with Moscow.[15] This ambivalence, together with the splintering of the two major parties, made policy formulation more difficult than it usually is.

The decision to send a delegation to Moscow did not receive the support of Petliura and the other Ukrainian military commanders (*otamani*). Vinnichenko later accused Petliura of desiring war with the Bolsheviks in order to qualify for aid from the victorious Allied Powers, who at the time were commencing to negotiate the peace settlement in Paris. Petliura allegedly severed radio communications between the Directory and Mazurenko, who was in Moscow negotiating with Dimitri Manuilsky; he was also accused of refusing to permit a courier from Mazurenko to pass through the lines and travel to Kiev. The resultant confusion led the Directory to declare war against Soviet Russia on January 16, 1919, and caused the resignation of Chekhovsky.

In the midst of the invasion, civil war, and internal party conflicts, a movement was initiated for the unification of East and West Ukraine. As early as December 1, 1918, Dr. Longin Cehelsky and Dr. Dmitro Levitsky, representing the Western Ukrainian Republic, signed a preliminary agreement with the Directory at Fastiv in which both governments expressed a desire to merge. It was also agreed that West Ukraine was to enjoy autonomy because of its cultural, social, and legal particularism. On January 3, 1919, the Ukrainian People's Council of Eastern Galicia unanimously approved the Fastiv Agreement and instructed its Secretariat to enter into further negotiations for the purpose of obtaining a final treaty of union. A delegation of sixty-five persons was sent to Kiev to inform the Directory of this decision, and the act of union was finally promulgated on January 22, on historic Saint Sophia Square in Kiev.

[15] *Ibid.*, IV, pp. 49ff. Cf. Halahan, *op.cit.*, IV, pp. 99f.

Sovereignty was to reside in the Directory, but the People's Council of West Ukraine was to exercise authority in Eastern Galicia until the convocation of the Constituent Assembly. This made the union more nominal than real and enabled two different and at times contradictory external and internal policies to develop. West Ukraine, although a region of the Ukrainian People's Republic, maintained a separate foreign ministry and diplomatic missions abroad. The divergence in policy was evident in the Directory's refusal to go to war with Poland although hostilities were in progress between the Poles and the West Ukrainian Republic.

The war with Poland was not going well from the Ukrainian point of view, and Lviv was held by the Galicians for but three weeks during November. In Bukovina the situation was even more unfavorable; there the local Ukrainian population in the northern part of the territory had planned to seize control of the government on November 4, 1918, but never actually made the attempt because of lack of strength. On November 11, Rumanian armed forces took Czernowitz and within a week succeeded in occupying all of Northern Bukovina. An attempt by the Directory to finance a revolt against the Rumanian military occupation in January 1919 ended in failure.

The failure of the Ukrainian Republic to annex Northern Bukovina was accompanied by an abortive attempt to obtain control over Carpatho-Ukraine, a region which had been ruled by Hungary for nearly a thousand years. The few intellectuals and politically minded persons in this poverty-stricken territory were divided on the question of the disposition of their homeland. Those who favored retention of the ties with Hungary met in Uzhorod, while those who advocated union with the Ukrainian People's Republic met in Khust under the leadership of Michael Brashchaiko, a local attorney. Both of these groups were compelled to acquiesce in the annexation of the region by the newly-formed Czechoslovak Republic on the condition of autonomy. This solution had the support of an assembly which was organized in Prešov on November 8, 1918; it met with the approval of most of the immigrants from the territory whose representatives gathered in Scranton, Pennsylvania, during the same month. The union with Czechoslovakia was consummated in the autumn of 1919 by the Treaty of St. Germain-en-Laye over the unheeded protests of the Ukrainian People's Republic.

These defeats on the irredentist front during the winter of 1918-1919 were symbolic not only of the failure of the Ukrainian Army to halt the Bolsheviks but also of the grave internal problems which confronted the Directory. These pressing matters were to be dealt with by the Congress of Toilers which was convened in Kiev on January 22, 1919. This body in theory contained 528 indirectly elected delegates from East Ukraine and 65 from the West Ukrainian Republic. More than seventy per cent of the East Ukrainian membership was peasant while the workers were represented by twenty-two per cent of the delegates. The organized railroad, postal, and telegraph workers were accorded special representation. From a territorial point of view Kiev province had the largest delegation, numbering 67, and that of Taurida was the smallest with only 18.

The first day of the Congress was a national holiday prompted by the formal proclamation of the union of the two Ukrainian republics; this prevented the first business session from being held until the following day. The rapid Bolshevik invasion kept fully half of the delegates from arriving. Sessions rarely commenced on time, and, in general, it can be said that the Congress met under very inauspicious circumstances. The Directory enjoyed little confidence on the part of the masses, and the chaotic aftermath of revolution was too widespread for men to have faith in the ability of an assembly to cope with the problems of the day. Professor Hrushevsky failed to obtain the presidency of the Congress which was conferred upon the Galician Social Democrat, Semen Vitik. The left wing of Hrushevsky's Social Revolutionary party immediately split

231

the Congress over the issue of what the nature of Ukraine's future government was to be.

The impact of social and economic issues was evident in the limitation on membership as well as in the name given to the Congress. One of the supporters of the Hetmanate described the dissatisfaction which he and his kind experienced when he later expressed the view that it was impossible to expect a new song from old birds. In short, the rightist elements of East Ukraine, who were not allowed to participate in the Congress, regarded that body as unrepresentative and as a duplication of the Central Rada. The left wings of the Ukrainian Social Revolutionary and Social Democratic parties as well as that of the Jewish Social Democratic "Bund" were also disturbed but for another reason. They regarded the Galician delegates in the Congress as conservative and frowned upon the close associations which many of the latter had had with the officialdom of the defunct Dual Empire. The left wing in the Congress advocated an independent Ukrainian Socialist Republic and the transfer of all authority to soviets of workers' and peasants' deputies which, it should be recalled, were not monopolized in Ukraine by the Bolsheviks at this time. Peace was to be concluded with Soviet Russia, and a congress of workers' and peasants' soviets was to establish the normal order of government for the Ukrainian Socialist Republic of Soviets.[16]

Understandably, Petliura and his colleagues in the Directory were not eager to have themselves legislated into the ranks of the unemployed. They branded the program of the left wing as "Bolshevik." M. Rafes, who represented the Jewish "Bund" in the Congress, joined the left wing and chided Petliura for allegedly having predicted that Bolshevism would cease to exist within six months.[17] He also stated that the Congress was but an episode in the history of the Ukrainian revolution, and his words were not

[16] The position of the left wing in the Congress is described in Khristiuk, op.cit., IV, p. 63.
[17] Rafes, op.cit., pp. 148f.

without meaning in the face of the Bolshevik advance into the territory. The unfavorable military situation, together with the disaffection of the left wing and the abstention of much of the center, enabled the Congress to adopt a resolution on January 28 expressing its "full confidence in and gratitude to the Directory for its great work in liberating the Ukrainian people from the landlord-hetman government." Supreme authority was conferred upon the Directory although the presidium of the Congress was to call a second session with the return of normalcy. Resistance was promised to the attempt of any external power to impose its will upon Ukraine.[18] The left-wing groups accused the Directory and the Congress of waging a struggle against the revolutionary masses and of favoring war with Soviet Russia. The resolution was worthless because the Congress was compelled to adjourn following its adoption. On February 4, 1919, Bolshevik forces entered Kiev and the Directory commenced its peregrinations, which were to continue until its final expulsion from East Ukraine.

The rout of the Directory is comprehensible only in terms of the dilemma with which it was presented as a result of the French intervention in Sevastopol, Odessa, Kherson, and Mikolaiv in mid-December 1918. It was under continuous attack by the local Bolsheviks whose clandestine, irregular organ, *The Kievan Communist*, branded the Congress of Toilers as a "kulak parliament" and accused the Directory of failing to oppose the Entente imperialists who had seized the Black Sea coast. If the Directory attempted to rely upon the French interventionist forces, it would merely corroborate the Bolshevik charges that it was selling the birthright of the Ukrainian people. Failure on the part of the Directory to collaborate with Paris meant that it would have to face the invading Bolshevik forces alone. The dilemma was never resolved, and Ukrainian foreign policy never clearly formulated. This might be regarded as sufficient grounds for unqualified condemnation of the Directory were it not for the fact that French policy during

[18] For the text of the resolution see Khristiuk, *op.cit.*, IV, pp. 66f.

these months was equally obscure. Indeed, the failure of the Directory cannot be understood if it is not viewed within the framework of the French fiasco in Ukraine.

The intervention had its origin in the Anglo-French Convention which was drawn up at Paris on December 23, 1917, while General Tabouis and J. Picton Bagge were busy in Kiev attempting to persuade the Central Rada to continue the war against the Central Powers. The negotiators at Paris included Clemenceau, Pichon, and Foch as well as Lord Milner and Lord Robert Cecil; the convention had as its purpose the delineation of "spheres of action" in Russia for France and England so that they could continue the war against Germany on the Eastern front and also combat Russians who disagreed with them. The French sphere included Ukraine, Bessarabia, and the Crimea; that of England embraced the Don and Kuban regions, as well as the Caucasus, Armenia, Georgia, and Kurdistan. The Treaty of Brest-Litovsk and the subsequent occupation of Ukraine by German troops rendered this document worthless, but the signing of the armistice at Compiègne caused the British War Cabinet to reaffirm its adherence to the convention on November 13, 1918. The French military intervention in Ukraine and the British seizure of the rail line from Batum to Baku late in 1918 were based on this convention.[19]

The beginnings of the intervention of the French in Southern Ukraine can be traced to a set of instructions which Clemenceau sent on October 27, 1918, to General Franchet d'Espérey, commander of French forces in the East, proposing the military action as part of the campaign against the Central Powers. The General expressed hesitancy in his reply and frankly stated that he could do no more than hold Odessa and some of the neighboring ports.[20] Apparently the rapid collapse of the Central Powers caused

[19] For the text of this convention, see Louis Fischer, *The Soviets in World Affairs* (Princeton University Press, 1951, II, p 836) Cf. Winston Churchill, *The Aftermath* (New York, 1929), pp. 167f.

[20] Jean Xydias, *L'intervention française en Russie, 1918-1919* (Paris, 1927), pp. 113ff.

the matter to be tabled until the withdrawal of German occupation forces from Ukraine made necessary a reconsideration of the Russian problem. The whole matter was complicated by the conflicting policies and programs of the numerous groups each of which claimed to be speaking for all or part of the former Russian Empire. ·

Ukraine became the focal point of such activity in November 1918 when Russian landowners, Duma members, and industrialists as well as such liberals as Miliukov gathered there and made overtures to the victorious Allies. A conference was called at Jassy, the temporary Rumanian capital, and was attended by the Allied representatives stationed there. An important role in these proceedings was played by the Russian ambassador to Rumania, Stanislav A. Poklevsky-Kozell, who had met as early as October 17 with Émile Henno,[21] the nominal French vice consul in Kiev. The decisive conference opened on November 16 and lasted for six days. The initial request of the Russian delegates was simple; they asked for military aid for the purpose of overthrowing the Soviet Government. For the time being they believed that their needs would be met if the Allies sent a few naval vessels together with troops sufficient to hold strategic places. This would aid morale, but it was their opinion that eventually 150,000 Allied troops would be needed in Russia.

Difficulties arose when the question of Russia's future government was considered. The whole delegation was profoundly disturbed by the Ukrainian Hetman Government as well as by the rising of the Directory; at the very first meeting it was unanimously decided that the unity of Russia must be restored. The delegates at Jassy believed that the Hetman's envoy in Sofia, Alexander Shulgin, had

[21] There is considerable disagreement regarding the spelling of this surname. W. E. D. Allen in his history of Ukraine, in dealing briefly with this period, refers to the consul as "Hainnot." Élie Borschak in his *L'Ukraine à la conférence de la paix* uses the form "Hennot," while one of the publications of the Ukrainian Press Bureau in Paris employs the form "Aynaud." Jean Xydias, who claims to have known the diplomat in Odessa, renders it as "Henno," which is the form used in this study.

appealed to President Wilson to postpone ordering the withdrawal of German troops from Ukraine until the Hetman's army could be organized. The Western Powers were warned that "only the immediate arrival of Allied armed forces can prevent a rising of anti-social and narrow nationalistic elements which will plunge the country into the chaos of anarchy."[22] The various Russian groups represented at Jassy agreed on the necessity of reunification, but differences of opinion arose over the type of government which was to be adopted. Some desired a military dictatorship but were disagreed on who should be given the command; others favored a collegial executive and a constituent assembly. The matter had to be tabled, but the multiplicity of groups and proposals was to plague the French military once the intervention got underway.

The Jassy Conference cannot be said to have been the cause of the intervention in Ukraine because the interests of the Allies would probably have led to it even if the meeting had not occurred. However, it is possible that the Conference hastened the intervention. The French envoy in Rumania, Saint-Aulaire, sent a radio message to Paris on November 21 in which he stressed the necessity of occupying Odessa, Kiev, and Kharkiv because of the rise of Ukrainian chauvinists who allegedly were aided by bands of anarchists and Bolsheviks. The role of the British and American envoys in Jassy was that of accessories; the latter, Charles J. Vopicka, was a prominent Chicago banker and a native of Bohemia. It was the French minister in Jassy and the Kiev vice consul, Henno, who manifested most of the interest in the intervention, and it was their government which had the only troops available for such a venture.

It was impossible to land forces in Ukraine immediately, but it was necessary to give publicity to the impending intervention for the purpose of impressing the "unstable" elements in the country. This task fell to Henno, who for

---

[22] Shlikhter, *op.cit.*, pp. 34f.

a brief period played the role of a satrap in Odessa. One of the Russian participants in the Jassy Conference later claimed that he proposed the appointment of Henno as a plenipotentiary of the Entente Powers in South Russia with authority to instruct the German occupation officials to maintain order.[23] This was mutually acceptable, and the three Allied envoys at Jassy signed the vice consul's credentials which, in effect, made him a proconsul. Henno took the original of his credentials as well as the copy and departed for Odessa; on the following day the French legation in Jassy attempted to obtain a copy of the credentials in order to determine what had been signed. Thus Henno's task commenced, as it was to end, in confusion.

Upon arriving in Odessa, he ensconced himself in the Hotel de Londres and announced that Allied forces would disembark in the very near future for the purpose of restoring order in the country. He then sent the Hetman's foreign ministry a number of telegrams which reveal that his initial policy included recognition of the Skoropadsky regime as well as issuance of a warning that all attempts against the existing government would be suppressed. Henno stated that questions pertaining to contentious social and economic problems, as well as the issue of national self-determination, were to be examined following the arrival in Kiev of Allied troops and political representatives. He instructed the Germans to maintain order and prevent the entry of Petliura and the Directory into Kiev.[24] This minor official was soon the leading topic of conversation and of newspaper headlines, and his arrival in Kiev was anticipated.

The newly-formed Directory Government was taken aback by this policy and on November 27 it announced the issuance of a note to "the democracy of all nations of the world especially the democracy of the Entente." The

23 M. S. Margulies, God Interventsii (Berlin, 1923), I, p. 38.
24 A. I. Gukovsky, Frantsuzskaia Interventsiia na iuge Rossii (Moscow, 1928), p 155. Cf. General A. I. Denikin, Ocherki Russkoi Smuty (Berlin, 1925), IV, p. 194, and Mints and Eideman, op cit., pp. 191f.

Directory inquired as to the legal basis on which the French Government was intervening in the internal life of Ukraine and why it was not prepared to recognize the republican government with which it had relations prior to the coming of the Bolsheviks and Germans. The Entente Powers were accused of supporting "bourgeois-landowner reaction," and the Directory promised to "fight to the last person in its ranks for the social and democratic rights of the toiling Ukrainian People and for that national-state form of existence desired by the Ukrainian People."[25] On December 10, Vinnichenko, who was in Vinnitsa prior to the entry of the Directory into Kiev, received a very rude telegram from Henno which declared that the Volunteer Army of General Denikin and the pro-Hetman Russian units in Kiev at the time enjoyed the moral and material support of the Allied Powers.

Actually no French troops had landed at Odessa; instead, forces under Petliura's command were advancing on the city and took Rozdilna, which lay between Odessa and Tiraspil, thus severing rail communications with Rumania. Henno in the meantime sent telegrams announcing that his arrival in Kiev was imminent. Appointees of the Hetman were still exercising authority in the port city three weeks after Henno's landing late in November. Approximately two thousand Russian officers who favored Denikin's Volunteer Army were also in Odessa but were weak and expressed skepticism regarding the intervention. One observer noted on December 11 that the city could have been taken by ten old market women armed with brooms. Such conditions made it possible for the forces of the Directory to enter Odessa on December 13 and persuade the Ukrainian forces which had been loyal to the Hetman to accept Petliura's government. Henno then allowed the Ukrainians to occupy three-quarters of the city and limited the Russian Volunteer Army forces and the Polish legionnaires to a special zone. On December 17, the French consul issued a statement declaring that Petliura, Vinnichenko, and the

[25] Khristiuk, *op cit.*, IV, p. 6, n. 1.

238

Bolshevik leaders would be held "personally responsible for any inimical manifestations and all attempts to disturb the peace in the country."[26] Such an arrangement was naturally resented by the Volunteers, who regarded Odessa as a Russian city and who were repelled by the very thought of a Ukrainian government or army.

Thus a stalemate of very brief duration developed until the first French forces, numbering 1,800 men, disembarked on December 18 under the command of General Borius. The Ukrainian troops in Odessa were not pleased with the existence of a French zone since it constituted a blemish on their capture of the city, but they were ordered by Kiev to avoid a clash with the French at any cost. It was assumed by the Directory at this time that the interventionist forces would be used only against the Bolsheviks. However, French policy lacked clarity. The military had been instructed by Paris to "faire cause commune avec les patriotes russes,"[27] but such a directive was of little use because there were so many species of patriotism. General Borius was faced with the necessity of making a decision with respect to which group of patriots he would support. He announced that France and the Allies had not forgotten the efforts made by Russia in the beginning of the war and that they had now decided to make it possible for well-intentioned elements and Russian patriots to re-establish order in the country. Borius then proceeded to appoint the young Volunteer commander, General Alexei N. Grishin-Almazov, to the post of military governor.

In this way the French allied themselves with a single local group and irreparably harmed the cause of a united anti-Bolshevik front. Their next step was to allow the Volunteer forces to move into those portions of the city which were held by the Ukrainians. The latter had not been forewarned and were unable to organize an immediate defense. The Ukrainians waged a valiant but losing battle; French forces accompanied the advancing Volunteers at

[26] Shlikhter, *op cit.*, p. 93.   [27] Xydias, *op cit.*, p. 163

a distance and protected their rear. By the evening of December 18, the Ukrainians attempted to obtain a truce; their sole condition was the removal of Grishin-Almazov from the military governorship. Borius, in replying, laid down his own conditions: the immediate cessation of hostilities and surrender of arms by the Ukrainians, followed by their evacuation of the city. The Ukrainians were warned that if they refused to accept these terms they would be regarded not as the armed forces of a belligerent but as bandits to be shot on sight.[28] The Ukrainian command protested the lack of an adequate period of time for ordering a cease fire. In the confusion the Ukrainian troops could not or would not obey an order to surrender and retreated from the city under fire after having suffered more than thirty casualties.

This was a humiliating experience, but the Directory Government was impressed with the great victory which the Allies had won over the Central Powers and was in no position to declare war on France. Instead, it sent General Michael Grekov and General Matveiev to Odessa for the purpose of establishing contacts with the French military and obtaining technical aid. When the mission of General Grekov failed to produce any immediate results, the Directory sent Dr. Osip Nazaruk, press chief of the Ukrainian Government, and Serhi Ostapenko, minister of trade and industry. Vinnichenko was aware of his own unpopularity with the Allies and informed Nazaruk that he was ready to resign if the French were to demand his removal as a condition of their aid to Ukraine. At this time the Directory was pursuing its dual policy of offering peace to the Moscow Council of People's Commissars and simultaneously attempting to deal with the French. This prompted the Russian foreign commissar, Chicherin, to accuse the Directory on January 6 of depending upon "Anglo-French and American imperialism" which he likened to the relations that had existed between the Rada and Imperial Germany.

[28] Shlikhter, *op.cit.*, pp. 111f.

Such accusations did not prevent the Directory from sending Nazaruk and Ostapenko to Odessa in order to learn what the specific conditions of French aid would be. In Odessa, Nazaruk, after cooling his heels in an ante-room for ninety minutes, obtained an audience with Colonel Freydenberg, the chief of staff for General d'Anselme. The Colonel insisted that Vinnichenko had to be ousted and the Directory composed of men acceptable to France. The Ukrainians were to sign an agreement with the Volunteer Army and with the small Polish Legion which was in the French zone at the time. The Directory was to be permitted to organize an army of 300,000 men which would receive ammunition from France, but Russian Volunteer Army officers were to be given commissions in it. This Ukrainian army was to have the central sector of the anti-Bolshevik military front and was to be flanked by the Volunteer and Polish forces; territory taken by the Directory's army was to be placed under Ukrainian civil administration. During the military emergency France was to control the Ukrainian railways and finances, but two Ukrainian representatives were to be sent to the League of Nations and France was to support their recognition.

The two emissaries, who were nothing more than diplomatic errand boys, told Freydenberg that they would have to inform their government of these conditions. The Directory responded by insisting upon immediate recognition, non-intervention in Ukrainian internal affairs, retention of part of the membership of the existing Directory, and participation in the war against the Bolsheviks only to the Ukrainian ethnographic frontier. When Nazaruk and Ostapenko returned with these counter-proposals, Freydenberg informed them that they obviously were not military people since it was impossible to wage war only to the ethnographic line. The Colonel now insisted that Petliura would have to go because France could not deal with a bandit chieftain; he ignored Nazaruk's argument that Petliura had been arrested during the German occupation because of his sympathies for the Entente Powers. Freydenberg again pointed out that Vinnichenko's Bolshevism made his removal necessary; he also recommended that Andrievsky be ousted on the grounds that he was a worshipper of Bacchus. The war with Poland in East Galicia was also to be terminated and the western frontier demarcated later at Paris. The Hetman's ministers and the Russian Metropolitan of Kiev, Anthony Khrapovitsky, were to be released before any aid could be granted.[29]

By this time the negotiations were becoming more meaningless with each passing day. During the last week in January as the Bolsheviks were advancing on Kiev the talks with the French in Odessa were under attack from the left wing in the Congress of Toilers. M. Rafes, who represented the Jewish Social Democrats, argued that support for the socialist revolution came from the north and warned that the Allies would not permit the Directory to continue in power once their forces entered Kiev. Yet the fact that the Ukrainian military succeeded in obtaining a declaration of war against Soviet Russia on January 16 rendered this debate meaningless since it presented the Congress with an accomplished fact. The Ukrainians were under pressure from all sides: the Bolsheviks were advancing from the north and the east, the Poles were attacking in Galicia, and it was assumed that the French would move northward from the Black Sea.

Under these circumstances there seemed to be little choice but to continue the negotiations with the French in the hope that tangible aid would be forthcoming. As a result another emissary, Justice Arnold Margolin, left Kiev for Odessa on January 26 but encountered difficulties at Kazatin, where local officials halted his train and refused to heed his statement that he was traveling on orders from the Directory. This event in itself was indicative of the extent to which the authority of the Directory had been limited. Margolin finally succeeded in arriving in Odessa,

---

[29] This account of the January negotiations is based largely on the memoirs of Dr Nazaruk, *op cit*, pp. 119ff. and on an article prepared by Ostapenko and published in Shlikhter, *op cit.*, pp. 260ff.

where he attempted a new approach by uniting the Ukrainian plea for aid with the requests of the representatives from the Don, the Kuban, and Bielo-russia. The joint memorandum presented to the French by the four delegations on February 5 commenced with the assertion that the imposition of federalism from above was made impossible by the events of the preceding eighteen months. It was claimed that history contained few examples of the direct transformation of a unitary state into a federation; the cases of the United States and Switzerland were cited in support of the contention that federal systems are normally established from below when a group of independent states forms a union. Despite opposition from the Russian groups in Odessa, the four delegations requested the Allies to aid their movements for independence on the grounds that Bolshevism could be combatted most effectively in this manner. It was argued that the various ethnic units would be willing to defend their homes and families if appealed to in the name of local patriotism. The delegates asked for heavy artillery, tanks, armored cars, firearms, and ammunition, in return for which they were willing to accept a general staff that would direct military operations on the basis of a mutual agreement without intervening in the internal political life of the new states.[30]

On the night of February 1, while this memorandum was being prepared, Vinnichenko left the Hetman's palace and drove through the poorly lighted, cold and empty streets of Kiev on his way to the railroad station. Three days later the Red Army entered the city, and the Directory was compelled to flee to Vinnitsa. There Chekhovsky and Vinnichenko resigned and Petliura left the Social Democratic party in an attempt to make himself acceptable to the French. By February 13, a new cabinet was formed by Serhi Ostapenko, the former minister of trade and industry, who had been negotiating with the French in Odessa during January. This cabinet was composed largely of moderates

[30] For the text of the memorandum see Margolin, *Ukraina i Politika Antanty,* pp. 114ff.

243

and was designed to win the confidence of the Allies. It failed to do this and succeeded only in antagonizing most of the population. The Directory never recovered from the shock caused by the loss of Kiev, and in desperation it fawningly oriented itself toward the Allies.

The Soviet Provisional Workers' and Peasants' Government of Ukraine was quick to capitalize upon the situation. It not only presented the Directory to the masses as a tool of the imperialist powers but throughout February its foreign commissar, Christian Rakovsky, issued notes protesting the French intervention. On February 6, Rakovsky sent a note to Pichon, the French foreign minister, and to the other Allied governments, in which he stated that their troops were in Ukraine against the will of the workers and peasants and enjoyed the support of but a small group of capitalists, landowners, and military officers. When rumor of a Franco-Ukrainian agreement became widespread late in February, Rakovsky, in another note, termed the Directory a "fictitious government" and informed Pichon that French efforts to galvanize its corpse were futile. Yet he also expressed a willingness to make peace with France on the condition that the latter cease regarding Ukraine as a new Madagascar or Indo-China.[81] Thus the Soviet Government of Ukraine made very effective use of Petliura's overtures to the Allies and accused him of selling the country to French capitalists.

No agreement between the Directory and the French military was ever signed although several proposed texts were discussed and circulated. These were utilized with considerable effectiveness by the Ukrainian Communists; while the Congress of Toilers was in session they published the text of an alleged agreement which supposedly committed the Directory to federate with a restored Russia following the extirpation of Bolshevism. The Russian Communists pursued a similar line. The intervention prompted Stalin on January 7 to refer to the armed forces as "cannibals of the Entente." On February 22, he published an

[81] For the texts of these notes see Shlikhter, *op.cit.*, pp. 285ff.

article in *Izvestia* entitled "Two Camps" in which he stated that a choice had to be made between socialism, as represented by the Communists, and imperialism.[32] From Stalin's point of view Petliura had chosen the latter. Nor were relations improved in February as a result of Petliura's refusal to participate in the proposed Prinkipo Conference of "every organized group that is now exercising or attempting to exercise political authority or military control" anywhere in Russia. The Ukrainians were willing to go to Prinkipo only on the condition that Moscow withdraw its troops from Ukraine.

This effort made by Lloyd George and Wilson to learn what was transpiring in Russia was doomed to fail because of the refractory nature of the problem and the intransigeance of the anti-Bolshevik elements. The intervention continued through the winter with the participation of more than forty thousand foreign troops, including two Greek divisions as well as some Rumanian army units. Another twenty thousand Greek and French troops, including Senegalese detachments, landed in the Crimea. Under the circumstances this would have constituted a formidable military force if it had not been permeated with demoralization and if it had been utilized in the interests of a particular policy. The French could have decided to support either the Directory or General Denikin's Volunteer Army officers in Odessa. Instead, in attempting to obtain a united military front of all anti-Bolshevik forces and in not committing themselves with respect to Russia's political future, they succeeded only in antagonizing both the Ukrainians of the Directory and the Odessa Russians.

[32] Several Soviet sources which appeared later contain the texts of treaties and economic agreements which the Directory had allegedly concluded with the French. These probably were not fabricated by Soviet students of the problem, and it can be said that they probably reflected the conditions which the French were insisting upon in return for aid. See Shlikhter, *op.cit.*, pp. 134f. and N. Filippov, *Ukrainskaia Kontrrevoliutsiia na Sluzhbe Anglii, Frantsii i Polshchi* (Moscow, 1927), pp. 63ff. However, the most prominent Soviet historian of the intervention, A. I. Gukovsky, has concluded in his thorough study that, in all probability, no treaty was ever concluded between the Directory and France.

This was accomplished by negotiating simultaneously with both parties. Such a procedure could lead only to antagonism. Most of the Russian organizations and officials in Odessa were unwilling even to recognize any Ukrainian government and declared, instead, that the Ukrainians were a political party and not a nation. Colonel Freydenberg's negotiations with the representatives of the Directory were, from their point of view, nothing less than a betrayal of Russia.[83] Similarly the Ukrainians never recovered from the initial distrust which they experienced during their expulsion from Odessa by the Russians and French on December 18. Nor were relations improved by the Ukrainian allegation that the Volunteer Army had seized the Directory's currency plates in Odessa and was wilfully creating an inflation.

The vacillation of the French can be explained in terms of the political attitudes of the French officials on the spot. The replacement of Henno by Colonel Freydenberg in mid-January was marked by a willingness to negotiate with the Ukrainians, instead of the policy of unqualified support for the Volunteer Army which was followed by Henno. Dissatisfaction with the local Volunteer Army commander, General Grishin-Almazov, led to his dismissal on March 21 by the French. Many of the Russians in Odessa believed that this was done by General Franchet d'Espérey, commander of all French forces in the East, who was visiting the city at the time and whom they regarded as a Russophobe. Yet it is significant that Grishin-Almazov's successor was not the Ukrainian General Grekov but another Russian, General Schwartz, who was not persona grata to Denikin.

Neither the appointment of a new local commander nor the numerous visits made by French officers and Allied men-of-war caused the mass of the local population to be more appreciative of the intervention. To the average per-

[83] Documentary evidence of the attitude of the Russian Volunteer Army is to be found in "K Istorii Frantsuzkoi Interventsii na Iuge Rossii," *Krasnyi Arkhiv*, XIX, pp. 3ff.

son in Odessa, the presence of the foreign troops only meant that the city was cut off from the surrounding countryside and from sources of raw materials. As a result economic life was crippled and the percentage of unemployed ranged from twenty-five in the case of printers to eighty in the metal and construction trades. Numerous factories were compelled to close because of the fuel shortage. Between November of 1918 and the withdrawal of the forces of intervention in April, the currency in Odessa declined to one-tenth of its former value because of the acute shortage of goods. By mid-January milk was unobtainable. Only the center of the city enjoyed a relatively steady supply of electric current; at night the streets were unsafe, and numerous crimes were committed.

The general unrest brought on by the wave of unemployment and the high cost of living provided the local Communists with excellent material for agitation among the workers. Nor did they neglect the French soldiers and sailors for whom they published a special French edition of their clandestine newspaper, *The Communist*. Morale had been low since the first day of the intervention. A prominent citizen and newspaper publisher in Odessa, who witnessed the intervention and who was close to the French, has stated that General Borius, upon landing, recorded in his diary: "voici une entreprise qui, certes, tournera mal."[34] The officers and men regarded the war as having ended with the defeat of Germany and had no desire to see any more bloodshed. It is evident that the French military never intended to proceed beyond the littoral and occupy the interior of the country despite Henno's telegrams regarding his impending arrival in Kiev. Indeed, many of them saw no reason why the hundred thousand Russian citizens in Odessa were not capable of bearing arms. Each plea for additional French troops made by the numerous Russian groups in the city only served to intensify the general resentment of the French military.

Paris had ordered these men to land troops in Ukraine,

[34] Xydias, *op.cit.*, p. 171.

247

but it had failed to define the objectives of the intervention with adequate precision. Far too much authority was delegated to the reluctant and politically unschooled French officers in the east. Like most of the world, they failed to understand the economic and social aspects of the revolution in Russia. Circumstances had enabled a minor figure such as Henno to assume initially a position of importance in which he made decisions which had far-reaching consequences. Yet had his pronouncements been of a different nature, the intervention would probably have failed just as badly. It is idle but intriguing to speculate whether or not the Bolsheviks could have been defeated if the French had decided in the beginning to lend their support to the Ukrainian Directory.[35] The French knew very little about Petliura and, as a result, refused to aid him. It is probable that a policy of unlimited support of the Directory would not have created a solid anti-Bolshevik front.

The nightmare of policy implementation which the ranking French officers in Ukraine were experiencing was brought to an end when Paris suddenly and without explanation ordered the withdrawal of all troops. On April 3, all the Odessa newspapers published General d'Anselme's brief order regarding the evacuation which rationalized this step in terms of French inability to supply the city. It was widely and incorrectly rumored in the city at the time that Clemenceau's cabinet had fallen and had been replaced by one composed of socialists. The evacuation commenced under such a pall. The French had had some experience in such activity during March at the ports of Mikolaiv and Kherson which they were compelled to evacuate as a result of the advances made by Grigoriev, an independent local military commander who at the time was allied with the Red Army. In Odessa the large number of anti-Bolshevik Russians complicated the task since they competed with the French for all available space on ships which were in the

[35] Xydias advances this thesis and places much of the blame upon Henno for not insisting at Jassy upon the unity of all anti-Bolshevik elements, whether Russian or Ukrainian.

port. Workers called a general strike and refused to aid in the loading of vessels; the crews of many of the Russian ships sabotaged them so that they could not be used. Despite these difficulties, several thousand Volunteer Army men and thirty thousand Russian civilians managed to escape from the city. Thus the intervention ended in ignominy and in confusion similar to that in which it had begun.

The "conqueror" of Odessa was Grigoriev, a tsarist army officer who had supported Petliura against Skoropadsky but who quickly switched to the Bolsheviks following their invasion of Ukraine. For a brief period he enjoyed widespread popularity in the Mikolaiv region and was especially noted for his forthright manner: he had sent an ultimatum to General Grishin-Almazov in Odessa, ordering the latter to surrender or have his skin used in a drum. The withdrawal of the forces of intervention and the rapid southward advance of the main columns of the Red Army presented Grigoriev with a problem; since December he had been an authority unto himself, but now he was faced with the necessity of obeying the command of an army of which he claimed to be a part. When Grigoriev refused in May to follow an order to go to the Rumanian front and, instead, directed his men to attack the Red Army from the rear, Voroshilov compelled him to seek refuge with the anarchist band of Nestor Makhno. When the latter became convinced in July that Grigoriev was preparing to join the Denikin movement, he shot him at a public meeting and brought his meteoric career to an end.

Of the innumerable local military commanders who arose in Ukraine during this period, Makhno was by far the most colorful and prominent. Although Makhno was a peasant with little formal education, he was endowed with some organizational ability and with a burning desire to deliver orations. Released from prison following the March Revolution, Makhno returned to his native village of Gulyai Pole in the Katerinoslav province and engaged in anarchist agitation. He had little faith in the Provisional Govern-

249

ment and its "capitalist ministers" and still less in the Rada and its Secretariat, which he later branded as the tool of German Junkerdom and a "camp of Ukrainian chauvinists leading, behind its back, the bourgeoisie against the Revolution." By the summer of 1917 he concluded, in the fashion of a pure anarchist, that the revolution had "fallen into the noose of statehood." His formula was simply the transformation of all lands and factories into social property accompanied by the disappearance of the state "as a form of organized society." His enemies were the landowners, industrialists, officials, merchants, priests, and jailkeepers. From this it is evident that Makhno was not a Ukrainian nationalist although he never referred to his native land as "South Russia" but, instead, always employed its proper name. However, he was unable to speak Ukrainian well, and in his memoirs, which were written in Russian, he readily admitted that he mutilated the language in a most shameful manner.[36]

Makhno's political interests lay not in nationalism but in anarchism, and it was this which caused him to join the Bolsheviks against the Rada in January 1918, ostensibly for the purpose of saving the revolution and combatting the bourgeoisie. The rapid occupation of Ukraine by the Central Powers made it necessary for the peasant anarchist to seek refuge in Russia where he met with the venerable Russian anarchist, Peter A. Kropotkin. When Makhno failed to obtain the practical advice which he sought from the titular leader of Russia's anarchists, he decided to rely on his own devices, and returned to Southern Ukraine in July of 1918. There he reassembled his band and engaged units of the occupation forces in small-scale battles. The withdrawal of the German and Austrian armies made it possible for Makhno to obtain military equipment and fill a power vacuum in Katerinoslav province with his band of twenty thousand men fighting under a black anarchist flag. However, soon he found himself caught between the forces of the Bolsheviks and those of Denikin; Petliura

[36] Nestor Makhno, *Pod Udarami Kontr-Revoliutsii* (Paris, 1936), p. 153

constituted no threat to Makhno, who deserted the Directory with impunity at an early date.

Makhno's break with the Bolsheviks, which occurred in the spring of 1919, was made inevitable by his obsession with the notion that the spirit of the Revolution was to be found only in the village and that the city was, by its nature, the seat of counter-revolution. He regarded Moscow as the center of "the paper revolution"—a term which he believed described its artificiality and reliance upon decrees. This peasant could not discard his belief in the rectitude and straightforwardness of his class. He was convinced that its political needs could be fulfilled through "free soviets" without bureaucracy and payment of taxes. Soon he came to regard the Bolsheviks, with their nationalization of industry, as proponents of a state capitalism which militarized labor and subjected it to an exploitation as ruthless as any practiced by the bourgeoisie.[87] Makhno rejected political parties and statehood and, unlike Lenin, wasted his time and energy blowing up jailhouses; it was this which led to his ultimate defeat. The anarchist was brought to ruin because he lacked an organization, and yet if he had succumbed to this need he would have made the realization of his ultimate objective an impossibility. Lenin described the result of this dilemma when he saw Makhno in Moscow in 1918 and told him that the anarchists were so preoccupied with the future that they were unaware of the present.

Although anarchism failed to provide a satisfactory program for political action, the fact that Makhno obtained considerable peasant support indicates that the peasantry's loyalty was not to any blind nationalism but was directed rather to securing land. This was also true of the thousands of peasants who readily enlisted in the Directory's army during the march on the capital. Yet the inability of the Directory to establish a firm regime during its brief stay in Kiev meant that military freebooters of the type of

[87] P. Arshinov, *Istoriia Makhnovskogo Dvizheniia, 1918-1921* (Berlin, 1923), pp. 68f.

Grigoriev and Makhno were free to do as they pleased. Indeed, during the spring of 1919 the number of independent military commanders (*otamani*) became so large that Vinnichenko, upon resigning, stated that they, rather than the Directory, constituted whatever government there was. One of the most prominent Ukrainian commanders, Colonel Peter Bolbochan, had control of the Left Bank of the Dnieper during December 1918 until he was driven out by the invading Bolshevik forces. Petliura was the nominal commander-in-chief (*holovni otaman*), but he was unable to control the actions of his subordinates. Each *otaman* acted irresponsibly and became a veritable satrap in his own locale, requisitioning at his pleasure inanimate and animate objects, including women.[88] The forces of some of these commanders were part of the Directory's army, while those of others did not even pay lip service to any higher authority but were able to obtain supplies by disarming the German troops who were eager to return home.

The commanders, who were theoretically subordinate to Petliura, received large sums of money for supplying and indoctrinating their men. The deplorable financial administration of the Directory, which lacked a system of accounting and auditing, made possible lavish spending. Waste is seemingly inevitable in any military establishment, but in this case many commanders actually absconded with funds during the spring and took comfortable refuge in Stanislaviv, the temporary capital of West Ukraine. The rise of the *otamani* has also been attributed to the general mobilization which the Directory decreed despite the lack of an administrative apparatus capable of organizing and supplying the large number of enlisted men. Yet in all

[88] Some of the more prominent *otamani* were Zeleny, of Kiev and Poltava provinces (whose real name was Daniel Terpilo), and Struk who operated in Chernihiv province. Kotsur, a village school teacher and a former provincial official of the Rada Government, commenced to lead peasant uprisings in 1918 and continued during the following year. Anhel was prominent in Poltava province while Shuba led a band of plunderers in the Lubni district.

probability the real cause was the failure of the Directory to establish contacts between the capital and local authorities.

Two results of this anarchy were the decline of the Directory and an outbreak of anti-Jewish pogroms. Under the Rada Government and the Hetmanate, the Jewish population of Ukraine did not suffer oppression, but the civil warfare of 1919 released the latent anti-Semitism of the peasant. The Polonized landowners on the Right Bank of the Dnieper often employed Jewish stewards and in this way contributed to the development of antagonism. Peasants who become indebted to the Jewish tavern keeper in the village compensated themselves for their lack of willpower by blaming him for their pitiful plight. The religious differences which existed between Ukrainian Jewry and the peasantry provided another barrier and gave to the peasant a sense of exclusiveness which is evident in the Galician proverb: "He who eats the Jewish matzoth will not live to eat his own paschal bread."[39] This admonition was based on the peasant superstition that there was Christian blood in the matzoth. Anti-Semitism in Eastern Europe can be understood only when viewed in this historical context which is rooted in profound social, economic, and religious differences.

The circumstances of 1919 made it possible for this latent force to reassert itself. Many peasants who had their grain requisitioned by young Bolshevik commissars of Jewish descent hastily concluded that the movement was a Jewish phenomenon. This tragic notion was seemingly corroborated by the fact that many of the poorer Jewish workers and craftsmen in the towns and cities supported the Bolsheviks in the hope of obtaining some degree of economic justice. The Ukrainian nationalists were of the opinion that most of the Jewish population in Ukraine did not appreciate the national movement. This was correct because those Jews who favored the assimilation of their

[39] Ivan Franko, *Halitsko-Rus'ki Narodni Pripovidki* (Lviv, 1908), II, p. 505.

people were, for the most part, anti-Ukrainian and participated in the activities of the various Russian parties. However, two Jewish parties of this period were sympathetic with the Ukrainian cause.

The first of these, the Jewish Territorial Organization's Ukrainian section, was headed by Justice Arnold Margolin; the parent body was founded originally by Izrael Zangwill, the English Jewish author, who broke with the Zionists after 1903 in order to support the British offer of Uganda as a possible Jewish homeland. The other source of Jewish support for Ukrainian statehood came from the Poale Zion (Workers of Zion) which aimed to fuse socialism and Zionism; it differed from the Jewish Social Democratic "Bund" in that it held that the social and economic problems of the Jews could be solved only in Palestine, while the members of the "Bund" believed that a solution could be found only in the Diaspora. The "Bund" was not enthusiastic about Ukrainian separatism and regarded the 1917 revolution as an all-Russian event. Its representatives in the Rada were not in favor of proclaiming Ukrainian independence which they believed would be detrimental to the revolution. Thus the hesitancy of some Jewish groups to support the national movement probably helped to release a torrent of antipathy which had been accumulated over the centuries.

A catalogue of the resulting brutal and bloody massacres is not pertinent to this study. The most serious pogroms occurred in Zhitomir, Cherkassi, Rivne, Bobrinsk, Sarni, Fastiv, Korosten, and Bakhmach. Probably the most savage pogrom was perpetrated by Otaman Semesenko and his men in Proskuriv in February 1919. Upon taking the city Semesenko forbade all strikes and meetings and ordered the population to "cease its anarchistic outbursts because I have adequate forces with which to combat you, and I especially call this to the attention of the Jews." He cautioned them to "know that you are a people disliked by all nations and you are acting disgracefully amongst a

Christian people."[40] The commander also ordered all places of business in the city to change their signs from Russian to Ukrainian within seventy-two hours. The pogrom, which occurred shortly after the issuance of this order, brought death to more than three thousand Jewish persons in Proskuriv.

Faced with this and similar horrible outbursts, the Directory, beating a hasty retreat from Kiev, was not in a position to employ punitive or preventive measures. It could only remonstrate with the *otamani* and troops, as it did on January 11, 1919, when it condemned the pogroms and also called on democratic Jewry to combat "individual anarcho-bolshevist members of the Jewish nation." Military inspectors from the high command were often prevented from reviewing army units on the grounds that this indicated lack of confidence in the commanders and undermined discipline. The Directory attempted to persuade the Jewish population in Ukraine to support the government; it continued its ministry of Jewish affairs, which was headed by two members of the Poale Zion organization, A. Revutsky and P. Krasni. It also appropriated 11,460,000 *hriven* on July 30 for pogrom victims and in October almost doubled this amount.

While these were generous gestures, they in no way endeared the bulk of the Jews to the Ukrainian cause. Petliura attempted to retain the support of the Jews by reminding them that they and the Ukrainians had a common enemy in the Bolsheviks. The Ukrainian commander-in-chief was not an anti-Semite despite Vinnichenko's allegation to the contrary, but he became a helpless victim of this scourge of Eastern Europe because he headed a government which was responsible for the acts of officials over whom it was incapable of exercising effective control. Although Petliura issued a number of orders during the summer and autumn of 1919 censuring the instigators of pogroms, he was unable or unwilling to have such persons apprehended and brought to justice.

[40] For the text of Semesenko's order see Khristiuk, *op cit*, IV, pp. 105f.

This failure harmed the efforts which the representatives of the Directory Government were making to obtain aid from abroad. The appointment of ineffective investigating commissions could not correct the harmful impression which the pogroms created in Western European intellectual and political circles. Nor could it be undone by the publication of brochures abroad expressing the Directory's willingness to submit to an international investigation and attributing the pogroms to "the spirit of tsarist Russia." Yet despite this alienation of foreign support some broad-minded Jewish citizens of Ukraine continued to believe in the need for their participation in the government. Among these was Arnold Margolin, who had served as a justice of the Ukrainian General Court, the supreme judicial body under the Rada, and who continued in that capacity during the Hetmanate when it was reorganized as the state senate.

When the Directory came into power, Margolin became a deputy foreign minister although he was not fluent in Ukrainian. While in Odessa attempting to obtain aid from the French military authorities, Margolin learned of the February and March pogroms. He attempted in vain to persuade Colonel Freydenberg to make an official protest, but the latter stated, not without irony, that he did not wish to intervene in Ukrainian internal affairs. Margolin then tendered his resignation; it was not accepted, and he was requested, instead, to proceed to Paris and serve with the Ukrainian delegation which was gathering there. He complied and went to the peace conference with the conviction that only aid from the West could bring an end to the anarchy and pogroms. When the political atmosphere cleared several years later and the Directory was expelled from Soviet Ukraine, Margolin paid the exiled leaders a great tribute in stating that he would "never refuse to defend those who stood at the head of the Ukrainian movement."[41]

Such a statement absolves the Ukrainian leaders from

[41] Margolin, *Ukraina i Politika Antanty*, p. 338.

moral responsibility for the pogroms, but it cannot be said that these massacres, however reprehensible, were the cause of the Directory's defeat. The retreat from Kiev can be understood only in terms of the successful Bolshevik invasion which was made possible not only by superior Russian military forces but primarily because of the Directory's inability to satisfy popular demands. Early in December Petliura commanded no more than eight thousand men with thirty pieces of artillery, but following the taking of Kiev two weeks later he had thirty thousand troops in the capital and three times that number throughout the country. Yet within six weeks this army dwindled as rapidly as it had snow-balled despite the expenditure of 300,000,000 *karbovantsi* for military purposes during the Directory's brief stay in Kiev. This reflects the great hope which the Ukrainian peasantry had in the Directory and the ease with which it lost faith in that body's capacity to achieve results. Thus it is quite evident that the masses who joined in the revolt against the Hetmanate were fired not so much by national loyalty as by a desire to inflict vengeance upon the landowners who had been protected during the Austro-German occupation. The peasant demand for land was so great that the Directory found it necessary to promise army recruits allotments of seven *desiatinas* (nineteen acres) each.

Paper legislation was enacted on January 7, 1919, when all forests were nationalized without compensation; on the following day land was also "nationalized" in the same manner and the maximum size of a single holding was fixed at approximately forty acres (fifteen *desiatinas*).[42] The Congress of Toilers adopted these measures, which were drafted by agriculture minister Mikita Shapoval, but they never assumed reality because of the crushing military defeats suffered by Petliura's forces. Thus the men in the Directory were able to do little more than publicize the prison records which they had acquired previously as a result of their

[42] Mikita Shapoval, *Velika Revoliutsiia i Ukrainska Vizvol'na Programa* (Prague, 1928), p. 130.

political beliefs, and this was not enough to rally the masses against the Bolsheviks. The six-week period during which the Ukrainians were in Kiev was characterized by unbelievable inefficiency and padded public payrolls. Millions were appropriated for propaganda and the publication of additional newspapers, but with little tangible success. The chain of command was not clearly defined and competencies of administrative organs overlapped; deputations coming to the capital with petitions went to any ministry that would grant them a hearing.

These were factors which contributed to the rapid success of the Bolshevik invasion, but probably the most important cause lay in the growing demand for a soviet order, the fulfillment of which the Bolsheviks advocated, although on their own terms. The non-Communist leftists in the Ukrainian Social Democratic and Social Revolutionary parties, who desired a soviet order and who regarded the Bolshevik advance with more or less equanimity, soon found themselves unable to accept the new workers' and peasants' government. The reason for this was their conviction that it was not truly Ukrainian; Rakovsky was opposed to the use of Ukrainian as the official language and declared that such a step would be reactionary since more than two million Great Russians inhabited the cities. The Communists branded the Ukrainian leftists as bourgeois chauvinists and counter-revolutionaries because of their general peasant orientation and their desire to see the middle strata of the peasantry (*seredniaki*) participate in the organs of soviet authority. Seeing these organs bureaucratized and grain requisitioned impolitely by the Red Army, they had little choice but to oppose this particular species of sovietism being offered by the Communists.[43] The left Social Revolutionaries in their organ, *Borotba*,

[43] A Soviet writer, M. Ravich-Cherkassky, has admitted that in the spring of 1919 the Bolsheviks had succeeded in mastering the city but failed in the countryside. *Istoriia Kommunisticheskoi partii Ukrainy* (Kharkiv, (1923), pp. 123 and 126. For a vivid description of life in Kiev during this period of military occupation, see Volodimir Leontovich, *Spomini Utikacha* (Berlin, 1922), pp. 21ff.

pleaded in vain with the Bolsheviks to abandon the dictatorship of their own party, and at the same time the left Social Democrats accused the Directory of "national sentimentalism" and betrayal of the international solidarity and dictatorship of the toiling masses.

The monopolization of the soviet form of government by the Ukrainian Communists did not cause the other leftist groups to reject it as a desirable form. The popularity of the soviet political idea was so widespread that it prompted the Council of the Galician Sich Sharpshooters, meeting in Proskuriv, to issue a declaration on March 25 denying charges that the troops which it represented wished to serve reactionaries. Instead, it contended that they were fighting not only for an independent Ukraine but also for the soviet form of government on the local level. The Galicians, to whom Communism was completely alien, were attempting to keep abreast with events after having retreated from Kiev and having discovered the extent of anti-Directory feeling in the population. Yet by that time too much had transpired for the Ukrainian leaders to redeem themselves. The fall of Vinnitsa early in March caused them to flee to Proskuriv, and by the end of the month the Ukrainian army was divided as a result of the capture of Balta which enabled the Bolsheviks to cut the vital Zhmerinka-Odessa rail line. The fifteen thousand troops who were isolated in the south found it necessary to fall back on Odessa, where they obtained permission from General d'Anselme to pass through Bessarabia, where they were disarmed, and rejoin Petliura in Western Podolia. The advent of spring saw the Directory's army pressed into this narrow, shrinking pocket between the advancing Red Army and the forces of the West Ukrainian Republic who were retreating in the face of Polish military and diplomatic successes.

CHAPTER VI
The Debacle

Every kingdom divided against itself is brought to desolation; and a house divided against a house falleth.—*St. Luke, 11:17*

To have received from one, to whom we think our selves equall, greater benefits than there is hope to Requite, disposeth to counterfeit love; but really secret hatred; and puts a man into the estate of a desperate debtor, than in declining the sight of his creditor, tacitly wishes him there, where he might never see him more. For benefits oblige; and obligation is thraldome; and unrequitable obligation, perpetuall thraldome; which is to ones equall, hatefull.—THOMAS HOBBES
Leviathan (1651)

THE Ukrainian movement during 1919 and the following year was associated almost exclusively with the name of Simon Vasilievich Petliura, the former transport and insurance company employee who exchanged his bookkeeper's pen for a sword. Born in the heart of Ukraine, in Poltava, on May 5, 1879, the son of parents of modest means, Petliura spent ten years in an Orthodox educational institution receiving preparatory training for the priesthood. His preoccupation with Ukrainian nationalism led to his expulsion from the school. He sought refuge in Tiflis and in the Kuban, but soon went to Lviv, where he enrolled in several courses at the university and collaborated with some of the Ukrainian journalists. The 1905 Revolution in Russia enabled him to go to Kiev, where he edited a socialist newspaper, *Slovo* (The Word), and contributed to that city's first Ukrainian daily.

In 1911 Petliura took up residence in Saint Petersburg, where he obtained employment as an office worker and participated in the life of the capital's Ukrainian colony. During the following year he moved to Moscow and commenced publication of a monthly review in the Russian language entitled *Ukrainskaia Zhizn* (Ukrainian Life). With the outbreak of war in 1914 he joined the All-Russian Union of Municipalities, which provided medical and recreational facilities for the troops. Petliura was stationed on the Austrian front and ultimately attained the rank of colonel in this pseudo-military organization. In the days following the March Revolution his talent for oratory enabled him to become a delegate to the First Ukrainian Military Congress held in Kiev in 1917. He was included in the military representation in the Central Rada, where he was catapulted to a position of primary importance. Unlike Hrushevsky, the scholar, and Vinnichenko, the belles-lettrist, Petliura was a publicist and man of action. Upon this aquiline-nosed amateur soldier was placed the heavy responsibility of conducting military operations against the Red Army.

For this his enemies, including Soviet historians, have called him a bandit; his representatives abroad termed him the Ukrainian Garibaldi and savior of European civilization from Great Russian imperialism. Enemies of the Soviet Union who have acquired enough knowledge of Eastern European history to know of Petliura's existence have regarded him as a hero while Ukrainophobes have branded the national movement as "Petliurism." Calumny and eulogy have combined to make Petliura an extremely controversial figure. To appreciate his efforts, one must understand that in 1919 Russia had become a political kaleidoscope. This was a period in which railroad engineers often refused to move a train unless the passengers made a special collection on their behalf. The multiplicity of worthless currencies, together with the breakdown of transport, led to a reversion to the barter system. Authority was localized, and the few economic goods that were to be found were often hastily requisitioned by the possessors of superior force.

During such a period as this the great truth becomes apparent: what is legal is that which is supported by preponderant force. The ordinary individual caught in such chaotic civil strife is usually willing, in the hope of preserving his life if not his property, to pledge allegiance to whoever happens to be in immediate control. Eye witnesses of the civil war have contended that the swearing of allegiance became monotonous because it recurred so frequently as a result of rapidly shifting lines of battle. Men racked their memories, searching for unpaid non-financial debts incurred in the past by persons who were in power at the moment and who possessed the authority to deprive individuals of their life. Under such confusing circumstances, the Ukrainian national movement became but one of a number of participants in a ruthless competition for loyalty. In such a panorama of chaos the Directory was compelled, in Dmitro Doroshenko's words, to resort to a policy of "chronic evacuation."

While it was preparing to flee westward from Proskuriv, there met in Kamianets-Podilsk a second Congress of Toilers with more than one hundred delegates in attendance. There Social Democrats and Social Revolutionaries who were dissatisfied with the Directory met on March 21, 1919, under the leadership of Hrushevsky, hoping to be able to salvage some of the remnants of authority. To this end the Congress established a Committee for the Defense of the Republic under the presidency of Volodimir Chekhovsky, the former premier. On the following day, the Committee announced that it would serve as a "provisional representative of the central government of the Republic." It was willing to commence peace negotiations with Moscow on the condition that an independent Ukrainian Soviet Socialist Republic be recognized by the existing Ukrainian and Russian Soviet Governments. The Ukrainian character of the state was to be guaranteed, together with the legal existence of the Ukrainian socialist parties; Russian troops were to be withdrawn and a new Ukrainian government was to be organized at an all-Ukrainian congress of soviets of workers' and peasants' deputies.[1] The Committee intended to preserve military discipline and stabilize the fighting front until the completion of negotiations with the Ukrainian Soviet Government, but conditions in Kamianets and elsewhere were not conducive to the successful execution of this program.

The local garrison was small and the city was not immune to the ravages of the undisciplined military commanders and their marauding followers. Supporters of the Directory who were present in Kamianets regarded the Committee as illegal and usurpatory; a few unimportant "victories" won by Petliura led to a temporary stabilization of the front and enabled him to persuade the Committee to dissolve on March 27, although without renouncing any of its objectives. Andrievsky of the Directory ordered Otaman Khomadovsky to arrest several of the men

[1] For the text of the Committee's declaration see Khristiuk, *op.cit*, IV, p. 112.

in the Committee, including Isaac Mazepa, a Social Democrat. However, Petliura ordered that they be released and brought to Rivne in Volynia for the purpose of forming a new cabinet of the "left." This change in policy was prompted by the failure of Ostapenko's moderate cabinet to win French military aid. A comic situation developed in that two members of the Directory, Petliura and Makarenko, were in Rivne while two others, Andrievsky and Dr. Eugene Petrushevich, were in Stanislaviv, Galicia; the fifth member, Shvets, moved between the two wings. This division reflected the two alternative policies of perpetuating the Ostapenko cabinet or coming to terms with the Social Democrats and Social Revolutionaries; the members in Galicia favored the former, while Petliura now advocated the latter policy.

On April 5, the central committees of the two socialist parties presented Petliura with a plan which called for termination of the civil war in Ukraine, peace with Soviet Russia and the rejection of all aggressive alliances against that government, and the legalization of all parties not opposed to the sovereignty of the Ukrainian Republic. The proposed cabinet intended to walk a tight-rope between the Bolsheviks and the Allied Powers who had intervened in the South; on the one hand, it was to permit the organization of a soviet of working people for control purposes, and, on the other hand, it stated its willingness to conclude an agreement with the Allies if they were to recognize Ukrainian independence, withdraw their troops, and cease intervening.[2] This program was inadequate because it provided for peace with Moscow without including any concrete provisions for a settlement with the Ukrainian Communists.

On April 9, the new predominantly Social Democratic cabinet was organized by Boris Martos, who held the premiership as well as the finance portfolio; Isaac Mazepa, who had been arrested in Kamianets shortly before, was appointed to the interior ministry, and Nicholas Kovalevsky

2 *Ibid.*, IV, pp. 118f.

266

became minister of agriculture. This cabinet, unlike the short-lived Ostapenko government, hoped to arouse national sentiment by stating that it would not rely on foreign aid of any sort. Although it avoided social and economic issues, it was soon attacked by Andrievsky, who regarded it as radical. This member of the Directory, with the support of some of the former ministers in the Ostapenko cabinet, refused to recognize the Martos government. Opposition also developed in Rivne where a twenty-six-year-old *otaman*, Oskilko, expressed his willingness to protect Petliura's enemies in the temporary capital who accused the new cabinet of Bolshevism. When the commander-in-chief attempted to remove Oskilko, a coup was attempted on April 29, with the support of some local independentists-socialists, Socialist-Federalists, and popular republicans.[3] Oskilko proclaimed himself commander-in-chief, but before he could arrest Petliura and Makarenko, they, together with Shvets, fled south to Zdolbunovo. The men whom Oskilko sent to arrest Petliura turned against the usurper and overthrew him; Oskilko then fled to Poland with some of his aides and was interned there.

The significance of this abortive coup lay in the fact that it reflected the division which existed between socialists, extreme nationalists, and those caught in the intervening no-man's land. An immediate result was the weakening of the front which allowed the Bolsheviks and Poles to press closer to Rivne. The Martos cabinet retreated to Galicia in its railroad cars, fleeing from station to station and having the appearance of a gypsy band rather than that of a government. Vinnichenko later observed that "there were times when the only territory over which the Ukrainian *otaman*-'socialist' government exercised any authority was the few miles of railroad trackage on which its cars were temporarily located."[4] At Radiviliv Petliura ousted An-

[3] The popular republicans and the independentists-socialists were very small groups unworthy of being called parties They enjoyed no peasant or labor support and were composed exclusively of nationalist intellectuals and military personnel.

[4] Vinnichenko, *op.cit.*, III, p. 293.

drievsky from the Directory on the grounds that he had supported Oskilko. The cabinet then moved to Brodi, from which it had its cars pulled to Ternopil, which lay within the jurisdiction of the West Ukrainian Government.

Deprived of all semblance of military power, Petliura became increasingly dependent upon his diplomatic missions abroad. During January the Directory had decided to send an army of diplomats to more than twenty European governments. The Hetman Government had left a sizable treasury with considerable foreign valuta which made possible the financing of diplomatic, military, and commercial missions. These were not well-staffed since many insincere Ukrainians, who were incapable of speaking foreign languages, obtained positions with them. The foreign ministry became a veritable emigration bureau, providing passports, foreign currency, and rail accommodations for the hundreds of amateur diplomats whose confidence in the Directory was so great that many of them took their children and grandchildren abroad at government expense. In Vienna, where all of the missions stopped in order to obtain visas, many of the diplomats ate in the most exclusive restaurants, tipped lavishly, stayed at the best hotels, and rode about in automobiles.

Upon arriving at its destination each mission attempted to obtain recognition from the foreign office of the government to which the Directory had accredited it. Innumerable letters were written but few answers were received and fewer audiences were granted. While many of the diplomats enjoyed themselves, others, who regarded their work with greater seriousness, found their experiences to be very humiliating on occasion. Some had distressing encounters with cockroaches and put up with unbelievably slow and uncomfortable train service during their travels. Cut off from their fleeing government and unaware of what was occurring in Ukraine, they could do little more than attempt to present the Ukrainian case before world opinion. Huge sums were spent in publishing brochures dealing with Ukraine's culture, history, and political objectives;

economic opportunities and resources were described in glowing colors. An impressive Ukrainian choir, directed by Alexander Koshetz, was financed by the Directory and sent in January on a tour through Western Europe. The diplomats employed every conceivable argument in attempting to persuade the governments to which they were unsuccessfully accredited that it was in their interests to support Ukrainian independence.

As time passed, the fruitless task of the Directory's diplomats became encumbered by financial difficulties, especially in countries in which the rate of exchange was unfavorable. Mission staffs deteriorated because of lack of funds and uncertainty regarding objectives, as in the case of the military attaché in Sofia, General Bobrovsky, whom visiting Russian officers persuaded to join Denikin. The agents of the Russian Volunteer Army and advocates of Russian reunification were not satisfied with raiding personnel but even attempted to discredit the Ukrainian missions. In Sofia they accused the members of the diplomatic mission of being Bolsheviks and counterfeiters, and the Bulgarian Government, under French influence, regarded the personnel of the mission as private individuals and forbade them to contact their government by courier or post.[5] Far greater difficulties were encountered by Alexander Lototsky, the Directory's envoy in Constantinople. That city was governed by Allied high commissioners and was a military and political center for the anti-Ukrainian Volunteer Army. Lototsky arrived in the Turkish capital late in April after a tedious journey by way of Vienna, Trieste, and Venice.

After several weeks of letter-writing, Lototsky made the Turkish foreign ministry aware of his presence but never succeeded in obtaining recognition and an audience with the sultan. General Agapiev and other of Denikin's agents accused the mission of having ties with Bolsheviks, Germans, and Mustapha Kemal. These accusations led to a raid on the Ukrainian mission made by Allied police on

[5] Alexander Lototsky, *V Tsarhorodi* (Warsaw, 1939), pp. 121f.

September 25, 1919. The mission's funds were frozen, papers seized, and the building padlocked; in the correspondence regarding the matter the mission was referred to as "persons describing themselves as members of the 'Ukrainian legation.' "[6] Lototsky established an office in a hotel room and did not regain possession of the legation until November 8, after the charges brought by Denikin's agents were found to be false. Four months later he left for Ukraine in order to tender his resignation in person.

The Ukrainian mission in Athens, headed by Fedir P. Matushevsky, had somewhat less difficulty but was not more successful than that in Constantinople. After a circuitous five-week journey through Central Europe, the mission arrived in Athens on March 3, 1919. Matushevsky lost no time in calling on the Greek foreign minister, Alexander Diomides, with whom he discussed Ukrainian-Greek relations during the seventh century; Diomides read the letter of credence but refused to make any statement until the Ukrainian question was decided at the Paris Peace Conference. This did not mean that the Ukrainians were denied the hospitality of the country although on one occasion they escaped arrest only by reminding the policeman that there were 400,000 Greeks in Ukraine.

Matushevsky learned of events in Ukraine by reading garbled reports in week-old London and Paris newspapers. Accused by the former Russian ambassador, Prince Demidov, of being a Bolshevik, Matushevsky paid a visit to the Orthodox Metropolitan Archbishop of Athens in an effort to demonstrate the falsity of the charge. Hoping to obtain financial and material support from the United States and recognition of Ukrainian independence, he called on Garrett Droppers, American minister to Greece and formerly professor of economics at Williams College. While expressing sympathy for the Ukrainian cause, the American minister informed him that such policy was not made at that level. Although the English and Rumanian envoys were willing to converse with Matushevsky they did so only

6 *Ibid.*, p 171.

after reminding him that they were acting unofficially.[7] There was little that could be accomplished in Greece or elsewhere since the important diplomatic decisions were being made in Paris.

It was at the Paris Peace Conference that the Ukrainians had the greatest opportunity to win recognition and support from foreign powers. The delegation there was headed by Gregory Sidorenko and included Alexander Shulgin and Arnold Margolin; Professor Serhi Shelukhin served as legal adviser. The Galicians, there as elsewhere, had their own representatives; Dr. Vasil Paneyko, besides heading the Galician delegation, was vice president of the whole Ukrainian mission and was aided by Dr. Michael Lozynsky and Colonel Dmitro Vitovsky. Sidorenko bombarded the conference with letters requesting recognition and declaring Ukraine to be "an independent and sovereign state." On February 12, a note was sent to the conference accusing the Bolsheviks of desiring "to pass over the corpse of independent Ukraine in order to obtain control of the Dardanelles, the Suez Canal, and the Persian Gulf." Ukraine was depicted as a bulwark against Bolshevism and as the means of preventing Russia and Germany from directing their forces against Western Europe. These notes had no effect, and by April Sidorenko was hoping to entice the Allies by promising that Ukraine would assume her share of the Imperial Russian debt. Despite these persistent efforts Ukraine was not officially represented at Paris although delegates from Guatemala, Hedjaz, and Siam were accorded recognition.

The Ukrainian delegation was at a disadvantage because the conference never came to grips with the Russian question. This was due in large part to the conflicting reports which emanated from that country and to the innumerable spokesmen who claimed to represent it. Nor were the statesmen of the Great Powers in agreement regarding a solution. Clemenceau was unequivocally anti-Bolshevik and

7 See F. P. Matushevsky, "Iz Shchodennika Ukrainskoho Posla," *Z Minuloho*, ed. by Roman Smal-Stocki (Warsaw, 1938), pp. 138ff.

did not wish to see the border peoples represented while Wilson and Lloyd George were willing to examine all aspects of the Russian problem. As a result "decisions" were made on a segmental and piecemeal basis and only when a situation assumed the proportions of a crisis. Thus the conference never resolved the problem which was posed by the existence of the Directory, but it was compelled to give repeated attention to one aspect of the Ukrainian question: the disposition of Eastern Galicia. The Powers could not ignore events in that region because of the role played there by the new Poland.

Independence had been promised the Poles by President Wilson in his Fourteen Points, and a Polish National Committee had been established in Paris under the presidency of Roman Dmowski. Initially, this body defended Polish interests at the Peace Conference, and on November 13, 1918, while the Ukrainians were still holding Lviv, it protested West Ukrainian independence and claimed that the Galician forces were largely German. It employed the historical argument pointing out that Eastern Galicia had been a part of Poland since the fourteenth century and alleged that the Ukrainian movement was a German scheme to wrest the territory from Polish rule.[8] During December Dr. Eugene Petrushevich, president of the Ukrainian People's Council, appealed to the Allies in the name of the principle of national self-determination, requesting them to compel the Poles to evacuate Eastern Galicia.

To the Western European and American statesmen and diplomats who had gathered in Paris, Ukraine was but a vague region in that vast political vacuum which was Russia. Sweeping conclusions were often arrived at on the basis of fragmentary evidence. Such was the case on January 16 when Lloyd George, at a meeting of the Big Five, referred to Petliura as an adventurer and stated that Ukraine was not the anti-Bolshevik stronghold that some

[8] *Papers Relating to the Foreign Relations of the United States, the Paris Peace Conference, 1919* (Washington, 1942-1947), II, pp. 411f. Hereafter referred to as *U.S., Paris Peace Conference.*

had imagined it to be.[9] Five days later the Big Five, at Clemenceau's request, heard Harald R. de Scavenius, Danish minister to Russia, declare that Petliura was supported largely by Bolshevik troops; the minister was aware of the fact that landowners had been expelled in Ukraine and immediately assumed that anyone capable of condoning such a crime was, ipso facto, a Bolshevik.[10] With such opinions prevalent in the council room of the Big Five, the union of East and West Ukraine appears in retrospect to have been less desirable than the arguments of the nationalist polemicists made it out to be.

Although the conference was plagued with many thorny issues, it was able to attempt to initiate a settlement in Eastern Galicia during February, when it sent to Lviv a mission headed by General Barthélemy and composed of English, French, Italian, and American members. At that time the Ukrainians held most of the region, but the Poles held the rail line between Lviv and Peremyshl (Przemysl) and in this way were able to supply their forces in the capital and, by dint of great effort, prevent its recapture by the Ukrainians. The Commission met with both Polish and Ukrainian representatives in an attempt to arrange a suspension of hostilities. Fighting ceased on February 25, but soon a deadlock developed; the Ukrainians expressed a willingness to agree to the San River frontier if the Poles withdrew from the Lviv-Peremyshl bulge, and the Poles countered with a demand for the Zbruch River frontier, which lay 160 miles to the east of the San.

The Barthélemy Commission proposed a solution on February 28 and called for temporary Ukrainian sacrifices until the frontier could be delimited at Paris. According to a member of the Ukrainian delegation in Lviv, Dr. Michael Lozynsky, the French representative on the commission, warned the Ukrainians that their military advantage could disappear quickly once General Haller's Polish army arrived from France. The agreement drawn up by the commission was to be purely military and was

[9] *Ibid.*, III, pp. 581f.   [10] *Ibid.*, III, p. 640.

to be terminated when the Polish-Ukrainian frontier was determined. However, the Ukrainians rejected the proposed agreement, and the Allied Commission in Lviv warned that it would hold them responsible for the resumption of hostilities. The commission left Lviv, and on March 4 the West Ukrainian Government in Stanislaviv sent a radio-telegram to the Allied Powers, protesting the proposed armistice line because it allowed the Poles to hold half of the ethnically Ukrainian territory in Galicia including the Drohobich-Borislav oil fields.[11] The Stanislaviv Government charged the commission with being pro-Polish and requested that a new impartial body be appointed.

Hostilities were resumed during the first week in March, and the Ukrainians took some of the Polish positions along the Lviv-Peremyshl rail line. Dr. Vasil Paneyko sent a note of protest to the Peace Conference from Bern on March 13; he accused the commission of being haughty towards the Ukrainians and complained that his government was not able to employ its army against the Bolsheviks as long as they had to defend the western frontier. Four days later the Big Five heard Marshal Foch report on the situation in Poland; he stated that Poland was menaced by the Bolsheviks, Germans, and Ukrainians and warned that the fall of Lemberg (Lviv) would mean the end of the Polish State. The Marshal went so far as to advocate the use of Rumanian forces in support of the Polish claim to Lviv, but Lloyd George expressed the opinion that such a proposal would lead to the establishment of a huge and costly army for the invasion of Russia. The British prime minister was concerned with the problem of financing such a venture and argued that the Marshal's proposal would simply destroy Petliura who, he was now convinced, was fighting the Bolsheviks. Nor would he admit that Poland had a right to Lviv.[12]

The Ukrainian military successes in Galicia caused some

[11] For the text of the proposed armistice agreement see Michael Lozynsky, *Halichina v rokakh 1918-1920* (Vienna, 1922), pp. 79f.

[12] *U.S., Paris Peace Conference, op.cit.,* IV, pp. 379ff.

uneasiness in Paris. Upon the advice of Dr. (later Reverend) Robert H. Lord, a professor of history at Harvard University who was with the American delegation, the Big Five agreed on March 19 to have the conference ask both belligerents to suspend hostilities. It was hoped that such a request would be heeded more readily than one from the Inter-Allied Commission in Warsaw since the conference supposedly possessed greater moral authority. Dr. Lord, an expert on Poland and Russia, was apprehensive regarding the fate of Lviv and feared that the Ukrainians would surround the city.[13] In an effort to preserve the military status quo, the conference sent notes to General Omelianovich-Pavlenko, commanding general of the Ukrainian Galician army, and to the Polish commander in Lviv, requesting that fighting cease; the two armies were to retain their positions on the condition that the Allied Supreme Council would take up the problem and hear both sides. Although the Ukrainians possessed the military advantage at the time, they readily accepted the offer on March 22, even though it committed them to allow the Peremyshl-Lviv rail line to remain in Polish hands. Their motive in accepting such an unfavorable arrangement was their conviction that a fair hearing could be obained in Paris.

The French, fearing a German revival, were desirous of having as strong a Polish ally as possible. This was evident on March 19, when Arthur Balfour questioned how the Ukrainians could be invading Poland while their country was being overrun by the Bolsheviks; Foch ventured to say

[13] *Ibid*, IV, pp. 405ff. Professor Lord, while recognizing that the "Ruthenians" constituted fifty-nine per cent of the total population of Eastern Galicia, was convinced that the division between Russophiles and Ukrainian nationalists which existed at the time and the high proportion of peasants made them incapable of governing themselves. He alleged that the West Ukrainian Republic was "a sorry failure." In 1921, following the consolidation of Polish control over Eastern Galicia, Dr. Lord received an honorary doctorate from the University of Lviv and also became a member of the Polish Academy of Sciences. Cf. *Some Problems of the Peace Conference* (Cambridge, 1920), of which Professor Lord was co-author and in which he defended the Polish seizure of Eastern Galicia (pp. 189ff.).

that it might be assumed that the Ukrainians could be in agreement with the Bolsheviks. Lloyd George, however, doubted that the Ukrainians were aggressors and observed that those who were attacking Lviv could be fighting for national independence. At the time the British prime minister was under the impression that the French were supporting the Ukrainians in occupied Odessa and asked why they shouldn't be aided in Galicia. He correctly suspected that the Poles were demanding far more territory than they had any right to claim on an ethnographic basis and asked that the conference be impartial. The Poles, fired by a nationalism which was more highly developed than that of the Ukrainians and relatively certain of French support, demanded that the February 28 armistice recommendations made by the Allied Commission in Lviv serve as a basis for future discussion. The Ukrainians soon became convinced that the Poles were utilizing the period of inactivity at the front for the purpose of preparing an offensive. By the end of April the Poles, aided by General Haller's newly-arrived army, were able to launch a successful offensive and remove the Ukrainian threat to Lviv.

The next effort to negotiate an armistice between the Poles and Ukrainians was undertaken by a special Inter-Allied Commission which sat in Paris and was presided over by General Louis Botha; it heard the Ukrainian delegation at the Peace Conference on four occasions during the latter part of April and the first two weeks in May. The commission was especially interested in the Polish charge that there were German officers in the Galician army; the Ukrainian delegation admitted that a shortage of officer material had caused the command to utilize some Czechs, Croatians, Rumanians, and Austrians as officers, but it denied that Germans were being used. On May 12, the Botha Commission proposed a conditional armistice line which would have given the Ukrainians the Drohobich-Borislav oil fields and limited the Polish and Ukrainian forces in East Galicia to twenty thousand men each. The Poles rejected this offer because it gave them only a third

of the region, and the Allied Supreme Council in Paris
did nothing to compel them to accept it. The Poles responded by launching a general offensive on May 14, on
the pretext that the Ukrainians were preparing one.

The Ukrainian delegation in Paris sent a note to the
president of the Peace Conference on the morning of May
21, asking if the Allied Powers possessed the will and the
strength to halt the Polish offensive. The note contained
a veiled threat in the statement that the delegation would
regard its further presence in Paris as useless if it could
not obtain real and effective support from the Allies.[14]
Late in the afternoon of the same day the delegation obtained an audience with the Big Four and the Botha Commission. Sidorenko, the head of the delegation, denounced
the Poles but characterized the Bolsheviks as Ukraine's
worst enemies. In discussing relations with Poland, Lloyd
George asked Paneyko if the Ukrainian and Polish languages were substantially different. When Sidorenko categorically rejected the possibility of union with Poland,
Paneyko assured Lloyd George that if the war with the
Poles were halted the Ukrainian forces would be used
against the Bolsheviks. Paneyko also requested officers and
supplies from the Allies, and on that uncertain note the
audience was brought to an end.[15]

On the following day, all of the Ukrainian delegates, including Margolin, had an audience with Clemenceau, who
informed them that the Supreme Council was awaiting an
explanation from Pilsudski regarding the military situation
in Galicia. When asked by Alexander Shulgin to recognize
the Directory, Clemenceau declared that Petliura was "almost a Bolshevik." After this meeting it became obvious
that the Supreme Council was not able or willing to curb
the Poles. In Paris there was a great deal of fear that if the
government headed by Paderewski were to collapse Poland
would turn to Bolshevism. Yet General Botha recognized

---

[14] Lozynsky, *op.cit.*, pp. 134f.

[15] *U.S., Paris Peace Conference*, *op cit.*, v, pp. 775ff. Cf. Lozynsky, *op.cit.*,
pp. 135ff.

that the Ukrainians had been dealt with unjustly, and Lloyd George also understood that the Poles were utilizing the bogey of Bolshevism as a cloak for their imperialist aims. Wilson suspected the French military of attempting to erect a *cordon sanitaire,* and Botha believed that the consistent absence of the French representative on the armistice commission was deliberate and was designed to sabotage the work of that body.[16] Although Wilson and Lloyd George prevailed upon Clemenceau on May 27 to send a second note to Pilsudski, admonishing him not to predetermine the boundary by the use of force, the conference was for all practical purposes impotent.

On the following day the conference learned that the Poles had taken Striy (Stryj) and were moving on Stanislaviv; concerned over this use of force, it summoned Premier Ignace Paderewski for an explanation but did not hear him until June 5. In the interim the Poles advanced rapidly eastward while the West Ukrainians were presented by the Rumanians with a twenty-four-hour ultimatum demanding that they evacuate the southern part of their territory, including Kolomeia and Stanislaviv. The purpose of this demand was to obtain control of the Kolomeia —Marmarosh-Sighet rail line as part of the military campaign which Rumania was waging for the purpose of liquidating the Communist regime of Bela Kun in Hungary. The Galicians abandoned Stanislaviv, their temporary capital, on May 26, and retreated to Chortkiv, which became the new seat of government.

Prior to this an attempt had been made by Vinnichenko to save East Galicia from becoming a victim of imperialism by forging a united front of soviet republics extending from Russia to Hungary. The Communist government of Hungary, headed by Bela Kun, was aware of the fact that its future existence depended upon the Bolsheviks' crossing the Carpathians. The Directory's envoy in Budapest, Nicholas Halahan, wished to end the war between his government and Soviet Russia; he believed that he could

[16] *U.S., Paris Peace Conference,* VI, pp. 61f.

utilize the Hungarian Communists to this end by advising them to convince Moscow that its aid would never reach Budapest in time unless an accord were concluded with the Directory. Bela Kun was sufficiently interested in this proposal to send a special railroad car to Vienna for the purpose of bringing Vinnichenko to Budapest on March 31. The former premier and head of the Directory laid down a series of conditions which included full recognition of Ukrainian independence and sovereignty within the ethnographic frontiers, including East Galicia and Lviv, and the establishment of a military union of socialist republics each with equal rights. Vinnichenko insisted that the armies of any soviet republic in the projected union could remain on the territory of another soviet republic only with the consent of the latter; he proposed as a government for Ukraine a coalition of independent Social Democrats, left Social Revolutionaries and Communists. Each of the soviet republics was to agree to render all necessary material aid to any other member-republic defending its territory against imperialist aggression and especially against the Entente Powers, Poland, and Rumania.[17]

These conditions for a Russo-Ukrainian peace were relayed to Moscow by Bela Kun's government. Vinnichenko waited in Budapest for one week, and when no reply arrived he returned to Vienna. The Russian answer came later in the form of a reply from the Ukrainian Soviet foreign minister, Christian Rakovsky, who branded Vinnichenko as a typical representative of petit bourgeois ideology. The Hungarian Communists were unable to comprehend this response since they were collaborating with non-Communist Social Democrats. The former Ukrainian premier later commented that if his plan had been accepted and a common soviet front established, the regime of Bela Kun would never have been overthrown and the soviet government of Bavaria would have been saved.

[17] Vinnichenko, *op.cit.*, III, pp. 321ff. Cf. Halahan, *op.cit.*, IV, pp. 173ff.

However, such a proposal would not have received the support of Petliura, but its importance lay in its indication of the extent of Vinnichenko's flirtation with the Bolsheviks. In April, when the proposal was made, Petliura was retreating and the Bolsheviks advancing, but during May some of the Ukrainian Social Democrats and Social Revolutionaries, led by George Mazurenko, initiated armed uprisings in occupied Ukraine. Although the insurrection was not well organized, it did reflect peasant dissatisfaction with Bolshevik rule, and, when combined with the drive on Moscow launched by Denikin from the southeast, provided a serious threat to Lenin's government. During May the situation became so serious that Trotsky, Kamenev, and Joffe were ordered to Ukraine by the Central Committee of the Russian Communist party, and the separate Ukrainian front was absorbed into the military command of the Russian Soviet Republic. The resultant weakening of the Bolshevik position in Ukraine enabled Petliura to terminate his "exile" in Galicia and recross the Zbruch, taking Kamianets-Podilsk on June 4.

At this point Petliura's leadership was challenged by Colonel Peter Bolbochan, who had led the rising against the Hetmanate in the Kharkiv region. This commander had been approached as early as January 1919 by some of the leaders of the Democratic Agrarian party who appealed to him to aid them in preventing the establishment of a socialist government. Petliura acted swiftly and had Bolbochan arrested but relented somewhat and ordered him to Stanislaviv. Bolbochan remained in East Galicia until the eastward offensive commenced late in May. On June 9, he was arrested for having engaged in agitation among officers and for planning a coup. Two weeks later he was executed in Chorni Ostriv.

This was government by crisis, and that of West Ukraine was not an exception. There the military situation became so serious as the Poles advanced eastward that it became necessary to make Dr. Eugene Petrushevich dictator. The president of the Ukrainian People's Council of Eastern

Galicia was granted dictatorial powers by means of the following legal instrument[18] adopted on June 9:

"In view of the seriousness of the moment and the danger which is threatening the Fatherland, the presidium of the Committee of the Ukrainian People's Council of the Western Territory of the Ukrainian People's Republic and the State Secretariat, for the purpose of strengthening and consolidating state authority, have decided to grant to a fully empowered dictator the right to exercise all military and civil authority which has been exercised on a constitutional basis by the Committee of the Ukrainian People's Council and by the State Secretariat."

One of the Dictator's first acts was to remove General Omelianovich-Pavlenko from the command of the army and appoint in his place General Michael Grekov.

The change in command did not retard the Polish offensive. Paderewski, appearing before the Big Five on June 5, claimed that the Galicians were not real Ukrainians but were under the influence of Germany. Accusing the Ukrainians of having violated the suspension of hostilities on May 12, the pianist-premier also admitted that Poland wished to annex all of East Galicia. Lloyd George rebuked him for desiring national minorities and termed the Poles imperialists, observing that they should be content with a homogeneous population of twenty million.[19] Only Wilson was willing to agree with the Welshman in taking measures against Poland; in mid-May he even favored asking the Poles to withdraw from the Peace Conference unless they ceased their military operations on the Ukrainian front. On June 12, he joined Lloyd George in advocating a plebiscite for the territory, but it was decided to refer the matter to the Council of Foreign Ministers for further study and consultation with experts.

When that body took up the Galician question on June 18, Robert Lansing, the American secretary of state, stated that sixty per cent of the Ruthenian (Ukrainian) popula-

18 Lozynsky, *op.cit.*, p. 107.
19 *U.S., Paris Peace Conference, op.cit.*, VI, pp. 194ff.

tion of East Galicia was illiterate and unfit for self-government. He also reported that the Ukrainian regime was one of "force and brutality." Lansing joined Arthur Balfour of Britain in proposing that the League of Nations select a high commissioner for East Galicia and that the Poles be allowed to occupy the territory to the Zbruch River temporarily, pending a plebiscite. The high commissioner was to supervise the occupation and determine when the needs of common defense were such as to terminate it. This proposal was an attempt to mitigate the harshness of the fait accompli with which the Poles had confronted the conference in occupying the territory without its consent. The Poles had defenders in Baron Sonnino of Italy and in M. Jules Cambon, the president of the Conference's Commission on Polish Affairs. The latter stated that Polish control of the region was necessary since the Poles were the only neighbors possessing a high civilization; he contended that East Galicia could not be ceded to Ukraine because no one knew what Ukraine was or would be since its governments "behaved atrociously" and were untrustworthy.[20]

The original proposal made by Lansing and Balfour regarding the appointment of a high commissioner was soon under attack by Sonnino, Pichon, and Cambon. They wished to settle the matter once and for all in favor of the Poles, giving them a mandate which would provide autonomy for the Ukrainians. Balfour was dubious, but Lansing naïvely thought that the Ukrainians might be friendly to the Poles. This was a decisive meeting because the United States and Britain compromised themselves in discarding their original proposal for a high commissioner although Balfour requested that the Poles be given to understand that their occupation was not to prejudice the future status of the territory. The matter was reconsidered by the foreign ministers on June 25, apparently because the proposal for appointment of a high commissioner was still being pressed. Cambon, in an effort to quiet British fears, stated that sooner or later a plebiscite would be held, but the

[20] *Ibid.*, iv, pp. 828ff.

Marquis Imperiali, substituting for Sonnino, believed that the Powers should not commit themselves to a plebiscite. Sir Eyre Crowe, attending in the absence of Balfour, renewed the British proposal for a League of Nations high commissioner. Cambon proposed the appointment of a Polish commissioner to supervise the occupation, but Balfour, upon arriving, opposed this on the grounds that it would constitute recognition of the Polish claim to the territory. Yet Balfour and Lansing retreated as they had a week earlier after Pichon and the Marquis Imperiali assured them that there was no real hostility between Poles and Ukrainians. The Italian proposal for rejection of the plebiscite was opposed by Lansing; this meant that the Powers were at least paying lip service to ultimate self-determination.[21]

This decision confirming the occupation of East Galicia was embodied in the following note[22] which the Big Four sent to Warsaw on June 25:

"With a view to protecting the persons and property of the peaceful population of Eastern Galicia against the dangers to which they are exposed by the Bolshevist bands [sic], the Supreme Council of the Allied and Associated Powers decided to authorize the forces of the Polish Republic to pursue their operations as far as the river Zbruch [which separates Galicia from East Ukraine].

"This authorization does not, in any way, affect the decisions to be taken later by the Supreme Council for the settlement of the political status of Galicia."

The West Ukrainian Government did not learn of this note until July 11, shortly before its expulsion from the territory. On July 2, the Ukrainian delegation in Paris protested this authorization and declared that it was not based on right and justice. The delegation stated that the Ukrainians had had faith in the Allies, hoping that they would protect their right to national self-determination. It resented having the anti-Bolshevism of its government impugned by the Poles and accused the Supreme Council

---

[21] *Ibid.*, IV, pp. 850ff.   [22] *Ibid.*, VI, p. 677, n. 4.

of "delivering the Ukrainian people into the hands of its historic enemy and condemning the Ukrainian land to Polonization." A similar protest was made on July 13 by a number of deputies of the Ukrainian People's Council meeting in Vienna; they stated that the area between the San and Zbruch rivers was Ukrainian ethnically and historically and demanded that Polish forces be ordered to withdraw to the San.

These protests were ignored and were followed on July 11 by a note from the Secretary General of the Peace Conference informing the Ukrainian delegation that the Supreme Council had empowered Poland to establish a civil government in East Galicia. This was to be done only after the Poles had an agreement with the Allied and Associated Powers providing for as much autonomy as possible, together with political, religious, and personal liberties. The powers promised that the inhabitants of the region would exercise their right of self-determination after the expiration of a period of time, the length of which was to be determined at a later date. The Ukrainians protested in vain that it would be impossible to exercise this right while under Polish domination, but, as is usually the case, the side with the largest number of most effective divisions prevailed.

The Galician army had no recourse but to abandon its territory and retire across the Zbruch River. This operation, which began on July 16 and lasted three days, involved the movement of 100,000 troops into East Ukraine, but only 40,000 of these were available for combat duty. During the preceding six weeks Petliura had held a narrow but slowly expanding strip of territory along the east bank of the Zbruch, but he was unable to hold Proskuriv against the counter-attack of the Red Army which was launched early in July. At the time of the crossing, the Ukrainian Soviet Government appealed to Dictator Petrushevich to break with Petliura and join it in resisting Poland and Rumania, but he declined this offer because he believed that the Allies would ultimately comprehend the Ukrainian point of view regarding Galicia. The decision to join Petliura was a difficult one to make since he was without French support; this caused many Galician politicians to consider placing themselves under the protection of the Allies by crossing into Rumania instead. Petliura probably benefited more from their decision to cast their lot with him than they did. As a result of the crossing his decimated army was reinforced with 40,000 men who were eager to join in the march on Kiev in the hope that it would lead to the reconquest of Lviv.

The Ukrainian advance on Kiev from the east was cramped by Denikin's offensive, which brought him to Kharkiv in mid-June. This caused considerable consternation in the Ukrainian camp because Admiral Kolchak, who was recognized by Denikin, had received the full support of the Allies. In an effort to improve Petliura's position with the Allies, Arnold Margolin and Dr. Vasil Paneyko had obtained a futile audience in Paris with American Secretary of State Lansing on June 30. While Paneyko expressed the hope that the Polish occupation of Galicia would be temporary, Margolin asked for moral, technical, and economic assistance. He protested the Allied tendency to regard Kolchak and Denikin as spokesmen for the whole of Russia. Margolin argued that Ukraine should be recognized but readily admitted that the territorial governments would federate in the future if they were granted provisional recognition. In the hope of obtaining such recognition and aid he promised concessions to American capitalists and assured Lansing that they would receive consideration ahead of the French in this matter. Lansing was not impressed and stated categorically that the United States did not favor Ukrainian independence although it regarded a certain degree of autonomy as desirable. He made it clear that Petliura could receive aid only if he came to terms with Kolchak and Denikin.[28]

[28] *Ibid.*, xi, pp. 253ff. Cf. Margolin, *Ukraina i Politika Antanty*, p. 161. The American position, as stated by Lansing, is in contrast to a report which Major Lawrence Martin of the General Staff of the U S. Army made

An additional problem confronting the Ukrainian effort to regain control of the whole Right Bank of the Dnieper arose when some of the military commanders, especially the Galicians, wished to advance on Odessa and Kherson rather than on Kiev. Their reason for wanting to take the Black Sea port was to obtain a "window" for contact with the outside world and facilitate the procurement of military supplies from abroad. The Galicians were not eager to clash with Denikin and believed that the limited number of Ukrainian troops could be used most effectively in a southward march which would encounter only light resistance. But Petliura and the East Ukrainians could not bear the thought of having Denikin take Kiev while their forces would be marching on the cosmopolitan port city of Odessa, which was alien to the national movement. They won out because the psychological value of taking Kiev proved to be such an overwhelming attraction.

The Ukrainian march on Kiev was aided by Denikin's northward advance as well as by peasant dissatisfaction with the Bolshevik occupation which had been marked by requisitioning and other excesses. On August 30, the Ukrainian troops entered Kiev and were instructed by Petliura to avoid clashing with Denikin's forces which were preparing to enter the city from the the east. On the following morning they obtained access to the capital by means of an unguarded bridge crossing the Dnieper. Reluctantly, the Galician troops consented to share the city, and soon the Russian and Ukrainian flags were flying from the city hall. This apparent cordiality was interrupted when a Ukrainian officer hauled down the Russian flag and threw it under the hooves of Otaman Salsky's horse as the latter was leading a column of troops into the city.

---

in mid-May after having traveled through East Galicia and Volynia He termed the Directory Government competent and effectual and remarked that the differences between Russians and Ukrainians were distinct enough to make independence desirable. This report was forwarded from Paris to Washington in June but with a note that it should be read with reserve since Martin's information was supposedly limited.

Russians in the crowd protested, and soon Volunteer Army troops arrived on the scene and commenced firing. General Nicholas Bredov, Denikin's commander in Kiev, then ordered the Ukrainians to withdraw their troops to Fastiv, and in the face of superior force they had no choice but to comply.

Prior to this incident Petliura had hoped to obtain diplomatic recognition from the Western European countries by reshuffling his cabinet. In mid-August Isaac Mazepa became premier and minister of the interior while Boris Martos, his predecessor, assumed the finance portfolio. This change proved to be as ineffective as the simultaneous removal of Gregory Sidorenko from the presidency of the Ukrainian delegation in Paris. During July much dissatisfaction arose among the members of the delegation who regarded Sidorenko as incompetent in the diplomatic field although they were prepared to accept him as a qualified engineer. Upon the recommendation of Alexander Shulgin it was decided to appoint Count Michael Tyshkevich, a Kievan landowner and Ukrainian envoy to the Vatican, as the president of the delegation in Paris. The new head of the delegation was unable to accomplish any more than Sidorenko had.

The French foreign office was under the influence of the Russian diplomats V. A. Maklakov and Sazonov, who were opposed to the dismemberment of Russia. American policy towards Ukraine was stated with finality on October 29, in the following letter sent by Lansing to the American delegation at Paris:

"On the basis of past investigations the Department is disposed to regard the Ukrainian separatist movement as largely the result of Austrian and German propaganda seeking the disruption of Russia. It is unable to perceive an adequate ethnical basis for erecting a separate state and is not convinced that there is a real popular demand for anything more than such greater measure of local autonomy as will naturally result from the establishment in Russia of a modern democratic government whether federative or not. The Department feels, accordingly, that the policy of the United States, while leaving to future events the determination of the exact character of the relations to exist between Great and Little Russia, should tend in the meantime, rather to sustain the principle of essential Russian unity than to encourage separatism."[24]

Less than two weeks prior to this Frank L. Polk, American plenipotentiary at Paris, wrote to Lansing complaining of the flood of propaganda which had been emanating from the unrecognized Ukrainian mission. The United States Army's official observer in Ukraine, Brigadier General Edgar Jadwin, reported in September that Petliura had attacked Denikin and in that way was aiding the Bolsheviks. An attempt by Ukrainian agents in Paris to contract with the United States Liquidation Commission for the purchase of more than eleven million dollars worth of war surplus goods ended in failure when the State Department ordered the agreement annulled.

By October the lack of supplies together with the spread of typhus reduced the fighting capacity of the Galician Army to four thousand men and that of Petliura to half that number. The Galicians, barefoot, ragged, hungry, cold, and immobilized by disease, were not at home in East Ukraine and saw no purpose in continuing to oppose Denikin's forces. On October 24, one Galician officer recorded in his diary: "It is difficult for us to fight with the Denikinites. They are a valiant and well-trained army and we are decimated by typhus and miserably defeated."[25] During the long, sleepless, windy autumn nights the men comprehended the inevitability of an understanding with Denikin although they were still aware of his desire to restore a united and indivisible Russia.

As early as October 20, General Myron Tarnavsky, commander of the Galician Army since July, appealed to Dictator Petrushevich to send an armistice mission to Denikin.

[24] *Foreign Relations of the United States, 1919, Russia* (Washington, 1937), pp. 783f.
[25] *Mizh Molotom i Kovalom* (Lviv, 1923), p. 9.

When the Dictator forbade all thought of negotiation, the General, who felt the military pressure at the front, acted arbitrarily and sent such a mission, headed by Otaman Emil Lisniak. The mission was instructed to negotiate for the exchange of prisoners of war and to learn on what terms Denikin would be willing to conclude an armistice with *all* of the Ukrainian Army. The delegation, acting in complete secrecy, contacted General Slashchov of the Volunteer Army on November 1, after having crossed the front lines on the previous day. The Galicians were told that Denikin was ready to negotiate with them at any time because they were an extra-territorial army, but he was unwilling to deal with the Directory's army, which he regarded as a group of Russian traitors. Lisniak asked that the Galician Army retain its autonomy, be withdrawn from combat duty for several months, and not be used against any other Ukrainian units; he also requested that the Dictatorship act as the sole representative of East Galicia. Denikin was willing to agree to these conditions in principle, but Tarnavsky hesitated to take the final step.

He believed that it was possible to obtain official consent for such a treaty and waited until November 4, when a meeting of the leading political figures was held in Zhmerinka. Tarnavsky did not attend, but he informed Petliura, Petrushevich, Makarenko, Mazepa, and the other participants that he would take matters into his own hands if the meeting did not lead to positive results. At Zhmerinka everyone complained of the lack of supplies, clothing, and footgear, but no decision was arrived at regarding policy. However, Petrushevich assured everyone that the Galician Army would do nothing without first consulting the government and the High Command. On the following day the Dictator ordered the removal of General Tarnavsky and his chief of staff, Colonel Shamanek, but at the same time the General sent a plenipotentiary mission to the Volunteer Army.

On November 6, at Ziatkivtsi, a railroad junction west of Uman, a preliminary treaty was signed by which the

Galician Army agreed to "place itself [and its equipment and rolling stock] at the disposal of the Supreme Commander of the armed forces of South Russia." The army was not to be employed against the troops of Petliura, and the Galician Government was to suspend its activities temporarily because of a lack of territory. Thus the Galicians submitted to one of the most pronounced enemies of Ukrainian independence, but it cannot be said that they betrayed the ideal of Ukrainian statehood because the treaty was based on sheer physical survival and was the sole means available for the attainment of that immediate end. This decision was a difficult one to make since it made it possible for the already defeated East Ukrainians to regard the Galician Army as a scapegoat. As soon as news of the negotiations and the treaty leaked out in Kamianets the East Ukrainians accused the Galicians of treason and some even charged Petrushevich with treachery. Tarnavsky, Lisniak, and the others who negotiated with Denikin were arrested on November 9, and were acquitted a few days later.

The final Galician-Russian treaty was signed in Odessa on November 17, and was ratified within forty-eight hours.[26] It was similar to the November 6 agreement and was not precise in defining the Galician Army's political status, which was dealt with in the following clause:

"The political questions regarding the mutual relations between the Galician government and the government of the Volunteer Army and also the future fate of Galicia are not under consideration and await the decision of political negotiations. Pending the settlement of these questions, General Denikin upholds the right of the Dictator of Galicia to direct and control the internal life of the Galician Army."

However, Petrushevich did not choose to avail himself of Denikin's magnanimity and, instead, left Kamianets on November 16 for Rumania. From there he went to Vienna, where he continued to pursue the cause of Galician inde-

[26] For the text of the treaty see Lozynsky, *op.cit.*, pp. 198f.

pendence. On the following day Polish troops entered the temporary Ukrainian capital, and Petliura fled to Volynia, where he finally decided to seek refuge in Poland.

The break between the two Ukrainian governments, which was consummated in November, had its origin in significant differences which existed between Galicia and East Ukraine. In 1919 the Galician Ukrainian was still incapable of understanding the socialist-patriot of Kiev who did not wish to fight the workers of another nation but only the bourgeoisie. Galicia had not experienced the Russian Revolution, and the struggle which Petrushevich was leading was purely national rather than socio-economic as was the case in the east. Conversely, the Eastern Ukrainian Social Democrat found it a simple matter to hurl the epithet of "bourgeois" at the Galicians and accuse them of being priest-ridden. Relations between the Galician Secretariat and the Martos cabinet were not good from the very beginning when some of the members of the former accused Petliura and other Social Democrats of being Bolsheviks. Although there was but one Ukrainian Republic after January 22, the agrarian legislation which had been adopted by the Congress of Toilers did not apply to East Galicia because the law did not provide for the compensation of former owners, and it was thought that such radicialism would alienate the Allies. When Mikita Shapoval, the author of this legislation, became convinced that Petliura was betraying his social and economic program he retired to Galicia in February; there he agitated against the bourgeoisie and was jailed briefly for Bolshevik agitation but was released on the condition that he go into exile.

In addition to this disagreement over social and economic issues, there was a marked disparity in the development of the national movement in the two parts of Ukraine. There were also significant cultural differences between East and West Ukraine, and the percentage of persons holding doctorates was greater in Galicia than in Russian Ukraine. One Galician who was in East Ukraine

291

in 1919 observed that the two Ukrainian peoples had a different psyche, and, although Galicia was to be the Piedmont of the national movement, it can be said that at this time Galician provincialism proved to be a stronger force than Ukrainian nationalism. One of the most important sources of this cleavage between provincialism and nationalism lay in the religious differences which existed between the Orthodox Eastern Ukraine and the Uniate Western Ukraine. The essentials of ritual in the two Churches were identical because the Uniates retained the Byzantine-Slavonic liturgy of St. John Chrysostom, but there were differences with respect to several important doctrinal matters. The Uniates accepted the supremacy and infallibility of the papacy, a belief which was repugnant to the Orthodox; they also incorporated the doctrine of the *filioque* into their Creed, believing that the Holy Spirit proceeded from the Father and the Son and not merely from the Father, as in the case of the Orthodox Church. Unlike the Latin rite Catholics, the Uniates traditionally employed the Julian Calendar and enjoyed a married clergy as well as the privilege for the laity to partake of the Sacred Host in two forms rather than in the form of a wafer.

Thus in appearance the two Churches were not very dissimilar, but the question of the recognition of the papacy was of great significance, and it was the most important single factor in the cleavage. Historically speaking, the Uniate Church was young, having been established at the end of the sixteenth century as a phase of the Counter-Reformation. Its establishment was made possible by the fact that the Western Ukrainians had been under Polish rule since the fourteenth century and desired to obtain equality with the Roman Catholics.[27] Yet this Church,

27 For a brief account of the historical background of the Uniate Church. see J. Mirtshuk, "The Ukrainian Uniat Church," *Slavonic Review* (December 1931), pp. 377ff Cf. Very Rev. Stephen Gulovich, *Windows Westward. Rome, Russia and Reunion* (New York, 1947). The Uniate Church in Western Ukraine was incorporated into the Russian Orthodox Church in April 1946 and was placed under the jurisdiction of the Metropolitanate of Kiev and Galicia, which is subordinate to the Patriarchate of Moscow

which attempted to embrace Rome and Byzantium, was somewhat of an anomaly in the total stream of Ukrainian history. It was alien to the Zaporozhian Cossacks of the seventeenth century who fought valiantly for their Ortho- dox faith and who associated Roman Catholicism with their traditional enemies, the Poles. This association persisted in the minds of many twentieth-century Eastern Ukrain- ians who also saw the Uniate Church as something not truly Ukrainian.

The provincialism which resulted from these cultural differences manifested itself in the fact that two govern- ments of the same nation existed on a single territory. The separate military commands continued after the Galicians crossed the Zbruch, although a joint staff was established under General Iunakiv for the purpose of coordinating operations. In the diplomatic field the Galicians main- tained eight separate missions although the Directory had more than twice that number; where the two governments each had a mission accredited to the same foreign gov- ernment, as in Hungary, relations between the two groups of Ukrainians were far from cordial. In short, there was a state within a state, but this was understandable if not justifiable in view of Petrushevich's opinion that he as a constitutional dictator did not have sufficient authority to consent to a merger of the two governments.

Yet the Dictator and his colleagues were not prepared to tolerate the existence of a liaison agency in the form of a ministry for the Western Territory which was added to the Directory cabinet early in July. They as National Democrats were undoubtedly irked by the appointment of a Social Democrat, Semen Vitik, to this post, but their opposition to such an office resulted largely from their desire to prevent Poland from retaining control over Ga- licia. They hoped that they would be in a position to deal

and All Russia. For the religious aspects of the national movement in Eastern Ukraine see the author's article "Ukrainian Nationalism and the Orthodox Church," *The American Slavic and East European Review* (Vol. x, No. 1), February 1951, pp. 38ff.

with the Allies regarding Galicia's independence if they preserved a separate government. This meant that the Galicians wished to pursue a distinct foreign policy which they believed could not be conducted by the Directory, and, significantly, it was the question of relations with Poland which brought the diarchy to an end.

The Galicians, even after having crossed the Zbruch, were concerned with the future of their province and were more anti-Polish than anti-Russian. The Directory did not declare war on Poland after that nation had invaded East Galicia; although there supposedly was one Ukrainian People's Republic, it had two governments, each of which had a different policy towards Poland. Petliura was anxious to end hostilities between the Poles and Galicians since that could ensure aid from the Allies. Petrushevich, however, was apprehensive that Petliura would purchase the support of Warsaw at the price of sacrificing East Galicia. This caused some of the Galician officers to advocate a coup against Petliura, but Petrushevich, who was a graying lawyer of fifty-seven, feared that such a step would cause the Poles to cross the Zbruch in defense of the "legal" Ukrainian Government. In all fairness to Petliura, it must be said that during the summer of 1919 he was concerned over the possibility that the Poles might cross the Zbruch; in an effort to prevent this and at the same time obtain Polish aid against the Bolsheviks, a mission was sent to Warsaw in mid-August. On September 1, an armistice was concluded for a period of thirty days and was subsequently renewed for shorter periods.

This agreement undoubtedly added to the already widespread suspicion which existed between the two Ukrainian governments. On September 11, the organ of the Galician Army's supreme command openly accused the Directory of concluding an alliance with Poland. This did not prevent the sending of a diplomatic mission to Warsaw early in October, but the distrust soon reasserted itself when the Poles demanded renunciation of the Ukrainian claim to East Galicia as a quid pro quo for any diplomatic support.

Fully aware of how tempting such an arrangement could be to Petliura, many of the Galicians became convinced that they could regain possession of their province only with the aid of the anti-Bolshevik Russians. This new orientation was made more attractive by Denikin's rapid northward advance, which in October brought him to Tula, 220 miles from Moscow, and made the fall of the Bolshevik capital appear to be inevitable. Yet Makhno's increased activity behind the Volunteer Army's over-extended lines made it impossible for Denikin to continue the advance, and, ironically, it was then, when the tide of battle was turning against Denikin, that the Galicians decided to join him.

Petliura wrote to Nicholas Vasilko on November 27 that his army had lost its capacity to fight "mainly because of the treason of the Galician Command, concealed and possibly prepared earlier by the Government of the Western Territory of the Ukrainian People's Republic." He maintained that "this treachery occurred precisely at the time when, according to the plan of operations of my staff, our forces had every chance of surrounding and destroying the Volunteer Army."[28] Petliura claimed that he was compelled to give up a unified, solid front and substitute for it a segmental, insurrectionary front. Such an assertion appears to be more in the nature of a rationalization than an accurate description of events, especially in view of the fact that just prior to the conclusion of the Russo-Galician treaty Petliura admitted to Arnold Margolin that the Ukrainian armies were in a disadvantageous position.[29] Thus almost inevitably the two Ukrainian armies were driven to collaborating with that enemy which, in each case, appeared to be the lesser evil.

While these new orientations were being developed and both governments were commencing to work at cross-purposes, the fate of East Galicia was again being considered at Paris. During the summer the Commission on Polish

[28] Alexander Lototsky, *Simon Petliura* (Warsaw, 1936), p. 23
[29] Margolin, *Ukraina i Politika Antanty*, p. 191.

295

Affairs prepared a draft constitution for the region and on September 19 submitted it to the Heads of Delegations of the Five Great Powers.[80] This document provided for a unicameral provincial diet elected for a period of five years under proportional representation; its competence was to include such matters as public worship, education, public welfare, local transport, and taxes for the provincial budget. A governor, to be appointed and dismissed by the Polish Chief of State, was to enjoy the right to dissolve the diet and exercise an absolute veto with respect to public secondary and higher education; a veto of any other legislation could be overridden by means of a re-enactment by a two-thirds majority. Polish and Ukrainian were to be the official languages of the province on the basis of equality, but each commune or municipality was to determine whether one or both of these would be employed in the local school. The Orthodox Church was to be accorded the same rights as the Roman Catholic, and the Galicians were to have their own minister without portfolio in the Warsaw cabinet. While this draft constitution, in its original form, ensured a considerable measure of autonomy and provided for an ultimate plebiscite, it was amended beyond all recognition in the various meetings which followed.

The Poles were opposed to such a constitution and again presented all of their stock arguments against the Ukrainian movement. Paderewski appeared before the Heads of Delegations of the Big Five on September 23 and again charged that the Ukrainians were being led by Germans. The pianist-turned-politician waxed eloquent over Poland's past, when Poland extended from the Baltic to the Danube and from the Elbe to the Dnieper. He expressed resentment over the proposal that Galicia be granted a diet and falsely claimed that Germans who had killed Polish women and children would sit in that body. The Polish premier objected to the provision which exempted inhabitants of East Galicia from military service. In place

[80] For the text of the draft constitution see *U S*, *Paris Peace Conference*, *op.cit.*, VIII, pp. 280ff.

of the draft constitution, which provided only for provisional Polish rule, Paderewski hoped to persuade the powers to grant all of Galicia to Poland permanently on the vague condition that it be governed humanely and justly.[31] Although Sir Eyre Crowe, British assistant undersecretary of state for foreign affairs, argued that the door should be left open for Galicia to unite with Ukraine or a regenerated Russia, Paderewski was persuasive enough to cause the Conference to reject all references to a future plebiscite. The proposed constitution was also altered in a few days to permit Galicians to be drafted into the Polish army.

During October the matter was tabled, but on November 7 Sir Eyre Crowe again spoke out against any final union of East Galicia and Poland. He proposed a new solution—a Polish mandate under the League of Nations for a period of fifteen years, upon the expiration of which the League would determine the disposition of the territory. Mr. Frank Polk, the American representative, expressed the opinion that this arrangement would leave the territory in a state of ferment; he was unable to conceive of any alternative to the surrender of the province to Poland.[32] The French proposed an extension of the mandate to thirty years, and finally a compromise of twenty-five years was agreed upon. The Polish delegates in Paris would not hear of a mandate; they argued that Galicia had been an integral part of Poland and threatened that the Polish armies fighting Bolshevism would become demoralized if Poland lost Lviv. They again charged that German and Austrian money was the source of agitation and claimed that Galicia would help provide their new state with access to the Black Sea.[33]

The opposition of the Poles to the twenty-five-year mandate persisted. On December 22, the matter was reconsidered at the request of the Poles, who stated that this would help keep their army immune from Bolshevik prop-

[31] Ibid , VIII, pp. 330ff.   [32] Ibid., IX, pp. 20f.
[33] Ibid , IX, pp. 244ff.

aganda. At the meeting of the Council of the Heads of Delegations held that day, Clemenceau together with de Martino of Italy and Matsui pushed through a decision "that the execution of the recent resolution which accorded to Poland a 25-year mandate for Eastern Galicia should be suspended and that the question should be reexamined later."[34] This nullification of the mandate was undoubtedly due to the collapse of Kolchak's and Denikin's military efforts which prompted Clemenceau to express concern over the anarchy, crime, and revolt prevailing in Russia. At a meeting held at 10 Downing Street on December 12, the French premier conceded that intervention had failed; he proposed as a substitute the erection of a figurative barbed wire entanglement around Russia in order to isolate her and prevent a Russo-German rapprochement.[35] Poland, strengthened by its acquisition of East Galicia, was to be an important and well-barbed segment of the entanglement.

Certain of French support, the Poles moved into Volynia and Podolia during the autumn of 1919, and Petliura in desperation expressed a willingness to become their puppet. In Kamianets they imposed an early curfew, made numerous arrests, searches, and requisitions; the protests of Ivan Ohienko, the ranking Ukrainian official in the city, were ignored. Petliura remained on territory which was occupied by neither the Poles nor the Bolsheviks and proceeded northward into Volynia. The railroad cars of what remained of the government were attacked by local peasants between Proskuriv and Starokonstiantiniv; the state treasury was stolen, and the war ministry and military staff went to Husiatin, where they were seized and disarmed by the Poles. On November 26, Petliura met in Starokonstiantiniv with Premier Mazepa and some army officers. Less than two weeks before, Petliura had been given the right to act in the name of the Directory; this was done with the consent of the other two members, Shvets and Makarenko, who were sent abroad in an effort to revamp

[34] *Ibid*, IX, p. 626.   [35] *Ibid*, IX, p. 848.

Ukrainian foreign policy. While this made Petliura a dictator in theory, it did not prevent the fall of Starokonstiantiniv.

Petliura fled to Liubar, where three commanders, led by Volokh, informed him that his career was finished; they ordered the commander-in-chief to transfer his authority to them preparatory to joining the Red Army. Petliura quelled this attempted revolt and on December 4 was advised by Premier Mazepa to go abroad and seek aid. On the following day he appointed General Omelianovich-Pavlenko to the command of the Ukrainian Army and then left for Warsaw. On December 6, the fatigued Sich Sharpshooters meeting at Nova Chortoriia decided not to continue as an integral unit. Some of the men wished to participate in guerilla activities during the winter with other aggregations of armed Ukrainians, but the Poles advanced unexpectedly and in seizing the town captured most of the Sharpshooters and interned them in Lutsk. Thus the military activity of the Ukrainians throughout the winter of 1919-1920 was limited to a partisan campaign east of the Zbruch directed by Omelianovich-Pavlenko and George Tiutiunnik. Most of Ukraine, including the cities of Kharkiv, Poltava, and Kiev, was in the hands of the Red Army.

Petliura's effort to drive out the Bolsheviks in 1920 by means of his ill-fated alliance with the Poles is one of the most sordid pages in all Ukrainian history. Even before Petliura arrived in Warsaw, his diplomatic mission there, headed by Andrew Livitsky, had issued a declaration on December 2, without the consent of its Galician members. The essence of this announcement was a willingness to accept the Zbruch River as the Polish-Ukrainian frontier, thus acquiescing in the Polish seizure of East Galicia as well as Volynia. The three Galician members were joined by Mshanetsky, an East Ukrainian, who stated that his adherence to such a declaration would make him guilty of a crime; this left only four of the eight members of the delegation willing to consent to the Zbruch frontier.

The declaration aroused great bitterness in Vienna among the members of the Petrushevich Government who assembled all available Galician political émigrés on December 9. At the meeting it was decided to protest the December 2 declaration of Livitsky's mission in Warsaw as well as the Allied Supreme Council's draft statute for East Galicia. When Dr. Vasil Paneyko, the West Ukrainian state secretary for foreign affairs, returned to Paris, he and his colleagues withdrew from the Ukrainian delegation and established one of their own for the purpose of defending the interests of East Galicia. In January of 1920 they organized a Ukrainian National Committee in Paris which advocated the "complete resurrection of Ukraine within its ethnographic frontiers united federally with a strong Russia."[36] This new orientation, based on a policy of cooperation with anti-Bolshevik Russians in Paris, was a result of the tragic cleavage which existed between Petliura and Petrushevich.

Both men desired to influence the Allies; Petrushevich issued protests in Vienna while Petliura hoped that he could win French support by means of his new Polish orientation. Several pro-Ukrainian addresses delivered in the Chamber of Deputies during the late winter and spring of 1920 by M. de Gailhard-Bancel won the applause of the right and center but did not alter French policy. The deputy argued that an independent Ukraine, if recognized, would pay a third of the Russian debt to France and would join Poland and Rumania in an alliance to stop the Bolsheviks.[37] A plea made by Petliura to the Allied Supreme Council on January 22, 1920, asking that the blockade of Ukraine be lifted to permit the shipment of medical supplies, was met with cold silence.

While enjoying the hospitality of the Poles during the winter of 1919-1920 Petliura met with Pilsudski and became convinced that the sole means of obtaining Allied, and more specifically, French, support was by becoming

[36] Lozynsky, *op.cit.*, p. 206.
[37] Emmanuel Evain, *Le problème de l'indépendance de l'Ukraine et la France* (Paris, 1931), pp. 109ff.

a Polish satellite. Prior to this, K. Macievich, the Directory's envoy in Bucharest, warned Petliura not to depend upon any alliance with Rumania because its transport system was in very poor condition. The Polish-Ukrainian treaty of April 21, 1920, was largely the work of Andrew Livitsky, the head of the diplomatic mission in Warsaw. Although this political convention had the approval of Petliura it was concluded without the consent of Premier Mazepa and his cabinet which remained on Ukrainian territory occupied by the Polish Army. The following is the complete text of this significant treaty signed in Warsaw by Livitsky and Jan Dombski of the Polish foreign ministry:

The Government of the Ukrainian People's Republic and the Government of the Polish Republic, profoundly convinced that each people possesses the natural right to self-determination and to define its relations with neighboring peoples, and equally desirous of establishing a basis for concordant and friendly co-existence for the welfare and development of both peoples, have agreed as follows:

1. Recognizing the *right* of Ukraine to independent political existence within the northern, eastern, and southern frontiers as they shall be determined by means of separate agreements concluded with the respective border states, the Polish Republic *recognizes* the Directory of the Independent Ukrainian People's Republic, headed by the Supreme Military Commander Simon Petliura, as the Supreme Government of the Ukrainian People's Republic.

2. The frontier between the Ukrainian People's Republic and the Polish Republic is established as follows: northward from the Dniester river along the Zbruch [Zbrucz] river and continuing along the former frontier between Austria-Hungary and Russia to Vishehrudka, and proceeding from there in a northerly direction through the Kremianets Hills, and then in an easterly direction from Zdolbunovo and then along the length of the eastern administrative boundary of the district [*povit*] of Rivne and continuing from there along the administrative boundary of the former province of Minsk to the juncture with the Pripet river and terminating at the mouth of that stream.

The districts of Rivne, Dubno, and part of Kremianets which

301

are immediately ceded to the Polish Republic shall be subject to a more concise agreement to be concluded later.

The final delimitation of the frontier shall be accomplished by a special Ukrainian-Polish commission composed of responsible specialists.

3. The Polish Government recognizes as Ukrainian the territory east of the frontier, as defined in Article II of this agreement, and extending to the 1772 frontiers of Poland (prior to the partition) and occupied at present by Poland or acquired in the future from Russia by military or diplomatic means.

4. The Polish Government obligates itself not to conclude any international agreements directed against Ukraine; the Ukrainian People's Republic obligates itself similarly with respect to the Polish Republic.

5. The same national-cultural rights which the Government of the Ukrainian People's Republic ensures citizens of Polish nationality on its territory shall be ensured to citizens of Ukrainian nationality within the frontiers of the Polish Republic, and conversely.

6. Special economic and commercial agreements are to be concluded between the Ukrainian People's Republic and the Polish Republic.

The agrarian question in Ukraine shall be resolved by the Constituent Body. In the period preceding its convocation the legal status of landowners of Polish nationality shall be defined by an agreement between the Ukrainian People's Republic and the Polish Republic.

7. A military convention is to be concluded and is to be regarded as an integral part of this agreement.

8. This agreement shall remain *secret*. It shall not be revealed to a third party or published by it in whole or in part except with the mutual consent of both of the high contracting parties. An exception to this is Article 1 which shall be made public after the signing of this agreement.

9. This agreement shall enter into force immediately upon being signed by the high contracting parties.

Done at Warsaw this twenty-first day of April, 1920, in two copies, one in the Ukrainian language and one in the Polish language. Only the Polish text is to be regarded as authentic in the event of doubt.[38]

[38] This translation of the treaty was made from the Ukrainian text in

302

This treaty was in complete violation of the centuries-old animosity which prevailed between the Poles and Ukrainians, and Petliura in consenting to it issued his own political death warrant. In his fear of Russian imperialism he surrendered himself to a people whose extremists have been equally imperialistic in their demands for a Poland which would dominate the area between the Baltic and Black Seas. During the negotiations the Poles did not hesitate to remind the Ukrainians that they were not dealing with equals since the latter possessed neither territory nor *stabilité du gouvernement*.[39] Petliura had been at the mercy of the Poles since December when he sought refuge with them, and this treaty merely formalized that relationship in which he was an instrumentality to be utilized or discarded according to the circumstances. Unfortunately, an international political agreement made under duress is valid and binding when the stronger signatory wishes to enforce it, and it can also be declared null and void by that same signatory under the principle of *rebus sic stantibus*.

From a theoretical point of view, it is doubtful whether Petliura possessed the necessary authority to sign such a treaty in the name of the Directory. When his colleagues, Shvets and Makarenko, went abroad in November, a separation of functions was agreed upon and precisely defined in an act issued by the Directory on November 15, 1919. Point four of this act stated that their task was the "conclusion of preliminary agreements and political-military treaties with other states in the name of the Ukrainian People's Republic"; point three empowered them to exercise the final control over the acts of all official bodies of the Ukrainian Republic abroad as well as over those of individual officials. Petliura's sole duty was to remain on

Professor Serhi Shelukhin's *Varshavski Dohovir mizh Poliakami i S Petliuroiu* (Prague, 1926), pp. 13f. The italics are in the Ukrainian text. For a Russian translation of the treaty see N Filippov, *op cit.*, pp 71ff. This document was not registered with the Secretariat of the League of Nations or published in its Treaty Series. Significantly, it did not provide for any ratification, as is usually the practice in international agreements

[39] Isaac Mazepa, *Ukraina v Ohni i Buri Revoliutsii* (n p , n.d), III, p. 14.

Ukrainian soil and carry on the struggle there in the name of the Directory. Thus it is evident that they and not Petliura were to negotiate such a treaty as that of April 21. Professor Shelukhin has concluded that the agreement was in no way binding upon the Ukrainian Republic because the other members of the Directory had not been consulted.[40] This is a valid conclusion, and it indicates by contrast the extent to which the national movement had become personalized at this time.

The first article of the treaty provided for Polish recognition of the Directory as the government of Ukraine but with the qualification that it be headed by Petliura. Such a provision, while possibly flattering to the commander-in-chief, was an error on the part of the Ukrainians because it denied the fact that man is mortal and that he has a limited life span, while a particular state can transcend generations. Even if the treaty had been observed by Poland, which was not the case, Petliura's death or resignation could have been regarded legally as a violation of a condition implicit in the recognition. The surreptitious nature of Petliura's adventure with Pilsudski is illustrated by his attitude towards Shvets and Makarenko when they and Andrievsky invited him to discuss foreign policy with them in Vienna. They knew nothing of the content of the treaty but were not in favor of the Polish orientation. Petliura refused to discuss the matter and informed them that they were relieved of all authority and were to be considered as private citizens.

Such arbitrariness could be overlooked if the new policy and the treaty which it had spawned had provided some real advantages for Ukraine, but in each of the carefully worded articles of the Warsaw Treaty more was lost than was gained. Petliura's status as a junior partner was made clear in the first article, which did not provide for a mutual recognition between the two contracting parties; Poland recognized Ukraine's right to an independent political existence, but as the senior partner it apparently did not

40 Shelukhin, *op.cit.*, p. 16.

require Ukrainian recognition of Polish independence. The second article provided for the cession of East Galicia and Western Volynia to Poland, while the third article placed Ukraine in a subservient position because it recognized a prior claim of the Poles to their 1772 frontier and made the Ukrainians appear to be objects of Polish beneficence.

Article five, which dealt with national-cultural rights, was deceptive and unfair. Under it Poland agreed to grant to Ukrainians living within its frontiers the same rights which the Ukrainian People's Republic was to accord to Poles residing in Ukraine. The injustice lay in the fact that the Polish minority in the Kiev province and in Podolia was infinitesimal, while the Ukrainian population of East Galicia and Volynia was in a majority in each region. Article six was no exception to the textual poverty of the treaty; it provided for Polish intervention in an internal Ukrainian problem—the agrarian question—in order to protect the landholdings of the Polish minority of the Right Bank. The eighth article, which provided for secrecy and applied to all but the fact of the treaty's existence, was necessitated by the sweeping concessions acceded to by Petliura and not accompanied by any corresponding recompense on the part of the Poles.

Most Ukrainians who were abroad immediately expressed skepticism regarding the treaty. The Ukrainian foreign office did not inform its diplomatic missions of the treaty text, and they were compelled to rely upon newspaper reports and rumors. A number of the chiefs of missions met in Vienna and decided to send three of their number on an inconsequential journey to Warsaw and to the seat of government for information concerning the content of the treaty as well as the future plans of the government. The alliance with Poland did not bring French support, and it also removed the possibility of a shift in British policy, which could have caused London to replace Denikin with Petliura as the recipient of whatever aid it could spare in the struggle against Soviet Russia. As far as Britain was concerned, the Warsaw Treaty placed Petliura in the French camp since London regarded Poland as a Paris creation. This, together with the vexatious Irish question, domestic labor difficulties, and Lloyd George's belief that Bolshevism would come to its own logical end, meant that English intervention on behalf of Petliura was not even a remote possibility.

The one-time theological student had cast his lot with Pilsudski's Poland in a final futile effort to retain some of the vestiges of power. Although this was a marriage of convenience doomed to fail if only because each man believed that his country alone should dominate East-Central Europe, both of these nationalists had in common an early period of participation in socialist party organizations. Both were unrestrained egotists who surrounded themselves with servile aides and, despite their lack of professional military training, reached the highest ranks. Both desired to be chiefs of state transcending party lines and personifying the nation. Pilsudski succeeded where Petliura failed, not only because he had greater military and revolutionary experience and active French support, but also because Poland's right to independence was recognized by the Provisional Government of Russia and by Woodrow Wilson in his Fourteen Points.

Petliura's association with Pilsudski was regarded by Hrushevsky and many others as final proof of his betrayal of socialism in favor of a blind nationalism calculated to preserve and advance his personal interest. Vinnichenko, who at the time was in Vienna preparing to leave for Soviet Ukraine, branded his former colleague as a "pernicious and filthy gladiator-slave of the Entente." He summoned all the invective at his command, calling Petliura an "unhealthily ambitious maniac, soaked up to his ears in the blood of pogromized Jewry, politically illiterate, willing to accept all reaction in order to preserve his power."[41] On April 22, Vinnichenko also issued an open letter to the

[41] Volodimir Vinnichenko, *Ukrainska Derzhavnist* (Vienna, 1920), p. 22 and p. 27.

Communists and revolutionary socialists of Western Europe and America in which he declared Petliura's government and its diplomatic missions to be usurpatory. The former head of the Directory contended that that body had been nonexistent since February 1919, following the dissolution of the Congress of Toilers by which it lost its juridical basis; he also maintained that the Directory's failure to hold Ukrainian territory deprived it of even the right to call itself a *de facto* government. Vinnichenko came to the conclusion that Ukraine could be truly and most effectively liberated by means of a world revolution which would establish a world federation of soviet socialist republics.[42]

In an effort to refute this contention, Petliura joined Pilsudski in an invasion of Ukraine which followed the signing of the Treaty of Warsaw and a supplementary military convention.[43] The latter agreement was concluded on April 24, as an integral part of the political treaty of April 21. It provided for joint military operations under Polish command east of the existing Polish-Bolshevik front, but Polish participation was to end at the Dnieper River, a boundary which indicates that Pilsudski was prepared to underwrite no more than a rump Ukraine of the Right Bank. This convention, like its political counterpart, was more advantageous to the Poles than to the Ukrainians. The Poles promised not to divide the Ukrainian forces into any more small, isolated units than was absolutely necessary for operational purposes and agreed to merge them as soon as possible. The Ukrainians prom-

[42] See Volodimir Vinnichenko's *Politichni Listi* (Vienna, 1920). At the time of the writing of these letters, the former Ukrainian premier was convinced that his people were "on the threshold of a new era" following the expulsion of Denikin. He assumed that Communism could not permit one nation to dominate and exploit another; he was certain in 1920 that Lenin and his comrades had discovered their error. Upon returning to Ukraine he expected to find a higher type of human being in a reformed society but, instead, found only slogans and programs. Quickly disillusioned, he resumed his exile in Western Europe.

[43] For the Ukrainian text of this convention see Shelukhin, *op cit.*, pp. 33ff. For a Russian translation see N. Filippov, *op.cit.*, pp. 73ff.

ised to supply the Polish forces on Ukrainian soil with meat, fats, grain, fruits, sugar, oats, hay, straw, and other commodities, as well as horses and means of conveyance. The method of supply was to be by requisition and issuance of a bilingual receipt to the victim. The Polish Command was empowered to establish the rate of exchange between the Polish and Ukrainian currencies and set it initially at ten to one in favor of Poland, but later changed the rate to five to one.

The Poles were also empowered to operate the Ukrainian railways; they agreed to restore the Ukrainian management as soon as possible. Petliura was to organize his own civil and military organization, but Polish gendarmes and troops were to protect the rear and Polish liaison officers were to be attached to the Ukrainian civil administration. Following the completion of the general plan of joint operations, the evacuation of Polish forces was to commence upon the proposal of one of the signatories, but the technical execution of the evacuation was to be based on a mutual understanding between the Polish and Ukrainian Commands. This meant that Pilsudski could occupy the country for as long a period as he wished. The Poles agreed to arm and equip only three Ukrainian divisions and in this way limited the number of troops under Petliura's command since it was unlikely that he could obtain aid elsewhere. This humiliating military convention, like the treaty, was to be kept secret, and only the Polish text was to be regarded as authentic.

The invasion which the two agreements precipitated proceeded rapidly because of very light resistance by the Red Army, which retreated in an orderly manner. On April 26, Pilsudski issued a proclamation assuring the Ukrainian population that Polish forces would remain only until the regular government was able to assume authority. The apparent cooperation between the Poles and Ukrainians had already been marred on the preceding day when remnants of the Galician Army surrendered to the Poles after deserting from the Red Army. These units had been with Denikin since the preceding November, and in January they had joined the Red Army. In surrendering to the invading army they had hoped to participate again in the struggle for Ukrainian independence, but, instead, they were disarmed and interned by the Poles. Petliura was unable to obtain their release since his forces operating on the Polish right flank numbered only four thousand and were of no particular military value in the invasion.

The high-watermark of recent Polish imperialism was reached on May 7, 1920, when Kiev fell. Only three days earlier Vinnichenko in an open letter warned that "the 'aid' of Poland and her aristocrats is the kiss of Judas and with this kiss the Ukrainian nation is being surrendered to a new Golgotha."[44] He doubted whether his letter would influence the "coffee house patriots" who wasted their lives in foreign capitals, but he wanted to express his conviction that inequality was the root of all evil in society. Communism, he now believed, would serve as the catalytic agent which would amalgamate the national and the social. Although Vinnichenko later revised his views regarding Communism, he did not become an advocate of a Polish-Ukrainian alliance; in that matter his prediction was borne out by time.

Premier Mazepa soon commenced to recognize the folly of Petliura's diplomacy and tendered his resignation in order to escape full responsibility for the consequences of the alliance with Poland. A new cabinet was organized in Kiev on May 25, with Viacheslav Prokopovich, a Socialist Federalist, as premier and Andrew Livitsky as vice premier and minister of justice; Mazepa joined the new cabinet as minister of agriculture only after Stanislaus Stempowsky, his Polish predecessor at that post, was transferred to the health ministry. Although the cabinet contained Socialist Federalists and some Social Democrats, party lines in it were more formal than real. The cabinet's stay in Kiev was brief; on June 3 it issued an announcement regarding the convocation of a pre-parliament, but five days

---

[44] Vinnichenko, *Politichni Listi*, p. 22.

later it fled to Zhmerinka because of the rapid counter-attack launched by the Red Army. The Bolsheviks took the city on June 11. On June 18, the bankruptcy of Petliura's government was apparent when Christopher Baranovsky, the minister of finance, persuaded the cabinet to adopt his proposal to replenish the state treasury by selling supposedly nationalized lands. The government was as bankrupt in appearance as it was in character. Nicholas Halahan, after visiting its railroad cars in Zhmerinka during June, observed that Premier Prokopovich had a third-class car while that of the war minister, General Volodimir Salsky, was much better. Halahan as Ukrainian minister to Hungary naturally visited the car which housed the foreign ministry; there he found a lone employee leisurely perusing the text of the Treaty of Versailles.[45]

At the end of June Andrew Nikovsky, the foreign minister, received a report from Arnold Margolin proposing the immediate convocation of a meeting of all Ukrainian diplomats for the purpose of considering a radical change in foreign policy. Margolin, who at the time was head of the diplomatic mission in London, also wished to know the full text of the Treaty of Warsaw, but instead of being summoned to the meeting he was directed to proceed to Spa in Belgium. There he was to be joined early in July by Nicholas Vasilko, Count Tyshkevich, and Andrew Iakovliv; at Spa they were to attempt to present the Ukrainian case to a conference of the Great Powers. This meeting dealt largely with the German question, but Margolin was told by the British delegates that the Ukrainians must attain independence themselves.[46] Disturbed by pogroms which broke out in Ukraine during the summer of 1920, the diplomat decided to resign; the most important reason for this step was his inability to carry out a policy which he had had no voice in making.

At this late stage no change of policy, however radical, could save Petliura. In mid-July his bedraggled and deci-

[45] Halahan, *op.cit.*, IV, pp. 271ff.
[46] Margolin, *Ukraina i Politika Antanty*, pp. 236ff.

mated forces crossed the Zbruch together with the Poles in their westward retreat. He proposed to Pilsudski that an amnesty be granted to all Ukrainians who had fought for the sovereignty of East Galicia. Petliura's interest in the fate of interned Galicians lay in his hope that this would induce them to join the allied army and fight Bolshevism. Much of East Galicia was overrun by the Red Army, and in August Warsaw itself was threatened. Some of the former officers of the Sich Sharpshooters proposed to Petliura that the Ukrainians extricate themselves from the defense of Poland by withdrawing into the Carpathian Mountains. This new strategy was based on the assumption that the Red Army would defeat Poland and threaten to communize all of Central Europe; the Western European nations, it was argued, would then be compelled to launch an anti-Bolshevik crusade, and the Ukrainian armed forces would emerge intact from the Carpathians and renew their struggle on the side of the Western Powers. Petliura rejected this plan ostensibly because he did not wish to betray his ally, Pilsudski.[47]

Yet this did not prevent Pilsudski from betraying Petliura. The latter and what remained of his government established themselves in Tarnow, Poland. Although the so-called "miracle of the Vistula" halted the Red Army's westward offensive, Pilsudski was in no position to continue this war of fantastically ephemeral victories and constantly shifting lines of battle. As soon as it became apparent that the Poles were prepared to conclude a peace with Soviet Russia, Livitsky made overtures to Moscow in an effort to obtain a separate peace with the Bolsheviks on behalf of Petliura's government. Chicherin, the Soviet foreign minister, refused to negotiate with a regime which he regarded as nonexistent; he pointed out that the government of the Ukrainian Soviet Republic ,was already represented at the Riga peace negotiations.[48] Although the Russian delegation at Riga had the authority to represent both Ukraine and Bielo-russia, Dimitri Manuilsky partici-

[47] Konovalets, op.cit., pp. 42f.   [48] Mazepa, op.cit., III, pp. 48f.

pated in the negotiations as a Soviet Ukrainian delegate. Apparently the Bolsheviks were more adept negotiators than Petliura because they successfully insisted that the Ukrainian text of the Treaty of Riga be regarded as authentic.

The treaty itself served to establish Russo-Ukrainian relations during the period between the two World Wars. Both of the high contracting parties recognized the "independence" of Ukraine and Bielo-russia and agreed on a frontier which prevailed until September 1939. This boundary was substantially the same as that agreed upon in the Treaty of Warsaw, and the Polish delegation based its claim to it on the Ukrainian acceptance embodied in that agreement. In this way Poland obtained all of Eastern Galicia and Western Volynia without consulting the predominantly Ukrainian population of these regions. The exiled government of Petrushevich in Vienna sent a delegation of observers to Riga which included Dr. Constantine Levitsky, Dr. Luke Myshuha, Ernest Breiter, and Dr. Osip Nazaruk. This delegation could not participate in the negotiations because it represented an unrecognized government, but even before arriving in Riga it sent a telegram to the peace parley, protesting any consideration of the Galician question undertaken without its participation. Upon arriving in Riga, it made additional protests which were as ineffective as those made en route; its final contention was that the Galician question would be settled at the Paris Peace Conference.

The Galicians were not alone in believing that the Riga settlement was not definitive; supposedly informed opinion in many foreign capitals doubted its validity because Soviet Russia had not been recognized. It was also thought in some quarters that the Russian troops of General Peter Wrangel, operating on the Crimean front, constituted a serious threat to the Red Army. These assumptions were as incorrect as Petliura's hope that Poland would be a dependable ally. If the Treaty of Warsaw can be regarded as Petliura's political death warrant, it can be said that the

Treaty of Riga was his political obituary. The fourth article of the Warsaw Treaty contained a very convenient interchange of the terms "Ukrainian" and "Ukrainian People's Republic"; while Poland agreed not to conclude any international agreement directed against Ukraine, it insisted in April 1920 that the Ukrainian People's Republic promise not to enter into any agreement directed against the Polish Republic. Thus it can be argued that the Poles, in negotiating with the Ukrainian Soviet Republic and in signing the Treaty of Riga in March 1921, did not conclude an agreement directed against "Ukraine." The Poles at Riga on September 30, 1920, stated that Petliura represented only one of the parties struggling for power in Ukraine.

While the negotiations were being conducted at Riga during the autumn, Petliura did not lose hope; he had been able to retake Kamianets-Podilsk and hold it for a brief period. Because of the inactivity on the Polish front, the Bolsheviks had transferred many of their troops to the South in a drive to liquidate Wrangel; they were aided in this by Makhno, who made a temporary alliance with them. This alliance made Petliura confident that his aid was indispensable to the White Russian commander in the Crimea from whom he hoped to obtain clothes, arms, and ammunition for 44,000 men. At the same time he instructed Nicholas Vasilko, the Ukrainian envoy in Switzerland, to attempt to get ammunition from Germany. However, the military situation changed rapidly and the outnumbered Ukrainians again retreated across the Zbruch on November 21, with an army of 30,000. With the conclusion of the Treaty of Riga in its final form in March 1921 the Polish abandonment of Petliura was complete. It took the form of the following Polish commitment embodied in article five of the treaty:

"Each of the Contracting Parties mutually undertakes to respect in every way the political sovereignty of the other Party, to abstain from interference in its internal affairs, and particularly to refrain from all agitation, propaganda or interference of any kind, and not to encourage any such movement.

"Each of the Contracting Parties undertakes not to create or protect organizations which are formed with the object of encouraging armed conflict against the other Contracting Party or of undermining its territorial integrity, or of subverting by force its political or social institutions, nor yet such organizations as claim to be the Government of the other Party or of a part of the territories of the other Party. The Contracting Parties, therefore, undertake to prevent such organizations, their official representatives and other persons connected therewith, from establishing themselves on their territory, and to prohibit military recruiting and the entry into their territory and transport across it, of armed forces, arms, munitions and war material of any kind destined for such organizations."[49]

Petliura's exiled government established itself in hotel rooms in Tarnow with the consent of its Polish hosts. Although some of the Ukrainians in Tarnow were bitter over what they regarded as betrayal by the Poles, Petliura was able to maintain his composure. Defeat did not cause him to deny the validity and correctness of his Polish orientation and his willingness to sacrifice Eastern Galicia in return for real or imagined Polish aid. He renounced the policy of "territorial maximalism"—inclusion of all parts of the nation in the first state—because of his belief that no nation ever achieved its objectives by this method. Many of Petliura's fellow Ukrainians, especially the follow-

[49] *League of Nations Treaty Series*, VI (1921), p. 131. This provision in the Treaty of Riga became a source of considerable tension in Russo-Polish relations during the early 1920's. Rakovsky, the Soviet Ukrainian foreign minister, protested the presence of Petliura and Boris Savinkov, the Russian Social Revolutionary, on Polish soil and accused Warsaw of condoning the formation of diversionary units in Ukraine. For the texts of these notes of protest and Polish denials and counter-protests see N Filippov, *op.cit.*, pp. 41ff. and *L'Ukraine Sovietiste, quatre années de guerre et de blocus* (Berlin, 1922), pp. 148ff. A large-scale raid into Soviet Ukraine was made in November 1921 by the Polish-based armed forces of the Ukrainian People's Republic; more than 300 men were killed in an encounter with Bolshevik forces at the village of Bazar near Korosten.

ers of Hetman Paul Skoropadsky, accused him of betraying the principle of *sobornist* or indivisible unity of the
nation. His defense lay in the assumption that *sobornist*
can be attained only if Ukrainians strive for what is possible under given external and internal circumstances. Until the day of his death at the hands of an assassin, Petliura
regarded the liberation of East Ukraine from Soviet rule
as his primary aim, even if this were to be achieved at the
expense of East Galicia. To the very end he remained
convinced that East Ukraine must serve as the base for the
development of Ukrainian statehood.

Doomed to live the last six years of his life in exile,
Petliura remained in Poland until 1923, living in Tarnow
and later in Warsaw but always in fear of assassination. In
that year he moved to Paris, which at the time was a veritable museum of Eastern European political relics. There
he lived with his family in a small hotel on the Left Bank
in a manner not befitting a former chief of state. While
walking at the intersection of rue Racine and the Boulevard
St. Michel on May 25, 1926, he was assassinated by a Jewish watchmaker, Samuel Schwartzbard, who ostensibly desired to avenge the pogroms associated with Petliura's
name. The assassin had served with French forces during
the occupation of Odessa and later joined an international
unit which fought beside the Red Army during the Russian civil war. This prompted many émigré Ukrainian nationalists to conclude that Schwartzbard was a Soviet agent
acting on orders from Moscow.[50] Whatever the motive
for the assassination, it cannot be denied that it endowed
Petliura with the crown of martyrdom and added another
tragic page to the history of Ukraine.

Politics is a cruel, interminable, and fascinating game in
which the winners reap rich, albeit temporary, rewards,
while the losers must content themselves with the hope

[50] The émigré nationalists made the same charge when Colonel Eugene
Konovalets was assassinated in Rotterdam; the former commander of the
Sich Sharpshooters went to that city under an assumed name on May 23,
1938, for the purpose of meeting a supposed collaborator. There he received
a package containing a bomb.

that the fates will smile more favorably upon their successors. Petliura lost, but he retained his conviction that all political movements at some time in their development experience moments of defeat. It is to his credit that as an émigré, living in very modest circumstances, he did not desert the cause of independent Ukrainian statehood. He devoted the last nine years of his life exclusively to the national movement, apparently undisturbed by the far-reaching and seemingly unattainable nature of his goal. While it is possible to doubt whether Petliura's remains will ever be reinterred in Kiev's Saint Sophia Cathedral, it is impossible to impugn his sincerity and resolution which enabled him to pursue his objective till the very end.

CHAPTER VII
In Retrospect

The road to the liberation of every nation is covered with blood. This is no less true of our nation for it is covered with the blood of foreign enemies and with our own. Blood completes the profound processes of national emotions, consciousness, organized effort, ideological creativeness—all that the nation consciously and irrationally utilizes for the confirmation of its right to exist as a state. Blood which is shed for such a noble cause does not dry. It shall always be warmed by the spirit of the nation, and shall always serve as an activating force— a reminder of what is unfulfilled and a call to continue what has been commenced.—*Simon Petliura (1926)*

How far a people is able and worthy to form a state, cannot in the imperfect condition of international law be decided by any human judgment, but only by the judgment of God as revealed in the history of the world. As a rule it is only by great struggles, by its own sufferings and its own acts, that a nation can justify its claim.— JOHANN KASPAR BLUNTSCHLI, *The Theory of the State*

THE failure of the Ukrainians to achieve permanent independent statehood during the upheaval caused by World War I was, in large measure, a result of the underdevelopment of the national movement. Prior to the war their territory had been occupied by powers which, for the most part, were antagonistic to the cause of Ukrainian independence; the occupiers, both in the aggregate and individually, were more powerful than the active forces representing Ukrainian nationalism. The latter were almost exclusively intellectual and in Eastern or Russian Ukraine operated under an unfriendly government that was in marked contrast with thriving Western European nationalism, which at a much earlier date was buttressed and rationalized by the growing authority of the rising monarchs. Contacts with the West were limited, and this seriously retarded the growth of national consciousness. It also meant that the economy of the territory remained predominantly agrarian even into the twentieth century.

As a result Ukraine lacked a substantial middle class despite the not inconsiderable economic development which occurred in the nineteenth century. Since a national movement could not develop in the absence of a middle class, its formation was particularly difficult in Ukraine, where the bulk of the bourgeoisie were Russian-speaking and regarded the language of the Ukrainian peasants as crude and odd. Indeed, a middle-class Ukrainian who was at all conscious of his nationality would deny it in Imperial Russia if he wished to prosper. The relatively few who were willing and able to take risks identified themselves with the peasant masses and cultivated the village vernacular. Without such a nucleus the national movement could not have developed because the peasant, nationalism's raw material in Ukraine, would have remained in his torpor. Nationalism has usually been the concomitant of the rise of a commercial and professional bourgeoisie in a relatively urbanized and industrialized society.

The peasant, if left to himself, could not have acquired

an awareness of his membership in the nation. He was en-slaved by his locale and regarded the inhabitants of the neighboring villages as a species of foreigner. Convinced that "one's own blood is not that of a stranger,"[1] the peas-ant was truly autarchic and incapable of imagining a way of life which differed radically from his own. To a large extent this attitude can be attributed to the crushing pov-erty which compelled him to be preoccupied with his cow and the few other animals he might have been fortunate enough to possess. If he fared somewhat better than his fellow villagers, he was concerned with keeping what he already possessed and at the same time in acquiring greater wealth. This acquisitive aspect of peasant society left little time for ratiocination and speculation about the nation. Although the peasant village regarded it as proper for the priest and teacher to engage in book-learning, it usually frowned upon other members of the village who did so unless they were preparing for these professions.

The peasant's distrust of innovation was also reflected in his dislike for the state, which made life more expensive as well as unpleasant. The Galician gave expression to this fundamental fear when he said: "Where politics abounds sincerity is not to be found."[2] His ignorance of the law caused him to regard it as an ineffective and costly way of maintaining order when compared with the influence which was traditionally exercised by village opinion in en-forcing conformity to local mores. Later, compulsory mili-tary training deprived him of the labor of his sons when they came of age, and took them among strangers. Such an attitude made the peasant, as such, incapable of be-coming a nationalist since a nationalist inevitably became involved in political activity demanding the recognition of his people initially by advocating a grant of autonomy and later by joining in the demand for national independence.

Most of the men who undertook the propagation of the national idea in Ukraine were intellectuals with a middle-class background although many of them were of

---

[1] Franko, op cit., II, p. 313. [2] Ibid., II, p. 566.

peasant stock. Hrushevsky was the son of an official in the Russian ministry of public instruction, and Dmitro Doroshenko was the son of a military veterinarian. Colonel Eugene Konovalets and Volodimir Naumenko were the sons of teachers. Nicholas Mikhnovsky, Volodimir Chekhovsky, Valentine Sadovsky, Serhi Efremov, and Colonel Peter Bolbochan were the sons of priests. The village clergy, unlike the Russified princes of the Orthodox Church, remained relatively close to the peasantry, and this enabled their sons who refused to take holy orders to turn, instead, to the task of elevating the vernacular of their village boyhood into a fully developed language. The increased contact between village and city which made this endeavor possible during the latter part of the nineteenth century was also due to the rise in population and the lack of land, which made it necessary for many sons and daughters of peasants to seek employment in the growing cities of Ukraine. There they gave up the traditional native dress and were either overwhelmed by their contacts with the imported Russian workers or adopted an antagonistic attitude towards the Russified urban milieu.

The essentially agrarian character of late nineteenth century Ukrainian society, with its emphasis on the locale, tended to retard the development of that sentiment of group cohesiveness which transcends localism and is termed national consciousness. The peasant, because of his conservatism, was able to retain his language, peculiarities of dress, and local customs despite foreign rule, but initially he resisted the notion that all Ukrainians, whether living in Kharkiv province, in Volynia, or in Carpatho-Ukraine, belonged to the same nation. In part, the breakdown of this peasant parochialism was made possible by the more widespread acceptance of currency in place of land as a token of wealth; it was accompanied by the construction of railroad lines during the nineteenth century and a rapid increase in the dissemination of newspapers and periodicals. The growth of industry and beet-sugar cultivation and refineries in Ukraine also made the peasant somewhat less self-sufficient and extended his horizons. This was a protracted process, and it had not been consummated as late as 1917. So long as remnants of provincialism existed it was impossible to realize the idea of *sobornist*—translated in Orthodox theology as "catholic" and meaning that the whole is greater than the sum of its parts, with truth residing only in the collectivity.

Among the most important hindrances to the attainment of *sobornist* was the confusion regarding the names of various branches of the Ukrainian people. One of the first tasks which the nationalists faced in Eastern Ukraine was the elimination of the use of the term "Little Russian." The Galician or Western Ukrainians found it necessary to combat the widespread use of the term "Ruthenia" employed by foreigners in referring to Ukraine. When a sense of national consciousness finally commenced to make inroads in Carpatho-Ukraine following World War I, its proponents had to combat the acceptance of "Carpatho-Russia" and "Carpathian-Ruthenia" as names for the territory. At the turn of the century it was common for West Ukrainians to refer to themselves as "Rusins" (sons of Rus). Other terms used in identifying parts of the Ukrainian nation included "Galicians," "Bukovinians," "Uhrorusins," "Lemki," and "Hutsuli." The gradual abandonment of each of these synonymous names marks an important step in the breakdown of particularism which is prerequisite to nation-building.

Probably a greater threat to the national movement lay in the phenomenon of Russophilism: the belief that the Ukrainians, while endowed with a certain distinctiveness, still remained a part of the Russian nation. Some of the more ardent nationalists branded as "Russophiles" or as renegades even those moderates who recognized the existence of a Ukrainian nation but who believed that historical, linguistic, and religious ties with the Great Russians were profound enough to warrant a federative relationship. Small wonder then that the diplomats and statesmen of Western Europe and America were confused regarding the existence of the Ukrainian nation in 1918. Woodrow Wilson, while providing for Polish independence and for "the freest opportunity of autonomous development" for the peoples of Austria-Hungary, did not mention the Ukrainians in his Fourteen Points. Wilson's sixth point dealt with Russia but was predicated upon the assumption that Lenin's government was an ephemeral political aberration; it vaguely provided for a settlement which would obtain for Russia "an unhampered and unembarrassed opportunity for the independent determination of her own political development and national policy."

In the United States, Ukrainian immigrants added to the confusion by allowing themselves to be divided along provincial lines. Many from Carpatho-Ukraine refused to regard themselves as Ukrainians and, instead, joined with Great Russians and Bielo-russians in establishing Russian Orthodox parishes in American towns and cities. The Uniate immigrants came from East Galicia as well as from Carpatho-Ukraine, but those from the latter province preferred to call themselves "Uhro-Rusins" or Hungarian Rusins. The antagonism between the immigrants from these two provinces was so great that following World War I the Vatican found it necessary to discard its policy of having one Galician hierarch for both groups and, instead, established two separate ordinariates, each headed by a native of the respective provinces. Thus there were preserved in America very pronounced vestiges of a provincialism which was brought over by the first immigrants but which was rapidly weakening in the homeland.

Those immigrants in the United States and Canada who were conscious of their Ukrainian nationality were able to aid the cause of national independence by publishing brochures in the English language and by sending their own lobbyists to the Paris Peace Conference. They were not so successful as the Czechs and Slovaks in America who persuaded President Wilson that their brethren in Europe should unite to form one state; they did, however, succeed in making more people aware of Ukraine's existence. Much of this work was undertaken by the leading Ukrainian mutual aid society in the United States. This society was also able to finance the publication of a Ukrainian newspaper which contributed very decisively to the development of a sense of national consciousness among the immigrants in America. The very nature of immigrant life, with its opportunities for constant interaction, and hence clash, between groups, tended to make the former peasants conscious of the characteristics which set them off from other newcomers.

Yet despite the factor of common nationality there has not been an adequate consensus among the émigré Ukrainians regarding the most desirable means of achieving fulfillment of the national idea. It is this divisiveness in Ukrainian politics which has prompted wags to remark that wherever two Ukrainians gather there invariably arise three parties. Besides the disagreement over the question of whether there should be confederation or federation with Russia or absolute independence, there has been the problem of the best form of government for Ukraine. In the years immediately following the expulsion of the Directory from Ukrainian territory there arose at least four major political groupings. First, there were the Social Democrats and Social Revolutionaries who, like Hrushevsky, became Communists at least in name and returned to Soviet Ukraine after reconciling themselves to the victory of the Bolsheviks. The second group did not return to Ukraine but remained loyal to Petliura and his exiled government and hoped for a completely independent democratic non-socialist republic. The third group was that of the non-Communist Marxian socialists, led by Mikita Shapoval, and the fourth was that of the Hetmanites. The last two, because of their mutual antagonism, deserve special consideration.

Shapoval's nationalism was combined with his thesis that Ukrainian society was nonexistent because the nation constituted but one part of the society in Ukraine. According to Shapoval, the single-class Ukrainian nation, com-

posed almost exclusively of peasants, had to toil for landowners, capitalists, bureaucrats, and priests who were of
the ruling class or in its pay. Preaching a species of class
struggle, Shapoval condemned his people for thinking
religiously rather than scientifically. During a lecture tour
in the United States he warned the immigrants that the
fate of the Ukrainian may be the same as that of the American Indian, to be commemorated only by a statue similar
to those which he saw in Chicago and Boston. In his opinion
the national revolution could not avoid becoming social
because the casting off of alien rule would mean removing
the ruling class, which was composed of Russians, Poles,
Rumanians, Magyars, and Jews.[8] This émigré national-
Marxist movement attracted those Ukrainians who were
not sufficiently socialist to become Communist Party members and who were still nationalist enough to spurn Moscow's leadership.

Far to the right, the Hetmanite movement was perpetu-
ated in exile by some of General Skoropadsky's supporters
and aides. These were joined by others, like Dr. Longin
Cehelsky and Dr. Osip Nazaruk, who became dissatisfied
with Petliura's leadership, especially after he had sacrificed
East Galicia in the interests of an alliance with Pilsudski's
Poland. The theoretical framework for the émigré Hetmanite movement was provided by Viacheslav Lipinsky,
who, although born of Polonized parents in Volynia, redis-
covered his Ukrainian nationality and served both Skoropadsky and the Directory as envoy in Vienna. The débâcle
described in the preceding chapter prompted Lipinsky
to attempt to analyze the causes which underlay it and
propose a way by which the errors of that period could be
rectified. He published his reflections as a series of lengthy
letters addressed to his "brethren agriculturalists"; these
provided the ideological basis for modern Ukrainian mon-
archism. Although the writings of this little appreciated
idealogue aroused the ire of socialistically inclined intel-

---

[8] See Shapoval, *op cit*, *passim.*

lectuals, they could not be equalled in volume or erudition by the works of his opponents.

Lipinsky commenced his analysis with an indictment of the East Ukrainian intelligentsia, which he accused of lacking belief in the political independence of Ukraine. He charged the intellectuals with not being tied organically to any social class and with falsely believing that their failure to own land and buildings placed them above private interests and qualified them as spokesmen for the whole nation. As a separatist and opponent of socialism he could not adhere to their original conviction that the all-Russian revolution would free Ukraine. Lipinsky could not reconcile himself to what he termed the class hatred of 1917, which he regarded as a negation of national idealism. He contrasted Ireland with Ukraine, pointing out that the people in the former country did not unite around the slogan to "beat the landowners and seize the land" but, instead, rallied around the demand for home rule. Yet what Lipinsky seemed to forget is that the class struggle was something very real in 1917 and that it precluded his wish that the leaders of the nation regard each individual member of it, irrespective of his social class, as a valuable soldier and ally. His resentment over the view that all non-socialists were enemies rested on his refusal to recognize the extent of socialism's growth in Russia prior to the Revolution.

Although Lipinsky assumed that the social revolution could be separated from the national revolution and even postponed if not forestalled, he did not hesitate to advocate a program for the salvation of his country. His first proposal, embodied in his second letter, was that all foreign orientations be rejected and replaced with self-reliance: "no one will create a state for us unless we do so ourselves and no one will transform us into a nation."[4] According to Lipinsky, the social group capable of providing the strength required for self-reliance had to have a common tradition and culture. Since both the bourgeoisie and pro-

4 Lipinsky, *op cit*, II, p. 5.

letariat in Ukraine were unreliable from this point of view, only the truly Ukrainian class of agriculturalists (*khlibo-robi*) possessed such a heritage. Lipinsky had the curious notion that the distinctions which existed between the peasants and landowners could be erased not by one destroying the other but by a merger of the two. This was in accordance with his desire to elevate the nation to a position of supremacy.

Reacting to the chaos of civil war, Lipinsky concluded that only one form of government, a hereditary and non-elective monarchy, could guarantee the establishment of a Ukrainian state. He believed that it was monarchy which endowed the great states of Europe with patriotism; to him monarchy personified the mystic, irrational, elemental sense of national individuality and symbolized the nation's strength, unity, and indivisibility by standing above all classes and parties. Theoretically, the monarchical form of government would enable the state to attract the most capable and talented public servants, while it was thought that elected republican government, because of its temporary nature and the clash of party loyalties, would allow public offices to fall into the hands of party men. Lipinsky believed that Ukraine's trials and tribulations commenced in the seventeenth century with the rejection of the principle of a hereditary hetmanate following the death of Bohdan Khmelnitsky; thus, in his view, all that was needed was a restoration of hereditary monarchy and propagation of the idea that the agriculturalists constitute the lifeblood of the nation.

While such a program may have appeared to be theoretically sound, it was obviously the work of a man who was oblivious of the revolution of 1917 and its consequences. Its existence side-by-side with Petliuran democratic-republicanism and non-Communist Marxian socialism illustrates the fissiparous nature of the Ukrainian movement. In the course of the short period during which the Ukrainians had an opportunity to establish and attempt to consolidate their independent statehood, events occurred with such lightning rapidity that there was hardly time to strive for a national consensus. In the end each émigré political group blamed one or all of the others for the failure. The democrats charged the Hetmanites with responsibility for the Rada's overthrow. The Hetmanites blamed the Social Democrats and Social Revolutionaries for having cooperated with Kerensky and for having encouraged peasant unrest. Petliura placed all blame on the Galicians because of their surrender to Denikin, and the Galicians accused him of sacrificing their homeland. All were equally vehement in denouncing the Soviet Government of Ukraine.

Such disputation may have soothed some consciences, but it threw little light on the more profound causes of the failure to achieve national independence. It neglected the fundamental fact that the period under consideration was one of inauspicious circumstances. For the most part, civil strife and foreign invasions were predominant. During 1919 trains operated sporadically and almost solely for military purposes; epidemics raged, and hospitals literally bulged with patients whose suffering could not be relieved much because of a lack of medical supplies and surgical instruments. The currency became inflated and thousands of units were needed to sustain a single life for but one month. Most educational institutions found it impossible to operate and more often than not had their buildings put to other uses. Scientific and scholarly research was barely tolerated, and the available newsprint and paper was usually employed for propaganda purposes. Living under such conditions ultimately became so unbearable that the bulk of the civilian population willingly accepted any government that would provide some measure of order and ensure a minimum of economic stability. In this way the Soviet regime in Ukraine gradually gained acceptance following its military victory.

In contrast with the iron discipline and effective organization of the Bolsheviks, the Ukrainians were plagued with an immature party system directed by inexperienced leaders who did not enjoy the support of a mass organization. Revolutionary leadership was to be found not in the peasant villages but rather in the non-Ukrainian urban centers. In the cities and towns "there were millions of nationally unconscious people . . . who cried for Moscow and Russia, who regarded themselves as Russians and who, in accordance with Muscovite propaganda, believed the Ukrainian movement to be a 'German creation.' "[5] Many young Ukrainians preferred at that time to aid humanity at large rather than their own nation. Even many who professed to be nationalists were infected by this tendency; before the Social Democrat Nicholas Levitsky could agree to the peace settlement at Brest-Litovsk he found it necessary to journey to Berlin in order to confer with German Social Democrats and make certain that a peace would not harm the interests of the German proletariat. Thus many Ukrainians did not possess that egocentric singleness of purpose which we associate with modern nationalism.

Another important factor which contributed to the downfall of the various Ukrainian governments was their inability to withstand the onslaught of the Bolshevik invaders. Ukraine lacked munitions plants and failed to obtain needed aid from abroad. Besides numerical and technical superiority, the Red Army enjoyed the use of the north-south rail line to Kursk, where a bifurcation enabled troops to move on Kharkiv and Kiev simultaneously. The Bolsheviks were aided indirectly by the Volunteer Army and the Poles, who were also attacking the quickly-formed, inexperienced, and somewhat traditionless Ukrainian forces. The Ukrainians had no well-known émigrés of Paderewski's or Thomas Masaryk's stature capable of eliciting sympathy abroad. Their immigrants were not numerous nor well enough established in their adopted lands to aid the struggle for national liberation in a manner comparable to that of the Irish immigrants. Divided by personal rivalries and basic disagreements, Ukrainians both at home and abroad were unable to organize an effective

[5] Shapoval, *op cit*, p. 107.

central political organization capable of defending the interests of the whole nation.

Probably the greatest single obstacle to the establishment of an independent Ukraine lay in the apparent difficulty which the Ukrainians have had in severing their ties with the Russians. Petliura as an exile recognized that such a severance was imperative if his conception of Ukrainian nationalism was to prevail. He gave expression to this view in the first issue of *The Trident* which was the organ of his exiled government:

"The logic of the development of the national movement in Ukraine leads to a repetition of the military deeds of the years 1918-1920. We desire that the inevitability of this be grasped . . . as well as the fact that this conflict shall occur irrespective of the form of government prevailing in Russia. For us, all Russian governments are equally burdensome and oppressive for they do not reconcile themselves to the existence of Ukrainian political independence and shall always struggle with Ukraine by political and military means. We see no distinction between tsarist and communist Russia because both are merely different manifestations of Muscovite despotism and militarism. The ideal of Ukrainian statehood cannot be restricted within the narrow confines of federalism, confederation or autonomy either with Russia or with any other state."[6]

Petliura and his diplomatic envoys contended that Ukrainian independence would ensure peace in Eastern Europe and provide a third force capable of coping with the imperialism of the Russians and Germans. If necessary, Ukraine was to serve as the nucleus for a Baltic-Black Sea buffer area, and Petliura was confident that Ukraine would play the leading role in such an East-Central European bloc because of her large population and tremendous resources. It is these resources—the manganese of Nikopil, the iron ore of Krivi Rih, the coal of the Donets Basin and the rich grainfields—which have attracted both Russian and Communist to Ukraine. Evidence for the raw ma-

[6] Lototsky, *Simon Petliura*, pp. 13f.

terials, fuel, and foodstuffs attraction theory is provided by Stalin in an article of his entitled "The October Revolution and the Nationality Policy of the Russian Communists," which was published in the November 6-7, 1921, issue of *Pravda*.

The seizure of Ukraine by the Soviet regime in 1920 was facilitated, in part, by the weaknesses which reflected the underdevelopment of the Ukrainian national movement at that time. Many of these weaknesses are no longer real because in the several decades since the national revolution Ukrainian nationalism has continued to develop even under Soviet rule although the process has been complex and has involved setbacks as well as advances. Ukrainian nationalism has become a vital factor in any analysis of Eastern European politics, and it is commencing to receive the recognition and attention which it rightly deserves in the field of Slavic studies. The last page in the development of the Ukrainian national movement has not been written. Only the future will determine whether the Ukrainian quest for independent statehood will be fulfilled.

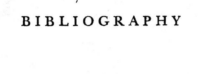
BIBLIOGRAPHY

Bibliography

GENERAL WORKS ON UKRAINE

Allen, William E. D. *The Ukraine*. Cambridge, 1941.

Brégy, Pierre, and Obolensky, Prince Serge. *The Ukraine—a Russian Land*. London, 1940.

Chamberlin, William Henry. *The Ukraine: a submerged nation*. New York, 1944.

Doroshenko, Dmitro. *History of the Ukraine*. Translated by Hanna Chikalenko-Keller. Edmonton, Alberta, 1939.

Fedortchouk, Yaroslav. *Memorandum on the Ukrainian Question in its National Aspect*. London, 1914.

Gambal, Marie S. *The Story of Ukraine*. Scranton, Pa., n.d.

Hrushevsky, Michael. *A History of Ukraine*. New Haven, 1941.

Krupnyckyj, Borys. *Geschichte der Ukraine*. Leipzig, 1939.

Manning, Clarence A. *The Story of the Ukraine*. New York, 1947.

Rudnicki, Stephan. *Ukraine, the land and its people*. New York, 1918.

Sands, Bedwin. *The Ukraine*. London, 1914.

Shumeyko, Stephen. *Ukrainian National Movement*. New York, 1939.

Simpson, George W. *Ukraine: a series of maps*. London, 1942.

Tiltman, H. Hessel. *Peasant Europe*. London, 1934.

Tisserand, Roger. *La vie d'un peuple, L'Ukraine*. Paris, 1933.

Tsarinnyi, A. *Ukrainskoe Dvizhenie* (The Ukrainian Movement). Berlin, 1925.

Ukrainska Zahal'na Entsiklopedia (The Ukrainian General Encyclopedia). 3 vols. Lviv, 1934.

Ukrainski Vopros (The Ukrainian Question). A handbook prepared by the editors of *Ukrainskaia Zhizn*. St. Petersburg, 1914.

Volkonsky, Prince Alexander. *La vérité historique et la propagande ukrainophile*. Rome, 1920.

Vowles, Hugh P. *The Ukraine and Its People*. London, 1939.

BOOKS AND PAMPHLETS

Anishev, Anatoli. *Ocherki Istorii Grazhdanskoi Voiny, 1917-1920* (Outlines of the History of the Civil War, 1917-1920). Leningrad, 1925. A general study.

Arshinov, Peter. *Istoriia Makhnovskogo Dvizheniia, 1918-1921* (A History of the Makhno Movement, 1918-1921). Berlin, 1923. The work of a prominent Russian anarchist.

Björkman, Edwin, et al. *Ukraine's Claim to Freedom*. New York, 1915. An early and disjointed collection of useful articles.

Borschak, Élie. *L'Ukraine à la conférence de la paix, 1919-1923*. Paris, 1938. A study which first appeared in article form in the French monthly, *Le Monde Slave*.

Bosh, Eugenia. *God Bor'by* (The Year of Struggle). Moscow, 1925. A fairly detailed account of Bolshevik activity in Ukraine prior to the German occupation.

————. *Natsional'noe Pravitel'stvo i sovetskaia vlast na Ukraine* (The National Government and the soviet authority in Ukraine). Moscow, 1919. Lacking in perspective.

Burnatovich, Oleksa. *Ukrainska Ideologiia Revoliutsiinoi Dobi* (Ukrainian Ideology of the Revolutionary Period). Vienna, 1922. Deals with the thought of Lipinsky, Vinnichenko, Hrushevsky and others.

Cehelsky, Dr. Longin. *Samostiina Ukraina* (Independent Ukraine). Vienna, 1915. A brochure dealing with Ukrainian history which was published by the League for the Liberation of Ukraine which functioned in Vienna during World War I.

Dnistrianskyj, Prof. Stanislaus. *Ukraina and the Peace Conference*. n p., 1919. A general treatment of Ukrainian history, culture and ethnography.

Dolenga, Sviatoslav. *Skoropadshchina* (The Skoropadsky Movement). Warsaw, 1934. An indictment of the Hetman's regime based largely on anti-Bolshevik Russian sources.

Dolinsky, D. *Bor'ba Ukrainskoho Narodu za Voliu i Nezalezhnist* (The Struggle of the Ukrainian People for Freedom and Independence). Winnipeg, n.d. Lacking in perspective.

Doroshenko, Dmitro I. *Istoriia Ukraini*. 2 vols. Uzhorod, 1930-1932. An excellent treatment of the Rada and the Hetmanate.

————. *Z Istorii Ukrainskoi Politichnoi Dumki za chasiv Svitovoi Viini* (From the History of Ukrainian Political Thought during the World War). Prague, 1936. A valuable study.

Dotsenko, Alexander. *Zimovi Pokhid armii Ukrainskoi Narodnoi Respubliki* (The Winter March of the army of the Ukrainian People's Republic). Warsaw, 1935. An account of the partisan campaign conducted during the winter of 1919-1920.

Dubreuil, Charles. *Deux Années en Ukraine (1917-1919).* Paris, 1919. A very brief eye-witness account.

Eideman, R., and Kakurin, N. *Hromadianska Viina na Ukraini* (The Civil War in Ukraine). Kharkiv, 1928. A brief and general pro-Soviet account.

Evain, Emmanuel. *Le problème de l'indépendance de l'Ukraine et la France.* Paris, 1931. A plea by a member of the Chamber of Deputies for French support of Ukraine.

Fedenko, Dr. Panas. *Ukrainski Hromadski Rukh u XX st.* (The Ukrainian Political Movement during the Twentieth Century). Poděbrady, Č.S.R., 1934. A very good general work

Felinski, M. *The Ukrainians in Poland.* London, 1931. A general pro-Polish study but with much valuable data on Galician parties.

Goldelman, Solomon. *Listi Zhidivskoho Sotsial-Demokrata pro Ukrainu* (Letters of a Jewish Social Democrat concerning Ukraine). Vienna, 1921. Sympathetic to the nationalist cause.

Gukovsky, A. I. *Frantsuzskaia Interventsiia na Iuge Rossii* (The French Intervention in the South of Russia). Moscow, 1928. This is probably the best Soviet account of the Intervention.

Heifetz, Elias. *The Slaughter of the Jews in the Ukraine in 1919.* New York, 1921. An indictment of the Petliura regime.

Hrihoriyiv, N. *Poliaki na Ukraini—pol'sko-Ukrainski vidnosini v istorichni perspektivi* (The Poles in Ukraine—Polish-Ukrainian relations in historical perspective). Scranton, 1936. An able account.

————. *Sotsializm ta Natsional'na Sprava* (Socialism and the National Question). Scranton, 1938. An exposition of the thesis that nationalism provides only partial freedom and is a step to complete freedom under socialism.

Hrushevsky, Michael. *La lutte sociale et politique en Ukraine*

(*1917-1919*). n.p., 1920. An apology written prior to Hrushevsky's return to Soviet Ukraine.

————. *Osvobozhdenie Rossii i Ukrainski Vopros* (The Liberation of Russia and the Ukrainian Question). St. Petersburg, 1907. A collection of articles by the noted historian.

The Jewish Pogroms in Ukraine. Washington, 1919. Statements issued by Arnold Margolin, Mark Vishnitzer, Israel Zangwill and others exonerating Petliura's government from having instigated the pogroms.

Kapustiansky, M. *Pokhid Ukrainskikh Armii na Kiev-Odesu v 1919 rotsi* (The March of the Ukrainian Armies on Kiev and Odessa in 1919). 2 vols. 2d ed. Munich, 1946. A military history.

Khit'kov, N. A. *Ukrainizatsiia shkoly s pedagogicheskoi tochki zreniia* (The Ukrainization of the school from a pedagogical point of view). Kazatin, 1917. A plea for the Ukrainization of education made during the administration of the Rada; the text of the pamphlet is in Russian and the preface is in Ukrainian.

Khristiuk, Paul. *Zamitki i Materiali do Istorii Ukrainskoi Revoliutsii, 1917-1920* (Notes and Materials for the History of the Ukrainian Revolution). 4 vols. Vienna, 1921-1922. Contains invaluable documents.

Kiselev, Michael. *Agitpoezd* (The Agitation Train). Moscow, 1933. A pedestrian account.

Kostomarov, Nicholas. *Deux nationalités russes*. Lausanne, 1916. A study in history and national character translated from the Ukrainian.

Kozelsky, B. V. *Shliakh Zradnitstva i Avantur, Petliurivske Povstanstvo* (The Path of Treason and Adventure, the Petliura Insurrection). Kharkiv, 1927. Deals primarily with the various *otamani* rather than with Petliura.

Kreizel, George. *Professional'noe Dvizhenie i Avstro-Germanskaia Okkupatsiia* (The Trade Union Movement and the Austro-German Occupation). Kiev, 1924. An economic study.

Kripiakevich, Ivan, and Hnatevich, Bohdan. *Istoriia Ukrainskoho Viiska* (A History of the Ukrainian Army). Lviv, 1936. A general work.

Kuchabsky, Vasil. *Die Westukraine im Kampfe mit Polen und dem Bolschewismus in den Jahren 1918-1923.* Berlin, 1934. A thorough study.

La Libre Ukraine. Constantinople, 1922. A collection of articles published by the Committee for the Salvation of Ukraine.

Likholat, A. V. *Razgrom Burzhuazno-natsionalisticheskoi Direktorii na Ukraine* (The Destruction of the Bourgeois-Nationalist Directory in Ukraine). Moscow, 1949. A partisan account.

Lototsky, Alexander. *Simon Petliura.* Warsaw, 1936. Especially valuable for the excerpts from Petliura's letters and articles which it contains.

Lozynsky, Dr. Michael. *Halichina v rokakh 1918-1920.* (Galicia between 1918 and 1920). Vienna, 1922. Invaluable for the work of the Ukrainians in Paris.

———. *Les "droits" de la Pologne sur la Galicie.* Lausanne, 1917. A refutation of the Polish claim to Eastern Galicia.

———. *L'Ukraine Occidentale (Galicie).* Paris, 1919. An indictment of the Poles for their seizure of East Galicia.

Maillard, Maurice. *Le Mensonge de l'Ukraine séparatiste.* Paris, 1919. An attack on the Ukrainian delegation at the Paris Peace Conference.

Manilov, V. (ed.). *Pid Hnitom Nimetskoho Imperializmu* (Under the Oppression of German Imperialism). Kiev, 1927. An account of the activities of the Bolsheviks during the occupation.

Margolin, Arnold. *The Jews of Eastern Europe.* New York, 1926. Of special interest because of its treatment of the Beilis Case in which the author was defense counsel.

Mazepa, Isaac. *Bolshevizm i Okupatsiia Ukraini* (Bolshevism and the Occupation of Ukraine). Lviv, 1922. A brief account.

———. *Pidstavi Nashoho Vidrodzhennia* (The Bases of Our Rebirth). n.p., 1946. A political treatise.

Megas, Osip. *Tragediia Halitskoi Ukraini* (The Tragedy of Galician Ukraine). Winnipeg, 1920. An indictment of the Polish invaders.

Miliukov, Paul N. *Istoriia Vtoroi Russkoi Revoliutsii* (The History of the Second Russian Revolution). 2 vols. Sofia, 1921. An anti-Ukrainian study.

339

Motuzka, M. *Ukrainska kontr-revoliutsiina emigratsiia* (The Ukrainian Counter-revolutionary Emigration). Kharkiv, 1928. A Soviet attack on the émigrés.

Myshuha, Luke. *Pokhid Ukrainskikh Viisk na Kiiv, serpen', 1919* (The March of the Ukrainian Armies on Kiev in August, 1919). Vienna, 1920. A brief but useful account of the ill-fated military campaign.

————. *Ukraine and American Democracy.* New York, 1939. A plea for greater American interest in Ukraine.

Pavlovich, M. (pseudonym of M. L. Vel'tman). *Ukraina kak ob'ekt mezhdunarodnoi kontr-revoliutsii* (Ukraine as an Object of the International Counter-revolution). Moscow, 1920. A polemic.

Pour l'indépendance de la Galicie. Vienna, 1921. A publication of the exiled Petrushevich government outlining the various phases of the Polish-Ukrainian War of 1918-1919 and including an account of Galician-Polish relations in the past together with a plea for Ukrainian independence.

Radziwill, Stanislas-Albert. *Les Ukrainiens pendant la guerre.* Paris, 1937. A doctoral dissertation.

Ravich-Cherkassky, M. *Istoriia Komunisticheskoi partii Ukrainy* (A History of the Communist party of Ukraine). Kharkiv, 1923. Useful collaterally.

Revyuk, Emil. *Trade with Ukraine.* Washington, 1920. Typical of the publications of the Ukrainian missions abroad.

Richitsky, Andrew. *Tsentral'na Rada vid Liutoho do Zhovtnia* (The Central Rada from February to October). Kharkiv, 1928. A pedestrian account.

Rudnitsky, Ivan (ed.). *Beresteiski Mir* (The Brest Peace). Lviv, 1928. A collection of various memoirs written by the participants of the peace conference.

Shapoval, Mikita. *Mizhnatsional'ne Stanovishche Ukrainskoho Narodu* (The International Position of the Ukrainian People). Prague, 1935. A sociological treatment of the relations between Ukrainians and other peoples.

————. *Velika Revoliutsiia i Ukrainska Vizvol'na Programa* (The Great Revolution and the Ukrainian Program of Liberation). Prague, 1928. A biased but useful series of lectures.

Shelukhin, Serhi. *Varshavski Dohovir mizh Poliakami i S. Pet-*

liuroiu (The Treaty of Warsaw between the Poles and S. Petliura). Prague, 1926. A trenchant legal analysis.

Shlikhter, A. G. (ed.). *Chernaia Kniga* (The Black Book). Ekaterinoslav, 1925. A collection of articles and materials relating to the French intervention.

Shulgin (Choulguine), Alexander. *Bez Teritorii* (Without Territory). Paris, 1934. An account of the activities of the government in exile of the Ukrainian People's Republic.

——. *L'Ukraine contre Moscou (1917)*. Paris, 1935. A highly useful personal account.

——. *L'Ukraine et le cauchemar rouge; les massacres en Ukraine*. Paris, 1927. An attempt to place the blame for the pogroms upon the Bolsheviks.

——. *L'Ukraine, la Russie et les Puissances de L'Entente*. Berne, 1918. Useful.

——. *Vers l'indépendance de l'Ukraine*. Paris, n.d. A very brief résumé of the Rada period.

Singalewycz, Wladimir and Kedrovsky, Volodimir. *The Ukrainian Problems*. Vienna, 1919. A series of five not very well prepared brochures aimed at obtaining Western support for Ukrainian independence.

Skoropis-Ioltukhovsky, Alexander. *Znachinne Samostiinoi Ukraini dlia Evropeiskoi Rivnovahi* (The Significance of an Independent Ukraine for European Equilibrium). Vienna, 1916. A polemic.

Stewart, George. *The White Armies of Russia*. New York, 1933. Thorough.

Timoshenko. *Ukraine and Russia, a survey of their economic relations*. Washington, 1919. A brochure which demonstrates the economic basis for Ukrainian national independence.

Vinnichenko, Volodimir. *Ukrainska Derzhavnist* (Ukrainian Statehood). Vienna, 1920.

——. *Politichni Listi* (Political Letters). Vienna, 1920.

Wheeler-Bennett, John W. *The Forgotten Peace: Brest-Litovsk*. New York, 1939. Thorough.

Xydias, Jean. *L'Intervention française en Russie, 1918-1919*. Paris, 1927. A personal account by a former résident of Odessa—not without bias but useful.

Zabarevsky, M. *Viacheslav Lipinsky i ioho dumki pro Ukrainsku natsiu i derzhavu* (Viacheslav Lipinsky and his thought regarding the Ukrainian nation and state). Vienna, 1925. An excellent résumé of Lipinsky's writings.

Zaitsov, A. *1918 God, ocherki po istorii russkoi grazhdanskoi voiny* (1918, outlines of the history of the Russian civil war). Paris, 1934. A general work.

Zolotarev, A. *Iz Istorii Tsentral'noi Ukrainskoi Rady* (From the History of the Ukrainian Central Rada). Kharkiv, 1922. A fairly frank account written by a Jewish "Bundist" turned Communist.

MEMOIRS

Alexeiev, S. A. (ed.). *Revoliutsiia na Ukraine po memuaram belykh* (The Revolution in Ukraine according to the Memoirs of the Whites). Moscow, 1930.

Andrievsky, Victor. *Z Minuloho* (From the Past). 2 vols. Berlin, 1921-1923. Strongly anti-socialist.

Antonov-Ovseienko, V. A. *Zapiski o Grazhdanskoi Voine* (Memoirs of the Civil War). Vol. I. Moscow, 1924.

Chernov, Victor. *The Great Russian Revolution*. Translated by Philip E. Mosely. New Haven, 1936.

Chikalenko, Eugene. *Spohadi* (Memoirs). Vols. II and III. Lviv, 1925-1926. Indispensable.

———. *Shchodennik (1907-1917)* (A Diary). Lviv, 1931.

Czernin, Count Ottokar. *In the World War*. London, 1919.

Denikin, General Anton I. *Ocherki Russkoi Smuty* (Sketches of the Russian Turmoil). Vols. III-V. Berlin, 1924-1925.

Dolnitsky, Myron (ed.). *Mizh Molotom a Kovalom* (Between the Hammer and the Anvil). Lviv, 1923. Memoirs of three Galician soldiers.

Doroshenko, Dmitro. *Moi Spomini pro Davne-Minule (1901-1914 roki)* (My Reminiscences concerning the Distant Past). These memoirs were published in serial form in the Winnipeg weekly, *Ukrainski Holos* (Ukrainian Voice), between April and September of 1948.

———. *Moi Spomini pro Nedavne-Minule (1914-1918)* (My Reminiscences concerning the Recent Past). 4 vols. Lviv, 1923-1924. Invaluable.

Goldenweiser, A. A. "Iz Kievskikh Vospominanii" (From Kievan Reminiscences), *Arkhiv Russkoi Revoliutsii.* VI (1922), pp. 161-303.

Goul, Roman. "Kievskaia Epopeia" (The Kievan Epos), *Arkhiv Russkoi Revoliutsii*, II (1921), pp. 59-86.

Gurko, V. I. "Iz Petrograda cherez Moskvu, Parizh, i London v Odessu" (From Petrograd to Odessa via Moscow, Paris, and London), *Arkhiv Russkoi Revoliutsii*. xv, 1924, pp. 5-84.

Halahan, Nicholas. *Z Moikh Spominiv* (From my Reminiscences). 4 vols. Lviv, 1930. Very useful.

Kachowskaja, Irene K. *Souvenirs d'une révolutionnaire.* Translated by Marcel Livane and Joe Newman. 3d ed. Paris, 1926.

Kedrovsky, Volodimir. *Rizhske Andrusovo, spomini pro rosiisko-pol's'ki mirovi perehovori v 1920 r.* (The Andrusovo at Riga, Memoirs from the Russian-Polish Peace Negotiations in 1920). Winnipeg, 1936. The memoirs of the unrecognized envoy of the Directory Government at Riga; the title is derived from the Polish-Muscovite treaty of Andrusovo (1667) which partitioned Ukraine.

Konovalets, Colonel Eugene. *Prichinki do Istorii Ukrainskoi Revoliutsii* (Supplements to the History of the Ukrainian Revolution). 2d ed. n.p., 1948. Valuable.

Leontovich, Volodimir. *Spomini Utikacha* (Reminiscences of a Refugee). Berlin, 1922.

Levitsky, Dr. C. *Veliki Zriv* (The Great Upheaval). Lviv, 1931. Useful.

Lototsky, Alexander. *Storinki Minuloho* (Pages of the Past). Vols. II and III. Warsaw, 1933-1934. Indispensable.

———. *V Tsarhorodi* (In Constantinople). Warsaw, 1939. Very useful.

Makhno, Nestor. *Russkaia Revoliutsiia na Ukraine* (The Russian Revolution in Ukraine). Paris, 1929.

———. *Pod Udarami Kontr-Revoliutsii* (Under the Blows of the Counter-Revolution). Paris, 1936.

———. *Ukrainskaia Revoliutsiia* (The Ukrainian Revolution). Paris, 1937.

Maliarevsky, A. (Sumskoi, A.). "Na pere-ekzamenovke P. P. Skoropadsky i evo vremia" (P. P. Skoropadsky and his Time on Re-examination), *Arkhiv Grazhdanskoi Voiny*. Part Two. Berlin, n.d., pp. 105-142.

Margolin, Arnold. *Ukraina i Politika Antanty* (Ukraine and the Policies of the Entente). Berlin, 1922. Very useful.

343

Margulies, M. S. *God Interventsii* (The Year of Intervention). Vol. I. Berlin, 1923. In diary form.

Mazepa, Isaac. *Ukraina v Ohni i Buri Revoliutsii* (Ukraine in the Fire and Storm of Revolution). Vol. III. n.p., n.d.

Mogiliansky, N. M. "Tragediia Ukrainy" (The Tragedy of Ukraine), *Arkhiv Russkoi Revoliutsii*. XI, 1923, pp. 74-105.

Nazaruk, Dr. Osip. *Rik na Veliki Ukraini* (A Year in Great Ukraine). Vienna, 1920. Valuable although pro-Galician.

Noulens, Joseph. *Mon Ambassade en Russie sovietique, 1917-1919.* 2 vols. Paris, 1933.

Oberuchev, Constantine M. *Vospominaniia* (Reminiscences). New York, 1930.

Petriv, General Vsevolod. *Spomini z Chasiv Ukrainskoi Revoliutsii* (Reminiscences from the Time of the Ukrainian Revolution). 4 vols. Lviv, 1927-1931.

Rafes, M. *Dva Goda Revoliutsii na Ukraine* (Two Years of Revolution in Ukraine). Moscow, 1920. Somewhat colored because of the author's conversion to Communism the year before; useful for clarification and corroboration.

Skoropadsky, Paul. "Urivok iz 'Spominiv'" (Fragments from "Reminiscences"), *Khliborobska Ukraina*. Vols. IV and V, 1923-1925.

Vinnichenko, Volodimir. *Vidrodzhennia Natsii* (The Rebirth of the Nation). 3 vols. Vienna, 1920. Biased but useful.

DOCUMENTARY SOURCES

Bunyan, James. *Intervention, Civil War, and Communism in Russia, April-December, 1918.* Baltimore, 1936.

Dotsenko, Alexander. *Litopis Ukrainskoi Revoliutsii* (A Chronicle of the Ukrainian Revolution). Vol. I, Books 4 and 5. Lviv, 1923-1924.

Foreign Relations of the United States, 1919, Russia. Washington, 1937.

Hryhorijiv, N. Y. *The War and Ukrainian Democracy: a compilation of documents from the past and present.* Toronto, 1945.

"Iz Istorii Frantsuzskoi Interventsii v Odesse" (From the History of the French Intervention in Odessa), *Krasnyi Arkhiv*, XLV (1931), pp. 53-80.

"Iz Istorii Natsional'noi Politiki Vremenogo Pravitel'stva"

(From the History of the Nationalities Policy of the Provisional Government), *Krasnyi Arkhiv*, xxx (1928), pp. 46-55.

"K Istorii Frantsuzkoi Interventsii na Iuge Rossii" (Toward a History of the French Intervention in the South of Russia), *Krasnyi Arkhiv*, xix (1926), pp. 3-38.

"K Istorii Iasskogo Soveshchaniia" (Toward a History of the Jassy Conference), *Krasnyi Arkhiv*, xviii, pp. 105-118.

Konstitutsiia Ukrainskoi S.S.R. (The Constitution of the Ukrainian Soviet Socialist Republic). Kharkiv, 1920. The text of the constitution adopted on March 10, 1919, by the Third All-Ukrainian Congress of Soviets.

Les documents les plus importants de la république ukrainienne de l'ouest. Vienna, 1918.

Lozynsky, Michael (ed.). *Décisions du Conseil Suprême sur la Galicie Orientale.* Paris, 1919.

Memoire sur l'indépendance de l'Ukraine présenté à la conférence de la paix par la délégation de la république Ukrainienne. Paris, 1919.

Memorandum to the Government of the United States on the Recognition of the Ukrainian People's Republic. Washington, 1920.

Mints, I. I., and Eideman, R. (eds.). *Krakh Germanskoi Okkupatsii na Ukraine* (The Crash of the German Occupation in Ukraine). Moscow, 1936.

Mints, I. I., and Gorodetsky, E. N. (eds.). *Dokumenty o Razgrome Germanskikh Okkupantov na Ukraine v 1918 godu* (Documents on the Collapse of the German Occupiers of Ukraine in 1918). Moscow, 1942.

Notes Présentées par la Délégation de la République Ukrainienne à la Conférence de la paix à Paris. Paris, 1919.

Papers Relating to the Foreign Relations of the United States, The Paris Peace Conference, 1919. 13 vols. Washington, 1942-1947.

Pervaia Vseukrainskaia Konferentsiia Profsoiuzov (The First All-Ukrainian Conference of Trade Unions). n. p., 1924.

Ravich-Cherkassky, M. (ed.). *Pervyi S'ezd Kommunisticheskoi Partii (bolshevikov) Ukrainy* (The First Congress of the Communist Party of Bolsheviks of Ukraine). Kharkiv, 1923.

————. *Revoliutsiia i K. P. (b) U. v Materialakh i doku-mentakh* (The Revolution and the Communist Party of Bolsheviks of Ukraine in Materials and Documents). Vol. 1. Kharkiv, 1926.

Salsky, General Volodimir (ed.). *Ukrainsko-Moskovska Viina 1920 roku* (The Ukrainian-Russian War of 1920). Warsaw, 1933.

Texts of the Ukraine "Peace." Washington, 1918.

L'Ukraine Sovietiste, quatre années de guerre et de blocus. Berlin, 1922.

Ukrainian Problems. London, n.d. A collection of notes and memoirs presented by the Ukrainian diplomatic mission in London.

Ukrainska Delegatsiia Skhidnoi Halichini v Rizi (The Ukrainian Delegation from Eastern Galicia at Riga). Vienna, 1920.

ARTICLES

Attwater, Donald. "The Ukrainian Church and Its Leader," *Studies, an Irish Quarterly Review*, XXVIII (1939), pp. 567-582.

Czubatyj, Nicholas. "The Modern Ukrainian Nationalist Movement," *Journal of Central European Affairs*, IV (1944), pp. 281-303.

————. "The National Revolution in Ukraine, 1917-1919," *The Ukrainian Quarterly*, October, 1944, pp. 17-39.

Dushnyck, Walter. "Russia and the Ukrainian National Revolution," *The Ukrainian Quarterly*, summer, 1946, pp. 363-375.

————. "The Russian Provisional Government and the Ukrainian Central Rada," *The Ukrainian Quarterly*, autumn, 1946, pp. 66-79.

Dziewanowski, M. K. "Pilsudski's Federal Policy, 1919-1921," *Journal of Central European Affairs*, X (July-October, 1950), pp. 113-128, 271-287.

Eudin, Xenia Joukoff. "The German Occupation of the Ukraine in 1918," *The Russian Review*, November, 1941, pp. 90-105.

Koenig, Samuel. "Geographic and Ethnic Characteristics of Galicia," *Journal of Central European Affairs*, I (April, 1941), pp. 55-65.

Mirtshuk, J. "The Ukrainian Uniat Church," *The Slavonic Review*, x (December, 1931), pp. 377-385.

Paneyko, Basil. "Conditions of Ukrainian Independence," *The Slavonic Review*, ii (December, 1923), pp. 336-345.

———. "Germany, Poland and the Ukraine," *The Nineteenth Century and After*, cxxv (January, 1939), pp. 34-43.

Reshetar, John S. "Ukrainian Nationalism and the Orthodox Church," *The American Slavic and East European Review*, February, 1951, pp. 38-49.

Rish, Arnold. "Iz Zhizni Spilki," *Letopis Revoliutsii*, No. 5, 1923, pp. 126-135.

Shemet, Serhi. "Do istorii Ukrainskoi Demokratichno-khliborobskoi Partii" (Toward the History of the Ukrainian Democratic-Agrarian party), *Khliborobska Ukraina*, i, pp. 63-79.

Shulgin, Alexander. "Ukraine and its Political Aspirations," *The Slavonic Review*, xiii (January, 1935), pp. 350-362.

INDEX

INDEX

Skrypnik, Nicholas, 223
Slashchov, General, 289
Slavinsky, Maxim, 82n
Slavs, 2, 7
Smal-Stocki, Roman, 11n
Smoliansky, Gregory, 171
Snip (The Sheaf), 17n
sobornist, 315, 322
Social Democratic party, All-Russian, 19, 26, 68, 71, 78; Mensheviks, 83, 113, 224
Social Democratic party (Galician), 213
Society of Ukrainian Progressives, 42, 43, 48, 51
Sokovich, Eugene, 196
Solf, Wilhelm, 195
Sonnino, Baron, 282-283
South Russian Democratic Union, 57
South Russians, 136-137
soviets, 97, 227-228, 232, 258-259, 265, 266, 278-279
Spa, conference at, 310
Spectorsky, Eugene V., 137n, 166
Spilka. See Ukrainian Social Democratic Union
Stalin, J. V., 92n, 136n, 224; on Russo-Ukrainian relations, 96-97; on the Rada, 102; attacks French intervention, 244-245; on raw materials attraction theory, 330-331
Stanislaviv, 252, 266, 278, 280
Starobilsk, 186
Starokonstiantiniv, 298
Stasiuk, Nicholas, 62
State Land Bank (of Hetmanate), 174-176
Statute for the administration of Ukraine (proposed), 68-70
Stavka (general staff headquarters), 91
Stebnitsky, Peter, 35, 59, 77, 170, 190, 194
Stefanik, Vasil, 30
Stempowsky, Stanislaus, 309
Steshenko, Ivan, 54, 62
Stockholm, 112
Stolypin, 175
Stolypin reaction, 41
Stolzenberg, Colonel, 121-122

Storozhenko, N., 7n
Striy, 278
Struk (Otaman), 252n
Suez Canal, 271
Sukovkin, Michael A., 49, 184
Sulkevich, Suleiman (General), 188
Swiss federal union, 25, 243
Switzerland, relations with Hetmanate, 196

Tabouis, General, 98-101, 105n, 234
Tahanrih, 178, 186; meeting of Ukrainian Bolsheviks at, 223
Tale of the Host of Igor, 5n
Taras Brotherhood, 12-13
Tarashchansk, district of, 174
Tarnavsky, Myron (General), 288-289
Tarnow, 311, 314
Taurida, 72, 73, 77, 178
Tereshchenko, Michael, 65, 67n
Ternopil, 159, 268
Terpilo, Daniel, 252n
Thomas, Albert, 98n
"Time of Troubles," 82
Tiutiunnik, George, 174, 299
Tkachenko, Michael, 85, 114, 127, 129, 228
Tolstoy, Leo, 210; letter to tsar, 25
Topchibashi, Ali M. B., 36n
Trident, 330
trizub (trident), 118
Trotsky, Lev, 101, 105-108, 113, 116, 136n, 280
Tseretelli, Irakli G, 65-66, 67n, 136n
Tula, 295
Turkey, recognizes Ukrainian Republic, 116; Ukrainian mission to, 269-270
Tyshkevich, Count Michael, 287, 310

Ukraina, 34. *See also* Kievskaia Starina
Ukrainian Democratic party, 21, 28
Ukrainian Democratic-Agrarian party, 120-121, 130-131, 147, 151, 174, 184, 194, 199n, 280
Ukrainian Democratic-Radical party, 28, 34, 41

CPSIA information can be obtained
at www.ICGtesting.com
Printed in the USA
BVHW062129310322
632891BV00005B/560